COLLECTIVE RESPONSIBILITY

Studies in Social & Political Philosophy

General Editor: James P. Sterba, *University of Notre Dame*

Social Contract Theories: Political Obligation or Anarchy?
Vicente Medina, Seton Hall University

Collective Responsibility: Five Decades of Debate in Theoretical and Applied Ethics
Edited by Larry May, Washington University (St. Louis) and Stacey Hoffman, Purdue University

COLLECTIVE RESPONSIBILITY

Five Decades of Debate in Theoretical and Applied Ethics

Edited by
Larry May and Stacey Hoffman

Rowman & Littlefield Publishers, Inc.

ROWMAN & LITTLEFIELD PUBLISHERS, INC.

Published in the United States of America
by Rowman & Littlefield Publishers, Inc.
8705 Bollman Place, Savage, Maryland 20763

British Cataloging in Publication Information Available

Library of Congress Cataloging-in-Publication Data

Collective responsibility : five decades of debate in theoretical and applied ethics / edited by Larry May and Stacey Hoffman
p. cm. — (Studies in social & political philosophy)
Includes bibliographical references.
1. Responsibility. 2. Social ethics.
I. May, Larry. II. Hoffman, Stacey, III. Series.
BJ1451.C64 1991
170—dc20 91-16441 CIP

ISBN 0-8476-7691-9 (alk. paper)
ISBN 0-8476-7692-7 (pbk : alk. paper)

Printed in the United States of America

™ The paper used in this publication meets the minimum requirements of American National Standard for Information Sciences—Permanence of Paper for Printed Library Materials, ANSI Z39.48-1984.

Acknowledgments

"Collective Responsibility" by H. D. Lewis originally appeared in *Philosophy: The Journal of the Royal Institute of Philosophy* Vol. 24, no. 83 (1948). Reprinted by permission of The Royal Institute of Philosophy and the author.

"Collective Responsibility" by David E. Cooper originally appeared in *Philosophy: The Journal of the Royal Institute of Philosophy* Vol. 43, no. 65 (1968). Reprinted by permission of The Royal Institute of Philosophy and the author.

"Collective Responsibility" by R. S. Downie originally appeared in *Philosophy: The Journal of the Royal Institute of Philosophy* Vol. 44, no. 167 (1969). Reprinted by permission of The Royal Institute of Philosophy and the author.

"Collective Responsibility" by Joel Feinberg originally appeared in *Doing and Deserving* (1970). Reprinted by permission of Princeton University Press and the author.

"Morality and Collective Liability" by Howard McGary originally appeared in *Journal of Value Inquiry* Vol. 20 (1986). Reprinted by permission of *The Journal of Value Inquiry*.

"Can a Random Collection of Individuals Be Morally Responsible" by Virginia Held originally appeared in *The Journal of Philosophy* Vol. 68, no. 14 (1970). Reprinted by permission of *The Journal of Philosophy* and the author.

"The Responsibility of 'Random Collection'" by Stanley Bates originally appeared in *Ethics* Vol. 81 (1971). Reprinted by permission of *Ethics* and the author.

''Why Corporations Are Not Morally Responsible for Anything They Do'' by Manuel G. Velasquez originally appeared in *Business and Professional Ethics Journal* Vol. 2, no. 3 (1983). Reprinted by permission of *Business and Professional Ethics Journal* and the author.

''The Corporation as a Moral Person'' by Peter A. French originally appeared in *American Philosophical Quarterly* Vol. 16, no. 3 (1979). Reprinted by permission of *American Philosophical Quarterly*.

''Ethical Responsibilities of Engineers in Large Organizations: The Pinto Case'' by Richard T. De George originally appeared in *Business and Professional Ethics Journal* Vol. 1, no. 1 (1981). Reprinted by permission of *Business and Professional Ethics Journal* and the author.

''Collective Responsibility and the Nursing Profession'' by James L. Muyskens originally appeared in the *University of Dayton Review* Vol. 15 (1982). Reprinted by permission of the *University of Dayton Review* and the author.

''Conduct and Responsibility in War'' by Richard Wasserstrom originally appeared in *Philosophy and Social Issues* (1980). Reprinted by permission of the University of Notre Dame Press.

''Guilt and Responsibility'' by Kurt Baier originally appeared in *Individual and Collective Responsibility: Massacre at My Lai* (1972). Reprinted by permission of Schenkman Books, Inc. and the author.

''Racism and Moral Pollution'' by Anthony Appiah originally appeared in *The Philosophical Forum* Vol. 18, nos. 2–3 (1987). Reprinted by permission of *The Philosophical Forum*.

''Metaphysical Guilt and Moral Taint'' by Larry May is previously unpublished.

''Measuring Responsibility'' by A. Zvie Bar-on originally appeared in *The Philosophical Forum* Vol. 16, nos. 1–2 (1985). Reprinted by permission of *The Philosophical Forum*.

''Organized Guilt and Universal Responsibility'' by Hannah Arendt originally appeared in *Jewish Frontier* (1948). Reprinted by permission of *Jewish Frontier*.

Contents

II. Applications

Introduction

There are few subjects today that elicit as much passion as the question of whether groups of people are collectively responsible for harms that their groups perpetrate. Let us begin by considering a few recent examples. Concerning a relatively small group, a court has ruled that John Metzger, head of a group calling itself the Aryan Youth Movement, must pay damages to the family of a man who was killed by several people who had been incited by Metzger's group. The Aryan Youth Movement sent an agent to Portland, Oregon to organize several so-called "skinheads" and teach them how to use violence against members of minority groups. The skinheads pleaded guilty to slaying two black men, and while they also had to pay damages to the victims' family, Metzger was told to pay ten times as much as the skinheads, on the theory that he headed a group which was responsible for provoking the violence.[1] The group, composed of those who committed the murders and those who organized and taught them was, in effect, held collectively responsible for the murders, as if each person had participated in a straightforward conspiracy. And as a result the leader of the group, Metzger, was told to pay the greatest share of the compensation owed to the victims of the action of the group. This conspiracy model is just one model of collective responsibility, but it is perhaps the most common.

Almost as common is the claim that a nation is responsible for what several of its members have done. In October 1990, some Israeli officials urged Jewish employers to fire Palestinian workers and replace them with Jewish immigrants from the Soviet Union. These officials acted in retaliation for various acts of violence that some Palestinians perpetrated against Israelis, and those Palestinian acts were themselves in retaliation for the killing of 20 Arabs by Israeli police outside a mosque that same month. In both cases, revenge was sought against people who had not themselves perpetrated any harm.[2] Rather, the people against whom retaliation was directed were simply members of a group, other members of which had committed violence. Implicit in all of this was the claim that the group, per se, was responsible for the harms, and that all of its members should pay compensation. As with many of the views we will examine, this is a misuse of the notion of collective responsibility. But the fact that such examples of guilt by association have been common in the history of human interaction may help explain why so many people have a visceral reaction to any form of collective responsibility.

Our final example concerns the recent discussions of German reunification which have raised again the question of whether the German people are responsible for the Holocaust. Syndicated columnist Linda Ellerbee described fears, which were being expressed around the globe, that a new united Germany would again perpetrate such horrendous violence. But she cautioned that the apprehensiveness should not be directed only at Germany.

> It is not enough to worry about what Germany might do. It's not enough to credit only that country with would-be Hitlers, or to think that one nation is made up of would-be followers. It really is not something dirty inside the German people. It's something dirty inside all of us, any of us who stand by, who say nothing, do nothing, when hatred speaks. The whole world will be watching Germany to see what happens next. But who will be watching us?[3]

Here we find collective responsibility spread to all members of the human race who fail to act to prevent various harms. Some believe that this so dilutes the notion of collective responsibility that it becomes indefensible. Yet several of our authors will support this version of collective responsibility.

In all three of the cases we have mentioned, what is asked is this: can groups, as opposed to individuals, properly be assigned moral responsibility? And, in addition, can one then translate group responsibility into the responsibility of every member of the group, even those who clearly took no part in a particular harm? Those who defend collective responsibility on philosophical grounds do so with reference to a number of features of groups which warrant assigning responsibility to the whole group.

The strategy employed most frequently is to assign collective responsibility to those groups which have decision-making procedures, such as exist in business corporations or nation states. The rationale for such a strategy is that some groups so greatly resemble individual persons that they can properly be treated as if they were individuals. In law, a corporation is treated as a person because a corporation has all of the relevant features of personhood, including a method for forming intentions and a capacity to act. Since it is legitimate to talk of corporate intentions and actions, it is also legitimate to talk of corporate responsibility. The decision-making capacity of certain groups melds the individual intentions into a corporate intention that is often different from the intentions of any of the members of the group. In addition, while the corporation cannot act except through its individual members, these acts are not understandable unless they are conceptualized as part of a larger process. Because both act and intention are best attributed to the group and not to the individual members, responsibility can also be attributed to the whole group.

A second strategy is to look to the common interests or needs of group members as providing a basis for group action. If the members of a group such as a family or a mob have enough in common, there may be sufficient solidarity to allow the group to engage in collective actions. Solidarity involves a sense that each member of a group has an interest in one another's interests and is motivated to act for the other's good. Group solidarity, in some situations, will focus the acts and intentions of various people into a common will. In addition, if a group has enough understanding of its common interests it may come to form a collective consciousness that allows the group to feel pride or shame for the group's conduct. Collective responsibility may be properly assigned to such groups once the group has sufficient cohesion to allow the group to take the kind of collective actions that are taken by groups with a decision-making structure.

A third strategy involves looking to the benefits which accrue to members of certain groups as a result of group membership. Professional groups provide their members with increased social status and recognized expertise. Along with such benefits of group membership there may be various costs, including the cost of being assigned responsibility for the harmful consequences of the actions of one's fellow group members. If one does not act to prevent one's fellow group members from doing harm, one may then share with them responsibility for these harms, even though one did not perpetrate the harm on one's own. Some people suggest that even if one cannot prevent one's fellow group member from doing harm, it is important that one distance oneself from the harm in some way so as break the connection between oneself and one's group and thereby to diminish, or eliminate, one's share in the responsibility for the harm. The benefit received from being a group member creates responsibility for the actions of one's fellow group members.

Once one has determined, if indeed this is ever justifiable, that a group is morally, politically or legally responsible for a consequence, then the next question concerns how, if at all, that responsibility is to be distributed or shared within the group. There are two opposed views about these matters and many positions in between. Some theorists maintain that collective responsibility is merely aggregated individual responsibility, that is, only the sum total of individual responsibilities of the members of a group. Others maintain that collective responsibility is truly non-distributive, that is, members of the group are not individually responsible but only the group as a whole is responsible. The most prevalent middle view is that the fact of group membership will play a major role in determining shares of responsibility among group members. Here, the fact that one was a leader, or could have played a leadership role in the group, is more important than whether one was the direct perpetrator of a particular harm, as was true in the case of the skinheads mentioned earlier.

I. The Concept of Collective Responsibility

We begin our anthology with one of the strongest challenges ever made to the very idea of collective moral responsibility. Just after the second world war, many philosophers urged that the German people be considered collectively responsible for the Holocaust. Writing in 1948, H. D. Lewis strongly rebuts this trend. He asserts the simple principle "that value belongs to the individual and that it is the individual who is the sole bearer of moral responsibility." There may be very good pragmatic reasons for assigning non-moral responsibility to groups and to institutions, but it would be unfair to the individual to merge his or her moral responsibilities with all other fellow group members. For this would fail to treat the individual person in terms of what "we can reasonably estimate could have been expected of the individual." We should not look to the attitudes or states of mind of individuals, but only to what they themselves intentionally bring about (through their agency) as the legitimate basis for moral blame. According to Lewis, we may be implicated in what others are doing, but this is not a moral implication. To think otherwise is to risk falling back into a barbarous, tribal way of thinking that loses any sense of personal accountability. Any defensible uses of the concept of collective or group responsibility are non-moral and purely pragmatic uses.

The most straightforward defense of collective responsibility against the charge of barbarism is that people in modern societies blame groups almost as frequently as they blame individuals. David Cooper begins his essay with this observation and then argues that it is quite difficult if not impossible to translate judgments of group blame into judgments of individual blame. One reason he advances is that it is possible to "hold collective X responsible for Y without thinking that each member of the collective bears responsibility." Since many groups have a varying membership, such as business corporations or civic clubs, one cannot reduce statements about group responsibility to statements about the responsibilities of the group's members. There are some cases where such a reduction or translation into individual responsibilities is possible, but there are many others where it is not, or at least where it is difficult to do so. Cooper concludes that those who have denied the legitimacy of collective responsibility need to rethink their understanding of responsibility in general.

The inability easily to translate statements about groups into statements about individuals weakens Lewis' case for thinking that responsibility should only be construed in individual terms. But more is involved than this. Cooper argues, for instance, that the ability to avoid causing a harm at a particular time may not be a necessary condition for being responsible for that harm. This can be seen in the case of groups, such as clubs, which cannot immediately change themselves into the kind of groups that avoid certain harms. A club may nonetheless be responsible for these harms if its inability to prevent the harm was due to the fact that the club failed to live up to a standard expected of such collectivities, for instance if the club lacked sufficient coherence to be able to act in its own behalf. This is also true of individuals, argues Cooper, for we often hold people responsible for harms caused while they are drunk, even though these individuals could not, at the time, have prevented these harms. Virginia Held takes up this issue in greater detail.

In a relatively short selection, R. S. Downie replies directly to the first of Cooper's arguments. Downie's main point is that while Cooper is right about the non-reducibility of certain judgments of collective responsibility to judgments of individual responsibility, he cannot sustain his thesis if he focuses on collective *moral* responsibility. Collectives do not have moral faults, since they don't make moral choices, and hence they cannot properly be ascribed moral responsibility. When a collective acts, some individual person acts. And while we sometimes cannot fully explain the aggregation of actions without some reference to a group's structure, for example, its operating rules, a group's decisions always stem from individuals' decisions. For there to be moral responsibility there must be blameworthiness involving a morally faulty decision, and this can only occur at the individual level.

Joel Feinberg focuses his essay primarily on the question of fault at the group level. Although he mainly examines legal cases, his emphasis throughout is on the *moral* justification of collective responsibility in the law. He begins by noting that the concept of collective responsibility involves a lessening or elimination of the notion of fault. But he argues that there are quite good reasons in many cases for just such a lessening. Feinberg's piece is a model of careful analytical classification. He first discusses those cases of vicarious liability where contributory fault is eliminated altogether, such as when a parent is held liable for the actions of his or her child, or when an employer is held liable for the actions of his or her employees. In such cases, civil liability may legitimately be assigned to the non-contributing party on the theory that the parent or employer was in a position to affect the child's or employee's conduct, and that the parent or employer is in a better position to pay. The kind of individualistic understanding of responsibility that Lewis advocated is not currently part of our common legal or moral notions. Collective responsibility is not merely a throwback to tribal times.

Unlike Cooper's defense of collective responsibility, Feinberg does not center on cases in which a group has a decision-making structure. Instead, Feinberg limits his discussion to those cases in which a group has a high level of solidarity, by which he means, among other things, that the members take a strong interest in one another's interests. By focusing on the common interests of the group, rather than its decision-making strategy, Feinberg offers a novel basis for justifying collective responsibility. Difficulties arise, though, when criminal liability is at issue. In such cases solidarity is not enough. It must also be true that "efficient professional policing is unfeasible," that the group expects that it will be held liable and that the individual members "have some reasonable degree of control over those for whom they are made sureties." While these conditions will rarely be met, Feinberg thinks that there will be some cases in which criminal liability can be legitimately assigned to a whole group for what (some of) its members have done.

Howard McGary takes issue with one aspect of Feinberg's views. McGary's main objection is that Feinberg requires too much for collective liability by demanding that a group display a high level of solidarity among its members. Some groups may not have much solidarity, but all of the members may identify themselves with their group sufficiently to be collectively liable for what (some of) the members do. Loosely structured groups, such as racial or ethnic groups, can provide enough support or benefit to their members to make the members identify with the group, even though the members do not see themselves as interested in one another's interests. If members of a group recognize the benefits they get by group membership, they should also recognize a corresponding cost of their membership. Most important, members of such groups should recognize a duty to attempt to prevent their fellow group members from doing harm.

McGary does recognize that the members of a group in which harm is occurring may relieve themselves of a share in the group's collective responsibility by disassociating themselves from the group. Of course, as he admits, even this may not be required if a group member's failure to disassociate from the group is "part of a reasonable strategy to prevent further or greater harm." In some cases, disassociation can only be accomplished by a complete break with the group that the member identifies with. In any event, like Feinberg, McGary argues strongly that collective moral liability is a justifiable notion.

Virginia Held considers one of the most controversial types of case, namely, collective responsibility ascriptions which are made concerning what she calls "random" groups. Held contends that valid moral judgments of responsibility require that a person be aware of the moral nature of an act and that the person "could have done something else." She argues that even such groups as the bystanders on a beach can, as a group, meet these requirements, and be held responsible for not doing what any reasonable person would think they should do. If a group is lacking in an organizational structure, and hence unable currently to do anything but remain passive, we might still be justified in holding the group responsible for not forming itself into the kind of group that could have done something else.

Held recognizes, though, that in most cases, holding a random group responsible for a harm means that every member of the group is morally responsible for that harm. The reason for this is that often the actions which are necessary to prevent a social harm are actions which only a group can take as a group. In such cases, apportioning responsibility is difficult because one cannot easily figure out what any individual could have done, on his or her own, to prevent the harm. In addition, it is almost always very difficult to figure out which members of a random group could have played the most important roles, and even which members could have been leaders in that group. As Held notes, many group actions cannot easily be broken down into component individual actions.

Stanley Bates begins by pointing out that each of us is a potential member of many "random" groups, for there are countless harms that we, acting with others, *could* have prevented. We are members of groups that could end world hunger, or that could end homelessness, or that could prevent the destruction of the Amazonian rain forest, at least if we conceive of "random" groups as loosely as Held does. Indeed, the vast array of groups we could form and the great diversity of harms which could be prevented by any one of us, acting in a group, is so immense as to be overwhelming. Surely, says Bates, Held would want to limit the groups that can be morally responsible to those which are "brought together in space and time," and not merely any collections of people which could act. In addition, Bates argues that even in the cases that are plausibly "real" groups it is not clear that each and every member of the group is responsible whenever the group is. If one person tried hard to get the group to act differently, that person may, as McGary also argued, be able to relieve himself or herself of the responsibility which the other group members have because of the group's responsibility.

II. Collective Responsibility in Application

In the second half of our anthology, we concentrate on the application of the concept of collective responsibility to detailed cases involving groups in contemporary events. The range of groups to which collective responsibility has been or may be attributed is quite broad, and our selections are chosen to represent as much diversity as possible, from highly structured groups, such as corporations and armies which operate as if they were persons, to groups with high solidarity, such as national and university communities, to groups as loosely connected as mobs, crowds, or even all of humanity.

We begin with a type of group which is perhaps the most commonly held responsible as a collective—the modern corporation. Manuel Velasquez argues that corporations, taken as a collective entity, and not simply as the individual members of the group, cannot be held morally responsible for any of their actions. His argument concentrates on the traditional notion of responsibility, both philosophical and legal, which holds that an entity can be liable to blame or punishment only for those actions which originate in its intentions (*mens rea*) and bodily acts (*actus reus*). A corporation, Velasquez argues, cannot meet either of these requirements for liability. On the one hand, the corporation cannot perform acts, only human persons can act autonomously. Since these acts are under the direct control of the individual, not the corporation, they cannot be attributed to the corporation. Further, in Velasquez' view, the corporation cannot be said to meet the *mens rea* requirement either. In order to form appropriately moral or legal intentions, the corporation must have a unity of mind and body which allows the intentions to be carried out by the acts of that same agent—and a corporation does not have this unity. Like H. D. Lewis, Velasquez believes that it is incoherent morally to blame or punish an abstract entity, as opposed to its members. Velasquez concludes that corporations cannot be held morally responsible for their "actions."

Peter French takes the opposite view, arguing that with regard to rights and duties, corporations should be considered moral persons, on the same footing as any other kind of moral agent. He begins by arguing that to be a moral person one does not have to be a biological entity, but only something to which rights and responsibilities may be attributed. The sort of responsibility in question, French suggests, is the liability of an agent to answer for an action. Like Velasquez, he interprets this as requiring that the agent actually perform the act, and that the agent intended the act. In French's view, the corporation's decision structure allows it to form intentions which are not attributable to any particular individuals within the corporation, although the intentions and acts of the members may contribute to the corporate decision. Like Cooper, French believes that a corporate action is not completely reducible to the actions of individual members of the corporation. Thus, corporations meet both the criteria for responsibility, since they can both form intentions and perform acts. For French, then, corporations qualify as moral persons and hence must be held accountable for their wrongful actions.

Richard De George deals with the responsibility of a more loosely structured kind of collective: the members of a profession taken not as individual practitioners but as participants in a group enterprise. He takes the faulty design of the Ford Pinto as his springboard. While the Ford Motor Company itself may be responsible for introducing an unsafe automobile, the question remains as to whether the group of engineers who designed the Pinto should be held responsible for defects in the design. De George maintains that engineers as professionals do indeed have a responsibility to design safe and efficient products, and to report on safety problems to their employers or supervisors. They are not, however, obligated to force management to accept their safety recommendations, nor to make these recommendations available to the public, although they are certainly morally permitted to do so. To make engineers morally responsible for the decisions of their employers is to give them obligations to do that which would take heroic efforts, and this is not a moral requirement for anyone.

James Muyskens considers the moral responsibility of the nursing profession taken as a whole. He recognizes that individual nurses are often treated as subordinates by doctors, and can do little to prevent breaches of procedure which result in harm. However, he notes, nurses taken as a profession hold a great deal of power in the modern hospital system, in that the system could not operate without nurses. Muyskens argues that professions may be held morally responsible for several reasons. First, one chooses one's profession in a way in which group membership is not often chosen, and this choice includes the agreement to assume certain responsibilities. Second, many professions, nursing included, have the legal right to establish and enforce basic procedures and standards for their members. Further, standards set for a profession, and so also for its members, often may exceed the standards which non-professionals are reasonably expected to meet. While the responsibility of nurses taken as individuals may be diminished, due to their relative lack of power to prevent some breaches of procedure, the profession as a whole should take collective responsibility for the enforcement of its standards.

While both Muyskens and De George argue that professionals have certain moral responsibilities over and above their obligations as individuals, they also recognize that the "system" as it stands provides many obstacles to carrying out these obligations. The job security of the individual nurse or engineer rides heavily on their loyalty to their employers, where this loyalty is usually perceived as "not rocking the boat." Muyskens and De George agree that concerns about job security may help to mitigate some of the professional responsibilities of the individual. But such concerns do not, however, absolve the profession as a whole. As a group which holds a great deal of power, both De George and Muyskens suggest, the profession must establish channels through which breaches of procedure or safety concerns may be called to the attention of higher-level superiors or the public, without endangering the careers of the individual professionals. Thus, in the end, both of these authors contend that there are collective responsibilities of the profession which do not necessarily reduce to the responsibilities of the profession's members.

The question of the responsibility of group members arises also with respect to wrongful actions committed by soldiers in wartime. Here, it is difficult to determine just where the responsibility should be placed—on the soldiers, whether carrying out orders or simply acting in accordance with military procedure; on the leaders, who gave the orders or otherwise allowed the wrongful actions to occur; or on the military as a whole, for being structured in such a way as to allow and even encourage such actions. In addition, one must decide what standards are to be applied to evaluate conduct in wartime. Are the actions of individuals in wartime to be governed by the same moral standards as actions in time of peace, or should they be evaluated in terms of special principles, like the international laws of war established by the 1949 Geneva conventions?

While he finds the laws of war conceptually problematic, Richard Wasserstrom uses them as a standard for the evaluation of conduct during war. He asks whether soldiers and military leaders may be held responsible for certain consequences of their joint action under these laws. He argues that it is difficult to satisfy the *mens rea* requirement for combat soldiers, since so many factors serve to weaken the responsibility of the individual soldier for those actions he or she commits. The emphasis on obedience in military training, combined with the actual fear of punishment for disobeying orders, reasonably leads soldiers to violate laws of war. In addition, even if the soldier could rationally evaluate actions in the midst of a combat situation, Wasserstrom suggests, the laws of war themselves do not provide a coherent system of principles by which individual actions may be evaluated by the soldier. Thus, he concludes, even when soldiers commit wrongful actions without being ordered to do so, their responsibility may be diminished by the stressful combat situations in which the acts are committed.

Wasserstrom also claims that it is questionable that military leaders themselves satisfy the appropriate *mens rea* requirement for culpability. For the necessities of war often require otherwise immoral actions in order to achieve another morally justifiable goal. Thus, one might say that the intention of the leaders was not to commit a wrongful action, but rather to bring the conflict to an end, or some other effect. Further, Wasserstrom argues, in order to hold a leader responsible for the wrongful actions of soldiers, one must show that the leader permitted these actions, by order or omission, and that the leader could reasonably be expected to foresee that the outcome of these orders or omissions would be a violation of the laws of war. This, he concludes, is the proper test by which to evaluate conduct in wartime, if one accepts the laws of war as a standard. Wasserstrom concludes that it is unlikely that many military leaders will satisfy these requirements.

Kurt Baier considers the responsibility of several increasingly broad groups for the massacre of villagers at My Lai during the Vietnam War. In Baier's view, it seems unreasonable to suppose that Lieutenant Calley, the leader of the battalion, was solely responsible for the massacre, although he may be in some sense guilty of the murders involved. Guilt for an action, he claims, should not be summarily identified with responsibility for that action. To make this distinction clear, Baier develops a notion of responsibility which distinguishes causal responsibility, in this case the actual shooting performed by the soldiers, from agent-responsibility. An agent may be held responsible if he or she fails to perform some assigned task in an appropriate way. Thus, the evaluation of Calley or his superiors and subordinates, must depend on whether they violated their responsibility to perform their tasks properly.

Anthony Appiah extends the notion of collective responsibility to wrongful consequences in which a group causally participates, but which that group could not prevent. He focuses on the case of universities that have invested in South African companies and which thereby support apartheid. He discusses the philosophical grounds for the divestment of universities and claims that if, contrary to fact, divestment would make no difference to apartheid then opposition to divestment is not consistent with modern moral ideals. That is, he argues that divestment can only be supported on the grounds that it frees the corporation or collective involved from a "taint" which arises from association with evil. In this sense, the action of divestment is performed merely to disconnect the group from a morally reprehensible system, rather than out of a sense of moral responsibility. Appiah urges that taint is not normally an appropriate basis for moral judgment of groups, since it requires that collectives be capable of integrity, and so of having a coherent moral plan of life—a requirement which corporations and universities cannot meet. In this respect, his argument resembles that of Velasquez. As an alternative, he suggests that the act of divestment should be seen as expressing a moral conviction. One should withdraw support from a wrongful regime not because the evil actions of the regime taint those who associate with it, but rather because divestment constitutes a meaningful public act which calls attention to the wrong.

Larry May, drawing on Karl Jaspers' notion of metaphysical guilt, argues that moral taint is indeed an important dimension of modern moral judgment. He begins by distinguishing metaphysical from moral guilt, suggesting that individuals as members of communities may be metaphysically guilty for many things for which they are not morally guilty. Metaphysical guilt arises from group membership. A group member may be metaphysically guilty for wrongful actions committed by the group (or members of the group) inasmuch as the individual member did not attempt to prevent the harm committed or to dissociate himself or herself from the group which committed the harms. But to be metaphysically guilty is not necessarily to be morally guilty, since metaphysical guilt does not concern those things one can easily change. Nonetheless, a category less severe than moral guilt, namely moral taint, is appropriately connected to metaphysical guilt. By emphasizing metaphysical guilt and the moral taint which arises from membership in a group guilty of some harm, May extends the range of actions for which an individual may, in some sense, be held responsible. Based on these considerations, he argues that metaphysical guilt is a legitimate motivation for disassociation from groups which participate in harms. On this point May's view is similar to McGary's.

The question of the collective responsibility of the German people is often raised in connection with the atrocities committed during the Holocaust. A. Zvie Bar-on argues that the German people should be held responsible in a qualified sense for harms committed. Also drawing on Karl Jaspers' division of guilt into several types, Bar-on suggests that only the actual participants in the Final Solution should be considered criminally guilty, for only they are truly liable to punishment and judgment by the courts. But this should not absolve everyone else of other forms of guilt and responsibility. Bar-on argues that each German who did not do everything in his or her power to stop the harms or to dissociate himself or herself from connection with the group committing the harms, bears moral responsibility, in at least a weak sense, for the crimes of Nazi Germany. This moral guilt, in Bar-on's view, arises from the failure to perform one's moral duty inasmuch as this moral duty is based on "the metaphysical fact of human solidarity."

Writing in 1945, Hannah Arendt also attempts to determine who was responsible for the atrocities of the Holocaust. She argues that while it is reasonable to hold the German people responsible in varying degrees for the harms committed, moral responsibility should not be limited to them. The actual participation in extermination of Jews or the maintenance of concentration camps is not all that is at issue, in Arendt's view. Rather, she claims, an important source of moral responsibility is the social system which forces people to participate in such harms, or to be unable to dissociate themselves from the group which does such harms. The scarcity of employment, according to Arendt, forces the individual to become little more than a breadwinner, willing to "undertake any function, even that of hangman." This social system was not limited to Nazi Germany, but rather infiltrates the entirety of modern civilization. In this respect, Arendt argues, we must consider the entire human race responsible for the crimes which are committed by fellow human beings. Not only the Germans, but all of humanity, must be held responsible for the Holocaust.

Arendt's point raises two related issues. If collective responsibility can be attributed to the group of all humans then its impact is greatly diffused. On the other hand, Arendt's extension of the discussion to universal collective responsibility resembles the discussion of the ordinary, noncollective responsibilities we, as humans, have to diminish harm where we can. Thus, far from being barbarous or primitive, collective responsibility can be extended so as to fit in with garden variety moral responsibilities. Of course, not everyone shares Arendt's view. But this much seems clear: when collective responsibility is extended to the group of all humans, it is hard to distinguish collective responsibility from the injunction that we should all be our brothers' and sisters' keeper.

Notes

1. The trial was reported in newspapers across America in late September of 1990. One newpaper had the headline "Racist ordered to pay $5 million."

2. Again there were many newspaper accounts of this incident. For instance see *The Chicago Tribune* story "Palestinians fired from jobs in Israel" which appeared on the front page of the first section of the October 29, 1990 issue.

3. Linda Ellerbee's column "Fear in united Germany belongs in every country" appeared in many newspapers in October of 1990, for instance see the Friday, October 12, 1990 issue of the *Purdue Exponent*.

I
Conceptual Issues

1

Collective Responsibility

H. D. Lewis
1948

I

If I were asked to put forward an ethical principle which I considered to be especially certain, it would be that no one can be responsible, in the properly ethical sense, for the conduct of another. Responsibility belongs essentially to the individual. The implications of this principle are much more far-reaching than is evident at first, and reflection upon them may lead many to withdraw the assent which they might otherwise be very ready to accord to this view of responsibility. But if the difficulties do appear to be insurmountable, and that, very certainly, does not seem to me to be the case, then the proper procedure will be, not to revert to the barbarous notion of collective or group responsibility, but to give up altogether the view that we are accountable in any distinctively moral sense.

On this matter more will be said below. In the meantime I should like to insist that the belief in "individual," as against any form of "collective" responsibility is quite fundamental to our ordinary ethical attitudes. For if we believe that responsibility is literally shared, it becomes very hard to maintain that there are any properly moral distinctions to be drawn between one course of action and another. All will be equally good, or equally evil, as the case may be. For we shall be directly implicated in one another's actions, and the praise or blame for them must fall upon us all without discrimination. This, in fact, is what many persons do believe, and it is very hard to uphold any form of traditionalist theology on any other basis. Of late this has been very openly affirmed by noted theologians who, if they seem to do very great violence to common sense, have, at any rate, the courage and consistency to acknowledge the implications of their view, and do not seek to disguise them by half-hearted and confused formulations. We have thus witnessed recently some very uncompromising affirmations of the belief in "universal sin" or the "collective guilt of man." This does not imply that there are no ethical distinctions of any kind which we may draw. Judgments may be passed upon the outward course of our conduct without prejudice to the view that guilt itself is "universal," and this is why Reinhold Niebuhr, whose influence on religious thinking today is very pronounced, is able to combine with his assertion of the doctrine of universal sin an account of the "relative moral achievements of history."[1] One action may be much more regrettable than another, it may be uglier in some ways, or it may do much more harm to our fellows, and thus we have "the less and more" of our day to day judgments, but where proper moral estimation is concerned there is not "a big sinner and a little sinner." We are all involved in the sins of all.

But this is not at all what we normally think. The distinction between what is outwardly right and the proper estimation of the worth of persons is not, one must admit, always very clearly drawn in our ordinary ethical thinking. And this is very frequently a source of great confusion. There is less excuse for this confusion today than in the past, since ethical writers have thrown the distinction in question into much prominence and stressed its extensive bearing on matters of practice. It has been shown, for example, that the facts of moral perplexity, and the diversities in our views about the problems of practice, admit of no reasonable explanation unless we allow that a person may do what is wrong in some outward sense without being morally to blame, and *vice versa*. For moral ignorance is not itself a moral defect. But while this shows that Niebuhr is perfectly justified in arguing that the "historical" judgments we pass on the effects of actions have little direct bearing on questions of properly moral worth, it gives no solid support to his view that there is "no less and more" where the latter are concerned. On the contrary, the more plainly we draw the distinction between the rightness of the act and the worth of the agent, the more will it also be evident that the main reason for stressing this distinction and the main consideration by which men may be induced to draw it, is that in *addition* to the distinctions we draw between the ethical qualities of actions in their "material" or outward aspect there are even more important distinctions to be drawn in respect of their moral value. We want to be sure that our estimation of moral worth is not prejudiced by considerations relating only to outward action, and it is the former that is usually uppermost in our ordinary ethical judgments. It seems therefore plain that, however prone we may be to confuse the two sorts of ethical judgments which have just been distinguished, we normally have little doubt that some of our actions are better than others, not merely in their effects, or in some other "material" regard, but in themselves and morally. All our usual ethical thinking presupposes this. And if it is to be argued that, in respect to properly moral worth, there is nothing to choose between the lives of various individuals, then it must be made very plain that this is diametrically opposed to all that we normally think, to the attitudes we adopt from day to day, and to the main body of philosophical reflection on ethical questions; for the latter has been mainly concerned with the problem under what conditions may distinctions between the strictly moral qualities of conduct be drawn. If there are no such distinctions, if the questions we ask about them are without substance, then the greater part of ethical controversy has been a peculiarly vain pursuit of a will o' the wisp.

II

This may be affirmed without prejudice to the further question of whether it is possible in practice to form reliable estimates of one another's moral worth. Subject to certain limitations, it seems to me not impossible to assess the moral worth of another person's conduct and there appear to be some occasions where censure is in order, not merely as directed to outward conduct, or as a means of inducing reconsideration of the rightfulness of the course pursued, but as directed to the moral choice itself. But if this is denied, and if it is also held that the difficulties attending the attempt to appraise one another's moral qualities rule out every prospect of success, it by no means follows that the distinctions themselves are suspect. We can know in a general way under what conditions moral censure is incurred without needing to determine how far those conditions apply in particular cases. There is nothing very disconcerting to ethical theory in having to admit, should that appear necessary, that we have no appreciable insight into the strictly moral struggles of other persons, even in the cases of our friends and acquaintances, or such understanding of the factors involved as would lead to reasonably certain conclusions. It may even be urged that the injunction of the Scriptures, "Judge not, that ye be not judged," holds without exception, and that it is none of our business to determine how any man fares in his inner moral life. For these are matters about which we may hold various opinions without seriously affecting the question whether there really *are* differences of value between different kinds of life. And what we need most to uphold is the reality of the moral distinctions themselves, not our ability to penetrate to the substance of them in particular cases.

Some comment may be added here on the reliability of the estimates we form of our own moral worth. Is fallibility in this regard also irrelevant to the question whether there really are moral qualities of conduct? This appears to me to be a most important question, but I will only venture here to make two observations. Firstly, the view which is commonly held, namely that we are usually wide of the mark in attempts to assess our own worth, seems to me very mistaken. To substantiate this in detail I should have to consider the main ways in which moral worth has been conceived. But it must suffice to note the two main alternatives. We may hold that moral distinctions depend mainly on our motives and characters, or we may relate them to some choice or free effort of will not determined by character. If we adopt the latter alternative it seems impossible that anyone should be in doubt about his own moral worth, for no one can really doubt whether he is making an effort to follow the course which his conscience requires. But if we adopt the former alternative there is room for deception of oneself in so far as we may be deluded about our own motives. But how far is such delusion possible, how far may a person persuade himself that he is contributing to a hospital from benevolent motives when he is really more concerned to ensure the esteem and gratitude of his fellows? It is often thought that we may be seriously mistaken about our motives in such cases, and that it is the business of the preacher and moral mentor to induce a deeper searching of heart and ensure a better understanding of our own characters. Literature seems to bear this out, but I am not sure that an alternative account of the facts usually adduced in this connection would not be possible if the matter were carefully investigated. But if this is denied, and if it is held that we can be widely astray in our understanding of the motives which move us to action, it seems to me that we have here a very formidable argument to advance against the first of the two main alternatives noted above, namely the view that moral worth qualifies character and motives. For, and here I come to my *second* observation, the nature of properly moral value seems to be such that it would be very strange to ascribe it to features of our conduct which we do not fully understand and bring within our control. To affirm that there can be serious delusion about our own moral attainments is thus in effect to cast very grave doubt on the validity of moral distinctions and the reality of moral responsibility.

The belief that we can be mistaken about our own moral worth owes its prevalence in no small measure to failure to distinguish effectively between questions about the "material" rightness of action and the question of the worth of the agent. In respect of the former we are indeed frequently subject to much error and perplexity, and persons of sensitive conscience have often incurred a great deal of mental pain because the very proper concern which they have felt about the "rightness of their act" became the cause of misgiving also about their own moral worth. But when the issue is clearly confronted, and it is understood that unavoidable ignorance may not be imputed to the agent, it is hard to see how we can entertain doubts about our own culpability or blamelessness in respect to conduct sufficiently recent for us to retain a clear impression of the way we responded to what seemed to be a duty. Nor is our own impression in matters of this sort easily dimmed in the course of time.

It is in respect to other persons that appraisement of moral worth is difficult. For the factors involved are not easily accessible to the outside observer. But there is no cause for misgiving here. For even if we never knew how others fared, our assurance that their actions, like our own, are subject to moral distinctions, would not be a whit affected. But if we surrender the view that there are such distinctions, and substitute for it the notion of some uniform moral quality pervading the whole of humanity, or even the whole of a particular group, we are left with nothing which we can recognize as our workaday ethical ideas; morality has suffered a complete transformation. We seem in fact to have, not morality at all, but the repudiation of it.

III

How, then, does this come about? Partly as a result of confusions which affect our ideas about value in general. We hypostatize abstractions and make them the bearers of value, forgetting that linguistic devices which make for succinctness of expression or poetic and rhetorical effect are not to be divested to their metaphorical and elliptical meanings, and taken as literal truth. We speak for example of sharing in the greatness of a nation, or we take pride in belonging to a musical or scholarly family even where we have no conspicuous claims to distinction in those regards ourselves. No objection can be taken to this provided we are clear what we are about. For the excellence generally attained by members of our nation or family warrants the presumption that we ourselves, having been subjected to the same influences, are not without a measure of the qualities for which others of our group are noted. The achievements of a relative, and especially of a son or daughter, may again reflect credit upon us, even when we have no part in what they have actually accomplished, to the extent that their success may be attributed to the devotion and discernment with which we have furthered their efforts. There is also the presumption that close association with persons of outstanding parts will have developed our own propensities, especially where general qualities of character are concerned. Men take legitimate pride in this way in their association with the great, or in erstwhile membership of a famous school or college. Our interest in those with whom we have special ties of affection will also enable us to follow their success with a glow of satisfaction as if it were our own. In these, and other ways, we participate in the excellence of others. But this does not mean that we can ever take credit directly for what others have become or accomplished. The worthwhileness of music does not become mine by my being the brother or parent of a gifted musician if I have no ear for music myself. What we are or achieve is affected by our relations to others, and we are emotionally involved in their lives, but what worth our actions and experiences have depends directly on their own nature. So that although we may be proud or ashamed of others, we add not a cubit to our stature; neither do we shrink, through our association with them except in the measure that we ourselves change under their influence.

This holds of all values. But it is peculiarly evident in the case of moral value. For failure may here be brought home to the individual in a very special way in blame and remorse. And this brings us to a further way in which men are apt to lose sight of the dependence of moral value on the individual.

IV

This turns on the definition of responsibility. The etymology of this word suggests that it means "liability to answer," this being, of course, liability to answer to a charge, with the implication that if the answer is not satisfactory a penalty will be incurred. This is certainly the meaning of responsibility in the legal sense, and there can be little doubt that the original meaning of the word must be sought along similar lines, for men have not always distinguished clearly between law and morality—in primitive life both are merged in communal custom. But we do distinguish sharply between them today. It is possible to be legally guilty and morally innocent, and *vice versa*. The question arises, therefore, whether the legal meaning of responsibility provides any analogy to the meaning of the term in the ethical sense. I do not think that it does. It would, no doubt, be easy to point to sanctions which societies impose on their members outside the sphere of State enactment, some of them, for example certain kinds of ostracism, taking very subtle forms, and there are also penalties which individuals are apt to impose on themselves, as recent psychology has shown so well. But these may also be out of accord with ethical requirements. No enactment is morally foolproof. A man may thus be morally guilty in respect of conduct to which no sort of penalty attaches. And this only helps to bring out in an indirect way what is in fact equally evident in cases where legal or quasi-legal requirements coincide with the moral law, namely that the mere fact of our liability to suffer a penalty is far too incidental a feature of conduct to constitute moral responsibility. Even if we hold, as do the advocates of the retributive theory of punishment, that wickedness calls for infliction of pain on the guilty agent, this is something *further* which we affirm about moral evil and responsibility, and not the essence of them. Such punishment presupposes the evil to which it is appropriate. We may thus reject the retributive theory of punishment, as I would certainly do, without impugning the validity of moral distinctions. What, then, does responsibility mean? It means simply to be a moral agent, and this means to be an agent capable of acting rightly or wrongly in the sense in which such conduct is immediately morally good or morally bad, as the case may be. But what do we mean by rightness, moral worth, and their correlatives? To this no answer is possible. For here we are dealing with ultimate ethical conceptions not reducible to natural fact. And the sum of this is that responsibility is an ethical conception not to be defined by reference to ideas which are not themselves distinctively ethical. It cannot therefore be conceived in naturalistic terms such as a threat of punishment and our liability to suffer it. But if we overlook this, and come to conceive of moral responsibility in ways not substantially different from our accountability before the law of our State, then it is easy to see how we come also to hold that there are some occasions, at any rate, when we share our responsibility with others and are immediately implicated in their wrongdoing.

This happens in the following way. Normally, the purpose served by the imposition of penalties require the penalties to be inflicted on persons presumed to have offended, and on no others. For if punishment were meted out without discrimination, its deterrent effect would be substantially lessened and, for the most part, reversed. For punishment would then have to be regarded as sheer injury or as "an act of God" unrelated to our own volitions, and, while thus little able to hinder crimes, it would often provoke them. But there are, however, exceptional cases where expediency requires proceedings to be taken against a group as if it were an individual entity. No account will then be taken of the guilt or innocence of individual members of the group. It is in this way that a teacher punishes a class of unruly children when he is not able to discover the real offenders, or when a meticulous apportionment of blame is not practicable. Such procedure may have effect in two ways, either (a) by directly deterring the main offenders or (b) by inducing the class to deal with them in ways not feasible for the teacher himself. The less recourse is had to such measures the better, both from the point of view of effective discipline and from regard to the ill-effects of a lingering sense of injustice. But there may also be some compensating factors, such as a deepening of the sense of community, which we might profitably investigate if we were concerned with educational problems or the general question of punishment. Suffice it for the present to note that, as a device for the achievement of practical ends, we have sometimes to accept collective responsibility. This is fully acknowledged in law, where a parent may in some respects be held to account for the conduct of children, or where a society or corporation may be proceeded against as a single entity or person. Extending our canvas still wider, we have the imposition of sanctions against a whole nation in the interest of international order, although it is plain that this involves quite as much suffering for the innocent as for the guilty, the former, in a case of this sort, being probably in a very great majority. Reparations and similar measures adopted against an aggressor among nations may also be mentioned here. Such measures may be needed both in the interest of immediate discipline, and as a part of political education, and they may provide means of redress to victims of aggression. But they will involve a great deal of suffering for persons who could not, by any streak of imagination, be held accountable for the culpable acts of the nation, most obviously in the case of infants and babes unborn. Something of this nature is, in fact, unavoidable in most forms of punishment and presents us with some of its most formidable problems. Locke, in consistency with his individualism, tried to show[2] that it could be avoided. He urged that, while the participants in an unjust war could fairly be punished with death, there should be no interference with their property, for that would involve a loss to their wives and dependents. But apart from the well-nigh impossible question of apportioning guilt for participation in an unjust war, once the leaders and authors of atrocities have been reckoned with (and that in itself is a notoriously complicated matter), it is obvious that a man's family may be much more seriously affected, even at the economic level, to say nothing of the deeper personal loss, by the death of a parent or husband than by confiscation of property. Punishment is therefore very likely, in most cases, to fall, in some measure, on the innocent as well as the guilty. But this unfortunate feature of punishment, and the fact that punishment has, in some instances, such as those mentioned above, to be deliberately inflicted, without discrimination, upon a whole group, serves only to show the limitations of the expedients by which society furthers its ends. Perfect justice is not attainable in practice, and even if measures which we normally consider expedient and just, in spite of their involving the innocent in the fate of the guilty, prove more easily avoidable than we are usually disposed to think, there will always be some intermingling of justice with injustice in human relations under any conditions we can anticipate. But what does this prove? Does it prove that the innocent share in the wickedness of the guilty, that the former are morally answerable for the ill deeds of the latter? Surely not. The question needs only to be stated plainly for us to see how foolish it is to allow our view of *moral* responsibility to be affected by imperfections in the ways in which members of society must deal with one another. And yet that is precisely what happens in a great many writings on ethics and jurisprudence, where the ideas of social and collective responsibility are put forward as properly ethical notions under cover of a false analogy with social enactments such as the enforcement of law.

An excellent instance of this may be found in two papers[3] by Professor Gomperz where the writer comes very frankly to the defence of the idea of collective responsibility along the lines just described. But Gomperz is only bringing out what is implicit in most accounts of responsibility in recent times. From Bradley's celebrated chapter on

"The Vulgar Notion of Responsibility" in *Ethical Studies* to the symposium on the problem of responsibility at a recent "Joint Session of the Mind and Aristotelian Societies,"[4] by far the most predominant tendency is to define responsibility in terms of a "liability to answer" and to incur blame or punishment. This is how Bradley, like Rashdall, and other thinkers, is able to reconcile responsibility with determinism. For blame and punishment would have significance even if our conduct could not be other than it is in the last resort, provided it conformed to certain other conditions. And in the symposium to which I have referred, while the first and second contributors eschew an unambiguously naturalistic theory of ethics, they both pass easily from the view that a man is responsible because "he can be called upon to answer" (the second writer adding, "by incurring blame or moral disapproval"[5]—a view which, even if it avoids being naturalistic, reverses the proper relation of blame and responsibility, for the latter is prior to the former—) to cases where one person takes responsibility for the action of another, in Mr. Falk's example[6] the case of a Prime Minister taking responsibility for the actions of his Chief of Staff by declaring his "readiness to take the blame." But this particular example serves to show very well on what a misleading course we are set when we conceive responsibility in the way described. For a Prime Minister can never be *morally* responsible for the act of a colleague, he simply cannot "take the blame" *morally*. It may be necessary for the conduct of a war, or for the normal functioning of Parliamentary government where, in our country at least, joint Cabinet responsibility seems to be established, for a minister to allow the action of another to be treated as if it were his own. But his willingness to share the blame in this sense, especially if he puts his own position and career in serious jeopardy, induces us to esteem him highly as a moral person even if it is also a reason for seeking to overthrow his administration. For his "implication" in the follies or misdeeds of his colleagues is not a moral one, but a requirement of certain governmental procedures, and his loyal acceptance of it, at personal inconvenience, redounds to his credit. It would, of course, be a different matter if he had encouraged or condoned the wrongful policy himself, or if he were sheltering a colleague for personal reasons or were retaining him against the interest of the public. He would then be morally responsible, but in respect of his own action. But to accept responsibility for others for practical purposes, to incur certain consequences for what another person has done, is one thing, to be morally accountable is another; and in this last regard we cannot answer for one another or share each other's guilt (or merit), for that would imply that we could become directly worse (or better) persons morally by what others elect to do—and that seems plainly preposterous.

V

The belief that guilt may be shared derives some plausibility also from the loose expressions which normally serve our turn when we need to refer to the contributions of several persons to a joint undertaking. Take a case of burglary. We have first the thieves who actually carried it out. One of these may be the prime mover, a confirmed criminal perhaps, another a novice pressed somewhat reluctantly to be his accomplice. The temptation may have been put in the way of these two, and the opportunity provided, by an acquaintance who bears the victim a grudge but takes no part in the actual robbery beyond supplying useful information. Yet another person may have covered the escape of the criminals or, by hindering the work of detection, have become an accessory after the fact. Finally, we may have a "receiver" who disposed of the stolen goods. Each of these persons is in some way implicated in the crime, and they may thus be said to share the responsibility for it. But it would be a great mistake to suppose that we have here a single criminal operation the blame for which rests equally on all concerned. Even the law would discriminate sharply in such a case, imposing the heaviest penalty on the habitual criminal, but, in his own case as well as that of the others, reviewing the judgment in the light of extenuating circumstances, previous convictions etc. The instigator who provided the original inducement might easily escape the toils of the law altogether. But at the properly moral level many further factors must be taken into account, several of them, as has been stressed, not easily accessible to the outside observer. And in this reckoning many roles may be reversed, the instigator, possibly, proving the worst offender. What has to be stressed is that the guilt of each is strictly proportionate to his part in the joint undertaking. It is not one crime that we have but many.

This seems very evident in the simple case described. It is just as true, however, in respect to complicated matters, such as social and economic injustices, where the lure of vague collectivist explanations is stronger. Reformers have often reminded us that we need, not merely to hinder the criminal, but also to remove the causes of crime, and, in this connection, it is frequently maintained that society shares the guilt of the criminal. Gomperz instances the case of a poor woman who steals a loaf to feed her starving children, and he contends that society is really as responsible as the woman herself, in as much as society failed to provide for her needs. He even goes so far as to speak of blaming the social "structure." But that, it seems evident, is only meaningful in a figurative sense and as a rhetorical device when concern is to be aroused at distressful social conditions. If taken in the literal sense, as Gomperz appears to intend, it is very misleading. For "a structure" cannot be the bearer of moral responsibility; neither can "society in general," for these are both abstractions which we must be careful not to hypostatize. What should be said, if we are to speak exactly, is this. The guilt of the poor woman is lessened, if not eliminated altogether, by her circumstances. But she alone is to blame, if blame there is to be, for what she herself has done. Others are also to blame, but *for something else*, namely for their part in allowing her to remain in desperate need. But they are responsible for this as individuals, and strictly in proportion to what each might have done, directly or indirectly, to ameliorate her lot.

It has also to be emphasized here that there are severe limitations on the power of the individual to modify social conditions, for normally he can only do so by concerted action, and concerted action, moreover, which requires a consensus of opinion on highly complicated social and economic questions. It is thus very foolish simply to look about us, as we are prone to do, and, having noted grave and persistent social ills, such as poverty, waste, unemployment, and war, straightway to take these as a measure of human wickedness. For ills of this sort, while they do in some ways reflect the moral life of a community, and provide the basis for *some* generalisations, can not be regarded as an indication of intentional evil until we have considered carefully just what could have been expected of the average individual when confronted with them. Allowance must be made for ignorance, for the need for leadership, and for the peculiar difficulties which attend the corporate effort required for effective social reform. This does not imply that the individual must simply surrender to the drift of events, or acquiesce passively in the policies of a handful of leaders. There is much that he can do, but ultimate success will depend on a great many factors wholly outside his control, no less in a democratic than in a totalitarian country. And therefore we need to be careful not to form exaggerated conceptions of human depravity by looking, not to what could reasonably be expected of the individual, but to society as a corporate entity directly accountable for social and economic ills.

This has a close bearing on the problem of war guilt. This question, it should be stressed, is only one aspect of the general question of the treatment of aggressor nations. For many factors besides that of moral guilt enter into the later problem. But so far as the properly moral issue is concerned, we do very serious damage to the prospect of eventual reconciliation if we allow a distorted conception of moral guilt to complicate questions which are already bewildering enough, the more especially as we shall not merely form a wrong estimate of the course we should pursue ourselves, but also encourage those pathological conditions to which vanquished peoples are prone, and which, however they may accord with our mood and the immediate requirements of a situation, are certain, if only by being an unhealthy condition unrelated to any rational assurance, to emerge at a later date in ways very little amenable to rational control—whatever the precise direction they take. What we need to ask, in the case, for example, of Germany, is not what is the record of Germany as a nation in the inter-war period or later—or our own record for the matter of that—but just what could have been expected of the average German citizen in the swirling tide of the events which engulfed him and others eventually in the deep vortex of war. This is not to suggest that he was helpless and must be exonerated altogether, and that questions of guilt concern only those who were in positions of power and authority. There were undoubtedly many things which the ordinary citizen might have done, and I can only leave it here for the historian in due course to attempt to determine what they were. But allowance must clearly be made for tradition, outlook, and environment, for the difficulty of anticipating the course of events (and it is easy for us afterwards, and from outside, to be wise about these), for the very limited influence which the individual, even if he is of a heroic mould, can normally have on the policies of a ruthless totalitarian government, and for the determined opposition to warlike and despotic measures which a certain proportion, at any rate, of the German people showed. Let us seek, by all means, to extend the influence of democratic principles which will enable the individual to give of his best to his State. But in the meantime, let us be fair to him, wherever he is found, by relating the question of guilt, not to some abstract entity in which he and all other individuals are merged, but to what we can reasonably estimate could have been expected of the individual, who is the sole bearer of guilt and merit, in the particular situation confronting him.

I should like to stress again what has already been noted, that no one is morally guilty except in relation to some conduct which he himself considered to be wrong. This seems plain enough in our ordinary encounter with one another from day to day, for circumstances force it more sharply upon us in close and immediate relationships. But it needs to be borne in mind very carefully when we are seeking to form ethical judgments about a vast concourse of people with whom individual and personal ties are slight. Otherwise we shall be inclined to arraign other peoples for follies and misunderstandings which, whatever the measures they may warrant in practice, are, I repeat, no direct indication of *moral* culpability. Again I do not imply that "to understand all is to excuse all." But I insist that we must first understand, and then we can have some indication of guilt. But to understand is very much harder, it calls for more wisdom and patience, when dealing with men in the mass than when we have to do with individuals in relative isolation, the more especially as the normal working of our imagination presents us with a simplified picture in which the nation or group is personified, and, having been given a mind and will of its own, is set to act on a stage very much simpler than the actual stage of history.

We are most prone to these false simplifications of complicated issues in times of confusion and change such as the present. For in such times there is apt to be a recrudescence of primitive ethical attitudes, as the recent history of Europe shows so well. And primitive peoples pay little heed to the individual; the unit is for them the tribe or the family. But reflection upon the affinity between the doctrine of collective responsibility and the undiscriminating "ethic of the tribe" should go a long way to discredit the former.

Failure to take due account of these matters will not only distort our vision in this or that particular regard, and poison our relationships. It will also give us in general an utterly misleading picture of man and "the human situation." Of this there is ample evidence already in the prevailing fashion of gloomy denunciation of all human endeavour, an indulgence which may show itself before long to be a more serious business than we are inclined to realise. Its immediate progeny are despair and its twin, irresponsibility. But worse may follow.

VI

How far these reactionary estimates of human activity owe their persistence to mistaken philosophical views is not easy to determine. But they have obviously derived much support from "organic" theories of society, such as the celebrated Idealist Theory of the State and the cruder forms of totalitarian theories which prevail today. These latter have not yet taken very deep root in democratic countries, and although the idealist doctrines, whose authoritarian aspect was, incidentally, qualified in important ways, were in the ascendancy towards the close of the nineteenth century in Western thought, they do not accord well with the main tendencies in European culture and civilization, much less with the temper and traditions of the British people. They have been very extensively discredited today so far as philosophical thought is concerned. It is therefore well to remind ourselves that the ideas of a pervasive communal guilt and of collective responsibility are simply the obverse of the tendency to set some abstract good of the community above the wellbeing of its individual members, a tendency whose natural terminus is the ruthless oppression and totalitarianism against which our face is so resolutely set in democratic countries. Most of the arguments which have recently been used so effectively to demolish the ideas of "a common good" and a "general will," as those terms are usually understood in philosophy, hold with undiminished force, *mutatis mutandis*, against any theory of communal guilt.

The advocates of collectivist theories of society, whether they be theories of human good or of human evil, are apt to hold their opponents in contempt on the score of an alleged individualism. But this is very largely a case of hitting at random, and making play with the meaning of a highly ambiguous word. Individualism may mean several things. It may mean that the good which human beings ought to pursue is always a private one, or it may mean, again, that individuals have unlimited and inalienable rights, this latter being, I think, its main meaning in Western philosophy, or it may indicate the general failure to appreciate the dependence of the individual on his social environment. In all these meanings the term stands for mistaken theories, and theories which have also, unfortunately, wrought very serious havoc in our thought and practice in the past, and which continue at the present time to obstruct very necessary positive reforms. But individualism in these reprehensible senses, has no necessary connection with the view that the individual is the sole bearer of value. We may insist, and the need to do so is as great in many regards today as in the past, that no one can have proper interests of his own unless he has also interests in others, that we are "members of one another" even with regard to properly moral struggles in so far as the attainment or failure of one person is a matter of concern to his neighbours who are *to that extent* involved in his moral attainment or failure. No one lives in a vacuum, no one is, or should be, unaffected by the destinies of others. And where natural sympathies reach their limit, or where the welfare of one is opposed, as in many ways it may be, to the welfare of others, there yet remain our duties to further the wellbeing of others independently of any advantage to ourselves. Although no one is "responsible for" others in the sense that he is answerable for the conduct of others, we are all extensively "responsible for" our fellows in the sense that we have duties towards them—most of our duties are of this sort. But all this may be fully allowed without affecting the principle that value belongs to the individual and that it is the individual who is the sole bearer of moral responsibility. This principle is not individualistic in any way which is incompatible with a true estimate of our essential social relationships. It is not "atomic" in any objectionable sense.

"But," it may be argued, "what of the individual's dependence on his society; is not our conduct shaped by our environment?" My answer here is that anyone who holds that the individual is never free to choose his action in a way not determined by factors outside himself should surrender the idea of properly moral responsibility; the position cannot be saved by extending our responsibility to our environment, and the attempt to do so is an excellent *reductio ad absurdum* of the view that morality is compatible with determinism. To bring this out fully would require careful discussion of the uniqueness of moral value and of other matters which cannot be brought within the scope of this paper. It must suffice here to note that the doctrine of freedom as "self-determination" makes no substantial difference to the present issue. For the fact that determination is of a special kind, and involves a peculiar assimilation into the character of the agent of the forces which affect him, still leaves the determinist with the view that factors from outside ourselves have gone to the shaping of conduct. And if the notion of responsibility is to be retained at all in such a case, it is hard to see how we can avoid extending it to these further factors,[7] an embarrassment that does not arise in connection with non-moral values which do not carry with them the notion of guilt and a correlative merit. The determinist thus finds himself extending the blame for wrongful actions to our environment, and eventually to the whole of reality. There arises in this way the notion of a principle of evil in the universe at large; and this notion has a wide currency at the present time. It derives much support from uncritical accounts of the findings of recent psychology, and it also encourages capricious play with the mythologies of primitive religion. This also contributes to the dissemination of irrational and despondent estimates of human attainment. But it seems evident that the quietus to such reactionary tendencies cannot be finally given until moral philosophers turn with much greater resolution than at present to the much neglected problem and moral freedom. This is the crucial problem today for religion as well as for ethics and politics. But here again I am touching on matters which cannot be effectively brought within the compass of this paper. Neither has it been possible to comment on the more specifically religious aspects of the problem of collective guilt, although these are in many ways the most important.

Notes

1. *The Nature and Destiny of Man*, p. 234.
2. *Of Civil Government*, Part II, Section 182.
3. "Some Simple Thoughts on Freedom and Responsibility" (*Philosophy*, January, 1937) and "Individual, Collective, and Social Responsibility" (*Ethics*, Vol. XLIX).
4. *Proceedings of the Aristotelian Society, Supplementary Volume XIX.*
5. Op. cit., p. 249.
6. Op. cit., 249.
7. Sir David Ross, for example, argues that a person's "responsibility for acts is divided" because "other people by teaching and example, the writers of the books he has read, and so on, have all helped to mould his character into that form of which his action is the expression." *Foundations of Ethics*, p. 248.

2

Collective Responsibility

D. E. Cooper
1968

I

Philosophers constantly discuss Responsibility. Yet in every discussion of which I am aware, a rather obvious point is ignored. The obvious point is that responsibility is ascribed to collectives, as well as to individual persons. Blaming attitudes are held towards collectives as well as towards individuals. (It should be noted that I am discussing that sense of Responsibility—moral or social—in which Responsibility is related to attitudes of blame, praise, indignation, remorse, reward, and punishment; not that sense of Responsibility in which even material objects can be responsible, and which is broadly equivalent to 'causally operative'.) Responsibility is often ascribed to nations, towns, clubs, groups, teams, and married couples. 'Germany was responsible for the Second World War'; 'The club as a whole is to blame for being relegated'. Such statements are not rare.

Now this may, or may not, be relevant to the proper understanding of the concept of Responsibility. It must not, though, be hopefully assumed to be of no relevance. Faced with the fact that we do ascribe responsibility to collectives, there are several alternatives open to us.

(1) We may take the tough line, and regard such ascriptions as misuses of the term 'responsible'. Or, if not as misuses, as merely rhetorical ways of stating what is more literally and clearly stated by making reference to individuals.

(2) Second, we may say that while such ascriptions are neither

mistaken nor rhetorical, that they are, nevertheless, reducible to statements ascribing responsibility to individuals. This would the answer of the 'Methodological Individualist'. It is faith in the rightness of this answer, no doubt, that has encouraged the neglect of Collective Responsibility. For, if statements of Collective Responsibility are equivalent to statements of Individual Responsibility, then any account of the latter will, *ipso facto,* be an account of the former.

(3) Finally, we may decide that Collective Responsibility is not reducible, in any sense, to Individual Responsibility. If so, then theories of Individual Responsibility either are, or are not, easily amended to cover Collective Responsibility. If they are not, then we may treat Collective Responsibility either as a different type of Responsibility—so leaving intact our theories of Individual Responsibility; or as showing that our theories are false as comprehensive accounts. We may decide that they should be altered, perhaps radically, so as to yield an overall account of Responsibility, both Individual and Collective. Indeed we may do more than this. We may see in Collective Responsibility not merely something that is recalcitrant to explanations in terms of our theories, but signals that these theories are false even *qua* theories of Individual Responsibility. We may, that is, treat cases of Collective Responsibility as salient, but not the sole, examples of the falsity of some theories of Responsibility.

The purpose in the following pages is two-fold. In section (II), I ask the question whether statements ascribing Collective Responsibility are reducible, in some sense, to statements ascribing Individual Responsibility. If, as I believe, the answer to this question is No, section (III) is devoted to analysing the relevance of Collective Responsibility to two current, and favoured, theories about Responsibility.

II

Are statements ascribing Responsibility to collectives reducible to statements ascribing Responsibility to individuals? I ignore the views that Collective Responsibility statements are mis-statements, or merely rhetorical. I see no reason whatever to suppose that 'responsible' is misused in 'the team is responsible for its own defeat'. As for such statements being rhetorical, I can see that sometimes they may—but hardly always. A person may say 'Patagonia is responsible for so much of the world's misery', and he may admit that this was simply a flamboyant and effective way of saying 'three Patagonian industrialists are responsible for the world's shortage of penicillin'; that no blame is meant to attach to Patagonia as a whole, nor indeed to anyone but the three corrupt industrialists. Equally, this might not be what he meant to convey by 'Patagonia is responsible for so much misery'. He may not be willing to single out individuals at all; and, if he is, he need not think that blame should be confined to them.

The 'Methodological Individualist', nevertheless, will insist that such a statement is reducible to statements about individuals. But what is meant by this claim? A schoolmaster saying 'The Third Form is responsible for my grey hair' may be using 'The Third Form' as a summary reference to Johnny, Mike, Charlie, and so on, all of whom are partially responsible for his grey hair, and all of whom happen to be in the Third Form. But, very often when Collective Responsibility is ascribed, the position is not at all like that. Very often the person who ascribes Responsibility is not willing or able to mention, explicitly, individuals. Nor, if he could, would his statements mentioning individuals be equivalent in meaning to his statement about the collective. This is because the identity of a collective does not consist in the identity of its membership. The local tennis club is the same club as it was last year, despite the fact that new members may have joined, and old ones departed. The expression 'the local tennis club' does not, except in rare circumstances, refer to a determinate set of individuals. So it is absurd to equate the meaning of a statement about a collective with the meaning of a statement about a number of individuals. This would have the bizarre consequence that, had one of the individuals belonging to the collective not been a member, the meaning of the statement about the collective would have been different.

The 'Methodological Individualist' may reply that the statement 'the local tennis club is responsible for its own closure' should be treated as a propositional function of the form, 'if anyone is a member of the tennis club, then he is partly responsible for the closure of the club'. Sometimes the maker of the statement will be willing to accept this interpretation—but he need not. For one may, in general, hold collective X responsible for Y without thinking that each member of the collective bears responsibility. In that case, it will be replied, we may treat 'the tennis club is responsible' as meaning 'if anyone is a member of the tennis club, and is not A, B, or C, then he bears responsibility'. But this is impossible, for this analysis lends a determinacy to the original statement that it does not possess. Once again we should be forced to accept the absurd conclusion that, had one of the 'innocents',

A or B or C, not been innocent, then the meaning of 'the tennis club is responsible' would have altered.

The problem so far is as follows; whether we regard statements about collectives as propositional functions or not, we cannot deduce from them statements about particular individuals. This is so because the existence of a collective is compatible with a varying membership. No determinate set of individuals is necessary for the existence of a collective.

The 'Methodological Individualist' may alter his position. He may agree that no set of statements about particular individuals is necessary for a statement about a collective, but he will insist that some such set of statements would be sufficient for making a statement about a collective. We could, that is, deduce the statement 'the tennis club is responsible for its own closure' from a number of statements describing the actions, or whatever, of several particular individuals, though not vice versa. This is, perhaps, all that is claimed in the 'Psychologism' of J. S. Mill.

What can we say of this claim? Undoubtedly, some of the motives behind this claim are shaky. 'Psychologism' is sometimes thought to be necessary in order to avoid the postulating of super-organic entities. Or it may be thought that it is justified because it is only individual humans, rather than collectives, that are 'directly' observed. These fears are unfounded. It is true, too, that there are several well-known objections to such reductionism. It is claimed, for example, that one can only deduce statements about collectives from statements about individuals if it is specified that the individuals are members of the collective. Statements about the banking-system cannot be deduced from statements about individuals unless it is made clear that we are speaking of the activities of the individuals *qua* bank-clerks, or *qua* writers of cheques. And making this clear involves reference to the whole banking-system. So we have not succeeded in eliminating reference to the collective.

I am not sure that the above objection holds against 'Methodological Individualism'. All it shows, I think, is that the set of statements about individuals from which we could deduce a statement about a collective must be infinitely more complicated than some advocates of 'Methodological Individualism' have supposed. For it will be necessary to analyse the rules and conventions binding men together in collectives into statements about individual behaviour, attitudes, and dispositions. We cannot deduce that a person is signing a cheque from a description solely of that person's physical movements and intention. For these will only amount to signing a cheque in circumstances which rules and conventions demand to be present. But I see no reason, in principle, why the existence of the rules and conventions themselves should not be deducible from a highly complicated set of statements about individuals, past and present.

Let us assume, anyway, that it is possible to deduce statements ascribing collective responsibility from statements about individuals. Does this solve our problem? Does it show that collective responsibility is reducible to individual responsibility? I think that it does not.

We agree that a set of statements referring to individuals, 'S1, S2, . . . Sn', does entail a statement 'C', referring to a collective, and ascribing responsibility to that collective. But it is not clear, that 'S1, S2, . . . Sn' must be ascribing responsibility to individuals, and that the responsibility ascribed to the collective in 'C' is, say, 'supervenient' upon the characteristics mentioned in 'S1, S2, . . . Sn'.

This is important and requires clarification. When a person says 'My stamp collection is very old' he may well agree to the set of statements, 'stamp X is old; stamp Y is old; stamp Z is old . . . etc.'. Here we may say that the predicate used to describe the collective is 'divisible'; that is, it is applicable to the members of the collective taken singly. Contrast the above case, though, with the following; A person states that the stew is delicious, but he certainly does not think that any of the ingredients, taken singly, are delicious. The stew's being delicious is, of course, the result of the ingredients having the qualities they do; but not one of them need be delicious. Here we say that the predicate used to describe the collective is 'indivisible' over the field of its members.

Now, it seems to me, that ascriptions of responsibility to collectives are sometimes divisible, as in the stamp-case, and sometimes indivisible, as in the stew-case. The important point is this; if collective responsibility is ever indivisible in the above sense, then ascriptions of it cannot be reduced to ascriptions of individual responsibilities. It cannot be so reduced, just as the description of the stew as delicious cannot be reduced to descriptions of each ingredient as delicious.

Let us consider a case where ascription of responsibility to a collective is indivisible. A man says, 'The tennis club is responsible for its own closure'. He may, it is true, be willing to single out various members of the club for blame, but he need not be. Consider how the speaker (B) might explain his position in the following conversation:

(A) Whom do you blame for the closing-down of the club?

(B) No one in particular. It was just the club as a whole one has to blame.

(A) Do you mean that each person, or almost each of them, is partly responsible?

(B) No. Not if by that you mean that I blame any of them. It's hard to explain if you weren't a member of the club yourself. The committee certainly tried. People were prompt to pay their subscriptions. In the early days everyone played a lot of tennis, and came along to the 'socials'. You can't blame them for not continuing to come; for they were always miserable failures. Everyone tried hard, for sure. There was just something missing—*esprit de corps,* if you like. People tried to be friendly, but it all seemed artificial. There was always a certain tension. No, I can't honestly say that any person failed to do what was expected of him. It was just a bad club as a whole. There was nothing for it but to close down.

(A) You mean that the characters of the members were to blame?

(B) Only in the sense that if they had been different people, the club might have survived. But this doesn't mean any of them can be blamed. I can't really say I hold any of them responsible. After all, if I was nine feet tall, I wouldn't need step-ladders. That doesn't mean I hold myself responsible, or to blame, for the expenditure on the step-ladders we've just bought. Not in the way that I would if I'd broken the old pair through carelessness, or something.

The viewpoint of (B) is not an uncommon one. It is often thought correct on the one hand to hold the collective as a whole responsible and to blame, and on the other to withhold ascribing responsibility to any members as individuals. For to hold particular individuals responsible would be to hold them blameworthy—and to refuse to ascribe responsibility to the collective might be taken to imply that some outside agency could be held responsible, and this might not be so. And it would fail to bring out that the collective has fallen beneath some standard expected of such collectives. Nor is there anything puzzling about this once we cease to assume that the standards used for judging individuals should be the same as those we use for judging collectives. A collective's falling below an expected standard might be quite different from an individual's falling below a standard expected of him. Certain things may be expected of a collective, and if it fails to live up to expectations then it will incur blame. This may occur without any individual failing to live up to what is expected of him.

This may be the position when a schoolmaster blames a boarding-house for its lack of spirit; or a captain blames the team for its lack of 'guts'. Individuals are not to blame for an individual cannot be expected, in the atmosphere of the boarding-house, or of the team, to do any more than he is doing. How can we expect a person to display spirit in a spiritless community? 'There's no *esprit de corps'*; 'there's some sort of malaise present, you know?'; 'There's something about the whole atmosphere that's wrong; can't you smell it?' 'the best of individual intentions can come to nought'. These may be some of the ways, loose as they are, in which we describe such situations.

It can only be an *a priori* insistance that where there is collective responsibility there *must* be individual responsibility that can make us deny the existence of such situations. But if we actually look; if we observe what is said; if we realise that people do employ different standards for judging collectives and individuals, we should free ourselves from this *a priori* insistence.

To conclude this section: I am not claiming that statements ascribing responsibility to a collective cannot be deduced from statements referring to individuals. It may well be that from a detailed enough set of descriptions of the behaviour, attitudes, dispositions, and so on, of the members of the tennis club, we could have deduced that the club would fail; that it would be a bad club. These descriptions of the individuals, however, need contain no ascriptions of responsibility to them. If this is so, then there is a practice of ascribing responsibility to collectives over and above the practice of ascribing responsibility to individuals. In the next section we will consider the implications of this conclusion.

III

Do the conclusions of section (II) show that there are two senses of Responsibility? There is no reason to suppose this. The fact that a stew's being delicious is not the same as each of its ingredients being delicious, does not tempt us to postulate two senses of 'delicious'.

The conclusions may, however, show that certain analyses of Responsibility are mistaken. To take an analogy: Professor Hart has shown how concentration on the Criminal Law alone has made at least one legal theory, the Command Theory, seem more plausible than it would have seemed if examples from the Civil Law had been considered too. Indeed, had Civil Law been taken into account, theorists may never have put forward a Command Theory at all. Similarly it seems to me that two commonly accepted pieces of analysis of Responsibility lose plausibility in the light of Collective Responsibility.

Someone may, of course, take the hard line and deny that such 'marginal' cases as I have discussed should have any bearing on theories which are adequate for explaining Individual Responsibility. But, in the first place, I do not think that the cases I have discussed are marginal—if by 'marginal' is meant 'rare' or 'fishy'. So, if such cases could be accommodated within an overall theory, this would be some conceptual gain. Second, as I shall argue later, I do not think the notions of Responsibility I wish to reject are to be rejected simply because they fail to cover Collective Responsibility. I think they fail as analyses of Individual Responsibility also. Cases of Collective Responsibility, therefore, may be regarded not simply as cases recalcitrant to certain analyses, but as salient examples of the failure of those analyses.

The two notions about Responsibility that lose plausibility in the light of our earlier conclusions are:

(A) The notion that 'X is responsible for Y' entails 'X could have avoided Y'.
(B) The notion that 'X is responsible for Y' entails that Y is an example of a type of behaviour, or state of affairs, which people may be deterred from performing or creating by blame or punishment.

Let us consider (A). When we held that the tennis club was responsible for its own closure, did we necessarily imply that it could have avoided the closure? I think not. For we are not attributing the closure of the club to any particular actions, or acts of negligence, on the part of the members. It is not the case that the club closed as a result of particular free decisions made by people. It is, therefore, unclear in what sense the club could have avoided closure. Quite what are supposed to be the avoidable happenings that 'could have been otherwise', and which resulted in the closure of the club? Of course, had the members been different ones, or the same ones with different characters, then the club may have survived. But if we make this uninteresting point by saying that, in some sense, the club could have avoided closure, we must realize that it is not the same sense as in 'John could have avoided upsetting his parents', where we do not mean simply that John might have been a different person. Rather we are implying that John made a number of unforced decisions which upset his parents. He could, while retaining his character, have chosen differently. The trouble with the tennis club, it will be recalled, was lack of *esprit de corps,* natural conviviality, and communal feeling. It is difficult to see where the question of avoidable decisions can enter into the account.

What is implied, I think, in the claim that the club was responsible for its own closure is that *not* closing, under similar circumstances, is what can be expected from most or many clubs. (By 'similar circumstances', I mean such factors as finances, state of the clubhouse and courts, and so on. I do not, of course, include the level of *esprit de corps.*) Staying alive is what most clubs can do, given favourable circumstances. Failure, avoidable or not, only belongs to sub-standard clubs.

Now I doubt that any more than this is implied when we speak of Individual Responsibility also. Consider Mr Kenner's example (*Mind,* April, 1967). We may agree that a certain driver could not have avoided a smash—given his lack of skill, bad nerves, the condition of the road, etc. We may, though, still hold him responsible for the accident. For avoiding the smash, given the condition of the road, is what we could rightly expect from most drivers. Our driver possesses sub-standard skill, and the accident was due to this lack of skill; and he is to blame for the accident. In general, when most A's can avoid B, then it is possible to hold a particular A responsible for an instance of B, even though he could not have avoided doing it at the time. Cases of Collective Responsibility are salient examples, but not the only examples, of this.

Let us consider notion (B). The notion that responsible actions are those amendable to blame, praise, punishment, and reward has been accepted from Bentham, through Bradley, to Nowell-Smith. According to Bradley we need make no distinction between responsibility . . . and liability to punishment' (*Ethical Studies,* O.U.P., 1962, p. 4). However, when a collective is held responsible, it is very often a completely unimportant, and irrelevant consideration as to whether blame or punishment would be effective in altering the behaviour of collectives. Let me give two examples to illustrate this claim.

First, the example of our tennis club again. We blamed the club—as far as we could discover—for lack of *esprit de corps,* of spontaneous warmth in the club-room, of natural conviviality and comradeship, and so on. Now blaming the club for such a state of affairs, chastising it by scrubbing its name off the official list of acceptable clubs, or whatever, is the last thing to improve the state of affairs, and the last thing to encourage other clubs to avoid such a state of affairs. Natural conviviality, for instance, is that last thing to be induced by threats. Those tyrannical jollificators at Holiday Camps only succeed with those who are already jolly. When it is the party as a whole's fault that each new arrival becomes gloomy after a few minutes, it will hardly help matters for someone to stand up and say, 'This is a terrible party. People must boycott parties like this one in the future.' Nor is the unspirited school boarding-house likely to have its spirit revived by being pilloried in front of the whole school on speech-day in the headmaster's speech, or by being kept in over half-term.

These considerations are even more obvious if we turn to a different type of example; that of ascribing responsibility to nations. We certainly do hold nations as a whole responsible; and we need not be ascribing responsibility to any particular individuals, and if we are, this may not exhaust our ascription of responsibility. For we may hold the nation as a whole responsible for supporting its evil public figures, without thinking that particular people have fallen below standards expected of them as individuals. We might, say, condemn the nation for its lack of spirit; its lack of principle; its lack of concentrated, concerted effort. We may do this in a way analogous to our condemnation of the tennis-club for its lack of *esprit de corps*.

The relevance of this is as follows: I am not even sure that it makes sense to speak of punishing nations. At least, this would hardly make sense in a world of national sovereignty. But even if it does make sense, it can hardly be claimed that the practice of 'blaming' or 'punishing' nations is of effect in altering the behaviour of nations, or their attitudes and internal structures. Censure and retribution have been notably ineffective in the cases of Turkey, in its 'sick man of Europe' days, and Germany over the last century.

Admittedly, the claim that Responsibility is analytically tied to the efficaciousness of blame and punishment does not require that blame and punishment should be effective in every case. This is so even when we are dealing with individuals rather than collectives. But surely the claim does require that the actions, states of affairs, and so on, for which we hold collectives or individuals responsible, should have a strong tendency to be effected by blame and punishment. Now in the case of nations at least, the examples of immunity to censure are so frequent that it is false to speak even of a tendency to be affected by blame and punishment. That is, we frequently hold nations responsible for X's (events, states of affairs, internal dissensions, etc.) where there is not even a presumption to the effect that nations may be deterred from X's by blame or punishment. If so, I can see little point in trying to explain responsibility in terms of the efficaciousness of blame and punishment.

As in our discussion of notion (A), this point can be generalised to cover Individual Responsibility also. That is, cases of Collective Responsibility are not the only cases recalcitrant to an analysis in terms of notion (B). As Professor Brandt has pointed out, Parricide is condemned more heavily than ordinary Homicide; yet evidence shows that Parricide is less amenable to blame and punishment than ordinary Homicide. In general I see no reason to suppose that A's being held responsible for B entails that B is the sort of action that is amenable to blame and punishment.

IV

If I am right, there is such a thing as Collective Responsibility that is not reducible to Individual Responsiblity. And if there is—though not only if there is—then at least two notions about Responsibility must be rejected. Therefore an analysis if Responsibility should be preferred which covers all ascriptions of Responsibility. However, such an analysis should also show why it is easy to have regarded notions (A) and (B) as part of the real analysis of Responsibility. The correct analysis, that is, should allow us to see why the points falsely expressed in notions (A) and (B) are nevertheless important.

What I wish to do is to agree with Brandt's definition of Responsibility. His is a definition which, unlike others, is easily amended to cover cases of Collective Responsibility. According to him, to say 'X is morally accountable on account of Z' means: 'Some trait (or set of traits) of X's character was responsible for Z in the sense that some trait (set of traits) was below standard, and all other traits of his personality having been the same, Z would not have occurred but for this fact; and it is on this account fitting or justified in itself for X to have some blaming attitudes, including . . . remorse towards himself, and for many other persons Y to have some blaming attitudes including retributive indignation towards X, and to express them in behaviour' ('Blameworthiness and Obligation' in *Essays in Moral Philosophy,* ed. A. Melden, p. 16–17).

This account can easily be amended to fit the example of the tennis club. The club's *esprit de corps* was below standard, and it was because of this that the club closed. It is thought quite fitting for members of the club to feel some shame, and for other clubs in the league to feel indignant towards the club for letting down the game of tennis.

The account also shows the importance of the points misleadingly expressed in notions (A) and (B). If it is for something 'below standard' that one is blamed, then it must, in general, be possible for the standard to be met. If nobody, or virtually nobody, could attain the standard, we would not speak of there being a standard so meet or fall below. So, while it is false to say that 'X is responsible for Y' entails 'X could have avoided doing Y', it is easy to see why the question of capabilities is relevant to Responsibility.

Even more obviously, Brandt's account shows the relevance of blame and punishment. These are 'fitting' and 'justified' where responsible actions are concerned. Now, presumably, blame and punishment are often effective. So it is easy to see why, in many cases, responsible actions are those belonging to a type amenable to discouragement via blame and punishment. Once again, though, there is no reason to suppose that 'X is responsible for Y' entails that Y is an example of a piece of behaviour, or state of affairs which people may be deterred from performing or creating by blame and punishment.

To conclude: It may be that my examples of Collective Responsibility have failed to convince. Someone may insist that there is only Individual Responsibility. It seems to me doubtful that the reduction could be carried through, however; and I feel that the failure to be convinced would be due to unwarranted preconceptions. But even if the reduction could be carried through, this would not affect the conclusions of section (III). Certain notions about Responsibility are false, with or without Collective Responsibility.

3

Collective Responsibility

R. S. Downie
1969

In his paper 'Collective Responsibility' (reprinted above) Mr. D. E. Cooper argues for the thesis that collectives can be held responsible in a sense not reducible to the individual responsibility of the members of the collective. And he uses this conclusion to support views of individual responsibility and of blame and punishment which he wishes to assert independently. I shall argue that although there is a sense in which the actions and responsibility of a collective cannot be analysed in terms of the actions and responsibilities of the individual persons who compose the collective, it is not *moral* responsibility which is involved. I shall then maintain that Cooper's account of collective responsibility does not support his account of individual responsibility; and that his account of individual responsibility is in any case false, if he means *moral* responsibility.

I

It is certainly the case, as Cooper rightly stresses, that sometimes the ascription of responsibility to a collective is to be understood as an indirect way of ascribing it to the individuals who make up the collective. Collective responsibility in this sense is what Cooper neatly calls 'divisible'. I shall not be concerned with this sense, however, but rather with what he calls 'indivisible' collective responsibility (p. 39).

Cooper's argument for the existence of indivisible collective responsibility is a simple one. He points out (pp. 39–40) that a collective, such as a tennis club, may close and be held responsible for its closure although no one member or group can be blamed for it. He allows that the future closure of the club could have been deduced from a set of statements describing the dispositions, attitudes and behaviour of the members, but stresses that these statements need contain no ascriptions of individual responsibility. The collective may incur blame because it falls below standards we normally expect of similar collectives, but no individual is to blame (p. 40).

In reply to this argument it is possible simply to deny that we would hold a collective *morally* responsible for its closure in these circumstances. We are asked to accept that no member ever failed in his moral duty to the club, but yet that the club as a collective is to be held *morally* responsible for its failure. Certainly, we may ascribe responsibility to the collective for its lack of *esprit de corps* while remaining unwilling to ascribe individual responsibility for this to any member or group of members (p. 40). But lack of *esprit de corps* is not a *moral* fault. It may be true (but it is trivial) that the club collectively is *legally* or *causally* responsible for its debts or bad atmosphere even when no individual or group is legally responsible: it would be exciting (but it is false) that the club collectively is *morally* responsible for its bad atmosphere or creating debts even when no individual or group (such as the committee) is individually morally responsible for creating them. Cooper's argument mixes the two claims, and he is able to continue stirring the mixture because he speaks only of 'responsibility' without making it clear in each context whether it is causal, legal or moral responsibility he means.

II

Cooper uses his (erroneous) account of collective responsibility to cast doubt on two commonly held moral views, which he wishes to reject independently. The first of these is that 'X is responsible for Y' entails 'X could have avoided Y' (p. 42). Now clearly, in Cooper's senses of collective responsibility, which I claim are non-moral senses, a collective can be held responsible for what it does although it could not have avoided acting as it did (for the tennis club could not have avoided closure granted the make-up of its members). But the reply to Cooper is, as I have argued, that he has not provided convincing grounds to show that *moral* responsibility is one of the senses to which his analysis applies. Hence, his account of collective responsibility has no bearing on the usual analysis of moral responsibility.

But he wishes independently to reject the usual analysis. His argument for rejecting the usual analysis is taken from Mr. Kenner (*Mind*, April, 1967). 'We may agree that a certain driver could not have avoided a smash—given his lack of skill, bad nerves, the condition of the road, etc. We may, though, still hold him responsible for the accident. For avoiding the smash, given the conditions of the road, is what we could rightly expect of most drivers' (p. 43). But this argument quite fails to show (*pace* Mr. Kenner) that there can be *moral* responsibility without avoidability. For, whatever is to be said about the driver's causal and legal responsibility in the situation, his *moral* responsibility for the accident consists in his being on the road at all granted his lack of skill, bad nerves etc. Certainly, he compares unfavourably with other drivers in these respects, but his moral responsibility does not consist in this, but in his *choice* to go on the road while knowing this. Hence, Cooper's view of responsibility (if he intends it as one of *moral* responsibility) is unconvincing independently of his account of collective responsibility.

Cooper discusses next what he takes to be the common view that responsibility is analytically tied to the efficaciousness of blame and punishment, a view which, once again, he wishes independently to reject (pp. 43–45). He points out that we certainly hold nations, say, collectively responsible, but argues that, far from being efficacious, it hardly makes sense to speak of punishing a whole nation (p. 44).

In reply it can be said that the lack of efficacy in blaming or punishing a collective has no bearing on the common view of the connections between moral responsibility and blame and punishment; for on the common view moral responsibility is not tied analytically to the efficacy of blame or punishment, but rather to *blameworthiness*. One can suggest that an individual person or a collective is blameworthy without suggesting that it ought to be blamed or punished. For 'X ought to blame or punish Y' is not deducible from the single premise 'Y is blameworthy'; the additional premise 'It will do some good for X to blame or punish Y' is required. A Utilitarian would be explicit about this, but even the Retributivist position involves the premise implicitly. Now it is certainly arguable that the additional premise is not always true of individuals, and that it is never true of collectives; but this in no way affects the analytic connection between 'Y is responsible for wrong action W' and 'Y is blameworthy on account of his performance of W'. The usual view of the connections between moral responsibility and blame and punishment (as I understand it) asserts no more than this. It is therefore undisturbed either by Cooper's account of collective responsibility or his independent arguments.

III

I wish to argue, positively, for the theses that the actions and non-moral responsibilities of some collectives are *not* analysable in terms of those of its members; but that if a collective is *morally* responsible for something it does, its moral responsibility *is* analysable in terms of the moral responsibilities of individuals, including some who may not at a given time be members of the collective.

An argument for the first thesis can be based on the claim that collectives are constituted by rules. When a collective acts individual persons act, but they are acting as its representatives—in roles, the rights and duties of which are to be defined in terms of the rules which constitute the collective. The actions of a collective cannot therefore be exhaustively analysed in terms of the actions of its members unless we stress that the members are authorised to act by the constitution of the collective.

Cooper considers this type of argument (p. 38–39) but rejects it because he sees 'no reason, in principle, why the existence of the rules and conventions themselves should not be deducible from a highly complicated set of statements about individuals, past and present'. But what does Cooper mean by a 'set of statements about individuals'? If he means a set of statements about how individuals *in fact* behave, he seems to be open to a well-known objection about the difficulty of deducing rules from factual statements. If he means statements about how individuals believe they *ought* to behave, then we can agree, but he is saying merely that individuals can accept rules. My point is simply that the actions and non-moral responsibilities of an 'indivisible' collective necessarily require institutional concepts for their adequate analysis; they cannot therefore be analysed solely in terms of individual actions and responsibilities.

But the *moral* responsibilities of a collective do stem although in a complex way, from the moral decisions of individuals. There seem to be three main ways in which the moral responsibility of a collective can be traced to the moral decisions of individuals.

In the first place, the rules which constitute the collective have been created or accepted by the decisions of individuals, who therefore bear moral responsibility for their decisions. If a collective tends to produce actions with a characteristic moral quality this will be partly because the decisions of the individuals who created the collective are to be morally praised or blamed. (Compare, for example, the moral decisions of those who created the collective 'The Gestapo' with those who created 'Oxfam'.) In the second place, whether or not the actions of a given collective tend to produce praiseworthy or blameworthy actions some individual person freely decided to become a member of that collective. The morality of 'role-acceptance' is, of course, complex—all sorts of pressures may force a person to join a certain collective—but we can still maintain that the decision to act as a member of a collective is basically an individual decision which carries moral responsibility with it. And a person can resign if he disagrees violently with the action he must take as a member of the collective. Finally, a person can bring various moral qualities of his own to his actions as a member of the collective. Thus the collective 'The Home Office' has often been morally criticised for the behaviour of its Immigration Officials. This is because some of them are alleged to bring their actions as members of the collective undesirable moral qualities—rudeness and so on.

The upshot, then, is that when collectives act their actions and non-moral responsibilities are *not* exhaustively analysable in terms of the actions and responsibilities of individuals; we must bring the institutional structure of the collective into the analysis. Secondly, the *moral* responsibilities of a collective *are* analysable in terms of those of individual moral responsibility, but in a complex way; the morality of the role-structure which constitutes the collective, as well as the role-acceptance and role-enactment of the persons who act in the collective are relevant.[1]

Note

1. I have developed these points in 'Social Roles and Moral Responsibility', (*Philosophy*, January 1964) and in *Government Action and Morality* (London, 1964). References to Cooper's essay are to the reprint of the article in this anthology.

4

Collective Responsibility

Joel Feinberg
1970

When we state that a person is responsible for some harm, we sometimes mean to ascribe to him *liability* to certain responsive attitudes, judgments, or actions. Some responsive actions require authority; of these some are punitive, and others force compensation of a harmed victim. In the typical case of individual liability to unfavorable responses from others, three preconditions must be satisfied. First, it must be true that the responsible individual did the harmful thing in question, or at least that his action or omission made a substantial causal contribution to it. Second, the causally contributory conduct must have been in some way *faulty*. Finally, if the harmful outcome was truly "his fault," the requisite causal connection must have been directly between the faulty aspect of his conduct and the outcome. It is not sufficient to have caused harm *and* to have been at fault if the fault was irrelevant to the causing. We can use the expression "contributory fault" to refer compendiously to these three conditions. Thus, in the standard case of responsibility for harm, there can be no liability without contributory fault.

Certain familiar deviations from the standard case, however, give rise to confusion and misgiving. All primitive legal systems, and our own common law until about the fifteenth century, abound with examples of liability without contributory fault. For three centuries or so these examples were gradually eliminated from the common law, but they have returned in somewhat different form, often via statutes, in the last century, to the great alarm of many critics. Some of this alarm, I think, is justified; but there is little ground for fearing a recrudescence of primitive tribalism. Much legal liability without fault rests on very solid rationales, which are quite another thing than primitive superstition. The cases I have in mind can be discussed under three headings.

Strict liability

What is called "strict liability" in the law is simply any liability for which the contributory fault condition is weakened or absent. This is the most general category; vicarious and collective liability are among its more interesting subspecies. For the most part, contractual liability has always tended to be "strict." Since this is liability that one imposes on oneself voluntarily, there is rarely any doubt expressed about its propriety. And no doubt can be expressed about its utility. Manufacturers brag about their warrantees and unconditional guarantees; and private bargainers quite often find it to their mutual advantage when one promises that, "if anything goes wrong, I'll bear the loss, no matter whose fault it is." In the law of torts, certain classes of persons are put on warning that, if they engage in certain ultra-hazardous activities, then they must be prepared to compensate any innocent parties who may incidentally be harmed, no matter how carefully and faultlessly the activities are carried out. There is always a risk of harm to others when one starts fires even on his own land, or keeps wild animals, or engages in blasting with high explosives. The law, of course, permits such activities, but it assigns the risk in advance to those who engage in them. This may seem to be a hard arrangement, since even if a construction company, for example, takes every reasonable precaution before dynamiting, it nevertheless can be found liable, if through some freakish chance a person at a great distance is injured by a flying rock set in motion by the blast, and can be forced to compensate the injured party for his losses. That the company was faultlessly careful in its operations is no defense. Still, this rule is by no means an arbitrary harassment, and its rigors are easily mitigated. The prospective responsibility imposed on blasters by law applies even to events beyond their control, but, *knowing this in advance* (an all-important consideration), they will be more careful than ever; and, further, they can guard against disastrous expenses by adjusting their prices and figuring compensation fees among their normal business costs.

Strict liability in the criminal law is much less likely to accord with reasonable standards of justice than in contracts and torts; but even penalties and punishments may, in certain circumstances, dispense with the requirement of fault, provided that prior assignments of risks are clear and that some degree of prior control is possible. Perhaps the best known strict liability statutes in the criminal law are those creating "public welfare offenses." Here the rationale for disregarding actual fault is similar, in part, to that supporting strict liability for ultra-hazardous activities in torts. All milk producers, for example, are put on notice by one statute that, if any of their marketed product is found to be adulterated, they will be subject to stiff penalty. The producers have the power and authority to regulate their own facilities, procedures, and employees. The law in effect tells them that, since there is such a paramount public interest in pure foods, they must give the public an unconditional guarantee of the purity of their product. If the guarantee fails, no questions will be asked about fault; the fine will be imposed automatically. Then it will be up to the company to exercise its control by locating and eliminating the fault. If this arrangement seems unfair, the company can be reminded that the risk is well known and is in fact the price producers pay for the privilege of serving the public for their own profit—a price they presumably have been quite willing to pay. Moreover, it really does protect the public by providing incentive to vigilant safety measures; and the penalties, in any case, are only fines. No perfectly innocent persons are sent to prison.

When criminal punishment involving imprisonment is involved, the case for strict liability, of course, is much weaker; but even here, in certain circumstances, the conviction of the "faultless" can sometimes be supported. Among serious crimes for which faultless ignorance ("reasonable mistake") is no excuse, the most celebrated example is the old English offense of taking an unmarried girl, under sixteen, from the possession of her father (for illicit purposes) without his consent. The rationale here, apparently, was that the harm done is so serious, and the opportunity and temptation so great, that any philanderer should be put on warning that, even if he has very good reason to believe his prey to be a thirty-year-old woman, he and he alone assumes the risk that she may be only fifteen—and a serious risk it is! The policy underlying the law was that philandery is a socially undesirable activity which it is the business of the law to discourage, but not the kind of moral offense that can properly (or practically) be prohibited absolutely. Hence young men are permitted to engage in it, but at their own peril. Understanding in advance where the risks lie, they will presumably be far more careful than they might otherwise be. The law here gives young sports a sporting chance. If they gamble and lose, even with the best of odds, they can blame no one but themselves. So interpreted, strict liability seems a relatively libertarian and humane means of social control.

In all the examples of plausibly just strict liability, the liable party must have had some control over his own destiny—some choice whether to take the risk assigned him by the law and some power to diminish the risk by his own care. When liability may be imposed even without such control, however, then it can "fall from the sky," like a plague, and land senselessly on complete strangers. Strict liability, when rational, is never totally unconditional and random.

Vicarious liability

Much, but by no means all, strict liability is also vicarious liability. There can be strict liability when *no one* is at fault, or where the question of contributory fault cannot be settled. There is vicarious liability, on the other hand, when the contributory fault, or some element of it, is properly ascribed to one party (or group of parties), but the liability is ascribed to a different party (or parties). In such cases we say that the latter party is responsible for the harmful consequences of a faulty action or omission of the former party. The person who did or caused the harm is not the one who is called upon to answer for it.

One familiar and surely unobjectionable type of vicarious liability is that which derives from the process of *authorization*. One party, called a "principal," authorizes another party, called the "agent," to act, within a certain range, for him. "He that acteth for another," wrote Hobbes, "is said to bear his person, or act in his name."[1] Acting in another's name is quite another thing than merely acting in his interests (also called "acting for him") or merely substituting for him, as an understudy, for example, replaces an indisposed actor (also called "acting in place of him"). An agent acts "for" or "in place of" his principal in a different sense. The agent is often given the right to act, speak, sign contracts, make appointments, or the like, and these acts are as binding on the principal as if he had done them himself. The relation of authorization, as Hanna Pitkin points out,[2] is lopsided: the rights go to the agent, and the responsibilities to the principal.

The relation of authorization can take two very different forms, depending on the degree of discretion granted to the agent, and there is a continuum of combinations between the extremes. On the one hand, there is the agent who is the mere "mouthpiece" of his principal. He is a "tool" in much the same sense as is a typewriter or telephone: he simply transmits the instructions of his principal. Thus messengers, delegates, spokesmen, typists, and amanuenses are sometimes called agents. Miss Pitkin points out that such persons are often called "mere agents," or (I might add) "bound agents" as opposed to "free agents."[3] The principal acts *through* his agent much as he might act through some mechanical medium. On the other hand, an agent may be some sort of expert hired to exercise his professional judgment on behalf of, and in the name of, the principal. He may be given, within some limited area of expertise, complete independence to act as he deems best, binding his principal to all the beneficial or detrimental consequences. This is the role played by trustees and some other investment managers, some lawyers, buyers, and ghost-writers. At the extreme of "free agency" is the Hobbesian sovereign; for each of his subjects has in effect authorized in advance *all* of his "actions and judgments . . . in the same manner, as if they were his own."[4]

It is often said that the very actions of agents themselves, and not merely their normative consequences, are directly ascribable to their principals, through "a kind of fiction";[5] but this, I submit, is a dangerously misleading way of talking. If *A* has *B*'s power of attorney, he may have the right to sign *B*'s signature; and if he signs it on a contract or a check, the pecuniary consequences may be exactly as they would be had *B* himself signed his name. The results are *as if B* had himself acted; but it is nevertheless true that *he* did not act—*A* acted for him. Even the Old Testament, which finds nothing objectionable in the vicarious criminal liability of children for the sins of their fathers, balks at the doctrine of literally transferred agency and causality. In Deuteronomy 24:16, Jeremiah and Ezekiel repeat that, if the fathers had eaten sour grapes, the children's teeth would not be set on edge (though if the fathers had *stolen* the grapes, the children, perhaps, would be punishable).

Another form of vicarious liability derives from the relation between superior and subordinate in hierarchical institutions, of which military organizations are perhaps the clearest model. At the lowest rank persons have no authority to command others and are responsible only for their own performances. Officers of the higher ranks have greater authority—that is, the right to command larger numbers of persons and make them "tools"—and correspondingly greater answerability for failures. A superior's failure may be the fault of some of his subordinates, but he must nevertheless answer for it to *his* superiors.

Subordinates, on the other hand, are not liable for the foolish or wicked commands of their superiors, since they are not "to reason why" but just to obey. In a way, a military hierarchy, then, can be viewed as a system of unidirectional vicarious liability. Something like it often exists in a less clear-cut form outside of military organizations. A recent press dispatch, for example, reports that there will no longer be automatic promotions of teachers in the Detroit public high schools and that teachers and principals will be held responsible for the academic performance of their students. Thus if students do poorly, their teachers will be "punished," and if they do well, their teachers will be rewarded. This liability is not entirely vicarious, of course, since there is presumably some causal connection between the teacher's performance and the students'; but it can approach pure vicarious liability when classes of students differ widely in ability. Its point, I think, is an interesting one, namely, to bolster the motivation of the *teachers*. (The students presumably do not care enough about the welfare of their teachers to be affected directly by the arrangement). In this respect, it is the very opposite of most forms of vicarious punishment (such as holding hostages, massive reprisals, family liability, blood feuds) whose point is to affect the motivation of the primary wrongdoers, not those who stand to be punished vicariously.

Another form of vicarious liability is the responsibility of employers ("masters") to compensate victims of the negligence or even, in some cases, the deliberate wrongdoing of their employees ("servants"), even when the employee is acting without, or in direct defiance of, the explicit orders of his boss, and the boss committed no negligence in hiring the employee in the first place, or in supervising, instructing, or outfitting him. Here, indeed, "the sins of the servant are visited upon the master." If my dog bites you, the biting is imputed to him, the liability to me.[6] Similarly, if the driver of my delivery truck, while doing his job, puts a dent in your fender or a crease in your skull, the liability to enforced compensation is mine, not his. (*His* liability is to *me*; he is now subject to being fired.) The rationale of this universal but once highly controverted practice is clear enough. If an accident victim has only a truck driver to sue, he may end up paying most of his disastrous medical expenses himself. The employer, having a "deeper pocket," is a more competent compensator; and, moreover, since he has *control* over the selection of employees for dangerous work, the rule will make him more careful in his assignment of tasks. It may be unfair to him to make him pay for an accident that was not his fault, but it would impose an even greater hardship and injustice to put the burden mainly on the shoulders of the equally faultless accident victim. And, again, there are means open to employers of anticipating and redistributing losses caused by their employees' negligence.

Still another form of vicarious liability derives from the relation of *suretyship*. A bonding company may insure an employer against the dishonesty of a new employee for a fee that may be paid by either employer or employee. If the employee commits embezzlement and makes his escape, the fault, guilt, agency, and causation all belong to the employee, but the liability to make good the losses is the innocent surety's. Similarly, the guarantor of another's debt pays if the other fails; and the poster of bail forfeits, if the bailed prisoner fails to make appearance.

Vicarious liability through authorization, hierarchy, mastership, and suretyship can thus be rational, in the sense that they rest on intellectually respectable, if not always convincing, rationales. Most of what has passed as vicarious criminal liability in human history is otherwise. Holmes traced the origin of both civil and criminal liability to certain animistic conceptions common to the Hebrews, Greeks, Romans, and Germans, and apparently to all human cultures at a certain stage in their development. The instrument of harm, whether it were a tool, a weapon, a tree, an ox, a slave, or a child, was regarded as the immediate and "natural" object of vengeance. It was "noxal," that is, accursed, and had to be forfeited to the victim, or his family, to be torn apart and annihilated. Later the principle of composition was adopted, and the owner of the noxal instrument could buy off its victim as an alternative to forfeiture. Nevertheless, in the early centuries of all major legal systems, inanimate objects and animals were "punished"; and the related practices of blood feud, noxal surrender, and substitute sacrifice flourished.

There are more refined forms of vicarious criminal liability for which a more plausible case can be made, although even these "rational" forms are rarely defensible as just. The imposition of punitive vicarious liability arrangements upon a community is always a desperate measure, justifiable at best only in extreme circumstances. I have in mind the taking of hostages by a wartime army of occupation (condemned by The Hague Convention of 1907 but practiced by Germans in two world wars) and stepped-up military reprisals for terrorism or atrocity directed at populations that surely include the innocent as well as the guilty. These cruel practices arouse angry resistance and thus tend to be self-defeating; and, in any case, they are examples of acts of war, rather than rules of a system of criminal law.

Could there be circumstances, in less desperate times, in which authorization, hierarchy, mastership, or suretyship, admittedly plausible bases for noncriminal liabilities, could also be the ground for criminal punishment? Under our present law, a principal will be coresponsible with his agent when the latter commits a criminal act at the former's direction or with his advance knowledge or subsequent ratification. The criminal punishment of superiors for actions done *entirely* on their own by subordinates, however, would be a barbarous regression in normal times. Criminal suretyship is a more difficult matter. I can imagine a voluntary system of suretyship that would permit fathers to arrange in advance to undergo punishment instead of their sons in case the latter committed crimes. Such a system could have some incidental merits among its preponderant disadvantages: deterrence and development of family solidarity. And it makes more sense than certain cosmic systems of criminal law in which the children answer for the sins of their fathers instead of the other way around.

There is an important point about all vicarious punishment: even when it is reasonable to separate liability from fault, it is only the liability that can be passed from one party to another. In particular, *there can be no such thing as vicarious guilt.* Guilt consists in the intentional transgression of a prohibition, "a violation of a specific taboo, boundary, or legal code, by a definite voluntary act."[7] In addition, the notion of guilt has always been essentially connected with the idea of "owing payment." The guilty party must "pay" for his sins, just as a debtor is one who must correct his moral imbalance by repayment. To be guilty is to be out of balance, or unredeemed, stained or impure. The root idea in guilt, then, is to be an appropriate person to make atonement, penance, or self-reproach, in virtue of having intentionally violated a commandment or prohibition. There have been extensions of this idea both through morbid superstition and natural analogy, but flawed intention, transgression, and needed atonement are still its central components.[8]

Now when an innocent man is punished for what a guilty man has done, he is treated *as if* he were himself guilty. There may be a rational point, and perhaps even justice, in certain circumstances, in doing this. Yet even though criminal liability can transfer or extend vicariously from a guilty to an innocent party, it obviously cannot be literally true that the guilt transfers as well. For guilt to transfer literally, action and intention too must transfer literally. But to say of an innocent man that he bears another's guilt is to say that he had one (innocent) intention and yet another (guilty) one, a claim which upon analysis turns out to be contradictory. I think that theologians and others have found it easy to talk of vicarious guilt only because the concept of guilt has always had the double sense of actual sin, on the one hand, and payment, atonement, redemption, and such, on the other; and of course it is at least logically intelligible for concepts of the latter kind to transfer. In short, liability can transfer, but not agency, causation, or fault (the components of "contributory fault"), and certainly not guilt.

Collective liability

In the remainder of this essay, we shall focus our attention on collective-responsibility arrangements. In principle, these can be justified in four logically distinct ways. Whole groups can be held liable even though not all of their members are at fault, in which case collective responsibility is still another form of liability without contributory fault similar to those discussed above; or, second, a group can be held collectively responsible through the fault, contributory or *noncontributory,* of each member; or, third, through the contributory fault of each and every member; or, finally, through the collective but *nondistributive* fault of the group itself. This section will be concerned only with the first of these forms, the collective liability that is one interesting subspecies of that vicarious liability which in turn is one interesting subspecies of strict liability.

Collective liability, as I shall use the term, is the vicarious liability of an organized group (either a loosely organized, impermanent collection or a corporate institution) for the actions of its constituent members. When the whole group as such is held responsible for the actions of one or some of its members, then, from the point of view of any given "responsible" individual, *his* liability in most cases will be vicarious.

Under certain circumstances, collective liability is a natural and prudent way of arranging the affairs of an organization, which the members might well be expected to undertake themselves, quite voluntarily. This expectation applies only to those organizations (usually small ones) where there is already a high degree of *de facto* solidarity. Collective responsibility not only expresses the solidarity but also strengthens it; thus it is a good thing to whatever extent the preexistent solidarity was a good thing. Where prior solidarity is absent, collective liability arrangements may seek their justification through the desperate prior *need* for solidarity.

When does a group have "solidarity"? Three intertwined conditions,

I think, must be satisfied to some degree. There has to be first of all, a large *community of interest* among all the members, not merely a specific overlap of shared specialized interests, of the sort that unite the members of a corporation's board of directors, for example, no matter how strong. A community of interest exists between two parties to the extent that each party's integrated set of interests contains as one of its components the integrated interest-set of the other. Obviously, this will be difficult to arrange in large and diverse groups. A husband, for example, might have as his main interests (whose fulfillment as a harmonious set constitutes his *well-being*) his health, his material possessions, his professional reputation, his professional achievement, *and* the well-being (also defined in terms of an integrated set of interests) of his wife and his children. His interests would thus include or contain the interests of several other people. If those other persons' interests, in a precisely similar way, were to embrace his, then there would be between them a perfect community of interest. Secondly, such "community" is often associated with bonds of sentiment directed toward common objects, or of reciprocal affection between the parties. (R. B. Perry defined "love" as an interest in the interests of someone else). Thirdly, solidarity is ordinarily a function of the degree to which the parties share a common lot, the extent to which their goods and harms are necessarily collective and indivisible. When a father is jailed, his whole family shares the disgrace and the loss of his provisions. There is no hurting one member without hurting them all; and because of the way their interests are related, the successes and satisfactions of one radiate their benefits to the others.

Individuals normally pool their liabilities when they share a common cooperative purpose, and each recognizes in the others complementary abilities of a useful or necessary kind. Thus salesmen combine with administrators to become business partners, pooling their talents and sharing their risks. Joint authorships are often cases of mutual ghost-writing, where each party stands answerable for the joint product of their several labors. Athletic team members must all win or all lose together: victory is not the prize of individual merit alone, nor is defeat linked to "contributory fault." Similarly, in underground conspiracies and desperate dangerous undertakings, the spirit of "all for one and one for all" is not merely a useful device; it is imposed by the very nature of the enterprise. What makes collective liability natural in such cases is that parties who are largely of one mind to begin with are led (or forced) by circumstances to act in concert and share the risk of common failure or the fruits of an indivisible success.

There have been times in the history of civilization when group solidarity was a more common thing, and more easily arranged, than today. In many places, including Northern Europe, the ultimate unit of legal responsibility has been not the individual, but the clan, the kinship group, or the immediate family; and only a couple of centuries ago the English common law still applied to married couples the "fiction of conjugal unity." Only since the passage of Married Women's Acts in the 1840's have married women in America had a legal identity separate, in many kinds of legal situations, from that of their husbands. The world has without a doubt been getting steadily more individualistic in this respect, and it is no wonder. Change is faster, leading at any given time to more continual novelty and consequent greater diversity. Political parties, religious groups, and fraternal associations can no longer count on perfect uniformity and general solidarity across a whole spectrum of attitudes and convictions. And how much harder it is today to be a marriage broker (even with computers) than in other more static ages, when persons were more easily interchangeable and common values could be taken for granted!

De facto solidarity, then, is less easily come by today, even within small family groups. And because it is, there is no longer much point in treating a wife, for example, as part of a single corporate person with her husband. Wives today can own their own property, bargain and trade with their husbands, sign contracts on their own, and sue and be sued in their own names. Still, some of the conditions making for *de facto* solidarity (such as the common lot, and indivisible goods and evils) are necessarily present in every marriage; and when these are reinforced by shared or contained interests and mutual affection, the solidarity that renders joint liabilities reasonable will also be present. When fates are shared, they must be pooled in any case. Where the plural possessive "our" more naturally comes to the lips than the singular "mine," then to enter joint bank accounts and other forms of collective liability is only to certify the given and destroy artificial inconvenience.

There is perhaps no better index to solidarity than vicarious pride and shame. These attitudes occur most frequently in group members on behalf of the larger group, or of some other member(s) of the larger group, of which they are a part. Individuals sometimes feel proud or ashamed of their families, ancestors, countries, or races; and all or most of those who belong to groups may feel pride or shame over the achievements or failures of single members of their groups. Some writers have in effect denied that pride (and presumably shame) can ever be authentically vicarious; and there is no doubt that the appearance of vicariousness can often be explained away. Parental pride in the achievements of a son may be the consequence of a belief that those achievements reflect the influence of the parent, so that it is really pride at "what I have created in my son." This sort of interpretation may be possible in some cases, but it obviously cannot explain the son's filial pride in the achievements of his parents or grandparents. In this connection, H. D. Lewis speaks of "the presumption that we ourselves, having been subject to the same influences, are not without a measure of the qualities for which others of our group are noted."[9] No doubt many occurrences of filial pride and shame can be traced to this source, but clearly it cannot account for the immigrant's pride in the "American way of life" or the war opponent's feeling ashamed "to wear the same uniform" as those he believes have committed atrocities. Of course, the latter may be something different from shame, namely, mortification at being associated by others with actions of which one disapproves and of which one is totally innocent. Normal embarrassment, like pride at what one has helped others to do or be and pride over one's qualities presumptively shared with conspicuously worthy other persons, is a self-centered attitude; an authentically vicarious feeling, if there can be such a thing, must be based on the doings or qualities of others considered entirely on their own account, unrelated to any doings or qualities of the principal.

H. D. Lewis provides a clue when he speaks of the phenomenon of sympathetic identification: "Our interest in those with whom we have special ties of affection will enable us to follow their success with a glow of satisfaction as if it were our own."[10] If this is what authentically vicarious pride is like, it is a phenomenon of the same order as sympathetic pain or compassion. Indeed, any feeling one person can experience can be experienced vicariously by some other imaginatively sensitive person. What we want, however, is not so much an account of vicarious or imaginative *sharing* alone as an account that will also apply to vicarious unshared or substitute feeling. Here too sympathy, I think, is the key. When someone near to me, about whom I care, makes a fool of himself before others, I can feel embarrassed for him, even though he feels no such thing himself. Yet when some total stranger or some person I despise behaves similarly, my reaction will be indifference or pity or contempt—reactions that are not vicarious. Compare "I am proud (or ashamed) because of you" with "I am proud (or ashamed) for you." The former is like taking partial credit (or blame); the latter is like congratulating (or condemning) from an internal or sympathetic judgment point. We are inclined to congratulate (or "condemn fraternally") only when we feel some degree of solidarity with the other parties. The solidarity is a necessary condition of the vicarious emotion, which is in turn an index to the solidarity.

I think this account helps explain some puzzling variations. It is natural, for example, that an American Negro should feel solidarity with all other Negroes and speak of what has been done to "the black man" by "the white man" and what the moral relations between "the" black man (all black men) and "the" white man (all white men) ought to be. But I, for one, am quite incapable of feeling the same kind of solidarity with all white men, a motley group of one billion persons who are, in my mind, no more an "organization" than is the entire human race as such. I certainly feel no bonds to seventeenth-century slave traders analogous to those ties of identification an American Negro must naturally feel with the captured slaves. Precisely because of this failure of imagination, I can feel no shame on *their* behalf. Similarly, a European, appalled by American foreign policy, will feel anger or despair, but not vicarious shame unless he has some sentimental attachment to the United States. An American with like views will be ashamed of his country. Indeed, one cannot be intensely ashamed of one's country unless one also loves it.

Collective-responsibility arrangements are most likely to offend our modern sensibilities when the liabilities are to criminal punishment. Yet there was a time when primitive conditions required that the policing function be imposed on local groups themselves through a system of *compulsory universal suretyship*. Among the early Anglo-Saxons, the perfectly trustworthy man was he who did not stray from the village where his many kin resided, for they were his sureties who could guarantee his good conduct. In contrast, the stranger far from his kindred had nothing to restrain him, and since his death would excite no blood feud, he had no legal protection against the assaults of others.[11] With the development of Christian feudalism, the ancient system of kindred liability broke down, for churchmen without kin or local tie began to appear among suspicious villagers, and "as time went on, many men who for one reason or another moved away from their original environments and sought their fortunes elsewhere . . . could not depend on ties of kindred to make them law-worthy and reputable."[12] Hence a new system of compulsory suretyship, based on neighborhood rather than kin was developed. Everyone was *made* "law-worthy and reputable" by being assigned to a neighborhood group every member of which was an insurer of his conduct. If an offender was not produced by his surety group to answer criminal charges, a fine was levied on each member of the group, and sometimes liability to make compensation as well.

Now this may strike us as a barbarous expedient of a primitive people who had no conception of individual justice; but I think that is too severe a judgment. The frank-pledge system was a genuine system of criminal law: there was nothing arbitrary, *ad hoc,* or *ex post facto* about it. It was also a system of compulsory group self-policing in an age when there were no professional police. Moreover, it reinforced a preexisting group solidarity the like of which cannot occur in an era of rapid movement like our own. And most important, the system worked; it prevented violence and became generally accepted as part of the expected natural order of things.

Yet surely there is no going back to this kind of collective responsibility. H. Gomperz concluded an essay by claiming: "that men can be held responsible solely for individual conduct freely willed is certainly wrong; it mistakes a principle characteristic of individualistic ages for an eternal law of human nature."[13] I agree that the principle of individual responsibility is not an "eternal law"; but Gomperz misleadingly suggests a kind of historical relativism according to which individualistic and collectivistic ages alternate like styles in ladies' skirts. On the contrary, the changes that have come with modern times have dictated quite inevitably that the one principle replace the other, and no "alternation" is remotely foreseeable, unless massive destruction forces the human race to start all over again in tiny isolated farming settlements. Under modern conditions the surety system would not work in the intended way, for the surety groups, being subject to rapid turnover, would lack the necessary cohesion and solidarity to exert much influence or control over their members. It is more difficult now to keep a watchful eye on our neighbors, since we no longer spend the better part of every day working in adjacent fields with them. Moreover, we no longer impose a duty on all citizens to raise the hue and cry upon discovery of a crime, drop their work, arm themselves, and join the hunt, on pain of penalty to their whole surety group. Now we say that detection and pursuit of criminals is the policeman's job. He gets paid for it, not us; and he is much more able to do it well. Besides, we all have other things to do.

But we have paid a price in privacy, which will get steadily stiffer, for the principle of individual criminal responsibility. The technical devices that make modern police work possible are reaching the point where they will make inspection of every person's life and history possible only minutes after a police official desires it. In olden times a man could not wonder for long whether he was his neighbor's keeper, for the voice of authority would instruct him unmistakably that he'd damn well better be. Today we prefer not to become involved in the control of crime, with the result that those who are charged with the control of crime become more and more involved with us.

In summary, collective criminal liability imposed on groups as a mandatory self-policing device is reasonable only when there is a very high degree of antecedent group solidarity and where efficient professional policing is unfeasible. Furthermore, justice requires that the system be part of the expected background of the group's way of life and that those held vicariously liable have some reasonable degree of *control* over those for whom they are made sureties. It is because these conditions are hardly ever satisfied in modern life, and not because individual liability is an eternal law of reason, that collective criminal responsibility is no longer an acceptable form of social organization.

So much for collective responsibility as a form of *liability without fault*. People often have other models in mind, however, when they speak of "collective responsibility."

Liability with noncontributory fault

Various faults can exist in the absence of any causal linkage to harm, where that absence is only a lucky accident reflecting no credit on the person who is at fault. Where every member of a group shares the same fault, but only one member's fault leads to any harm, and that not because it was more of a fault than that of the others, but only because of independent fortuities, many outsiders will be inclined to ascribe collective liability to the whole group. Other outsiders may deny the propriety of holding even a faulty or guilty person liable for harm that was not "his fault"; but for a group member himself to take this public stand would be an unattractive piece of self-righteousness. It would be more appropriate for him to grieve, and voluntarily make what amends he can, than to insist stubbornly on the noncontributory character of his fault, which was a matter of pure lucky chance.

In this kind of situation we have a handy model for the interpretation of extravagant hyperboles about universal responsibility. One man drinks heavily at a party and then drives home at normal (high) speeds, injuring a pedestrian along the way. The claim that we are all guilty of this crime, interpreted in a certain way, is only a small exaggeration, for it is a very common practice, in which perhaps *most* of us participate, to drive above posted speed limits at night and also to drive in our usual fashion to and from parties at which we drink. Most of us are "guilty" of this practice, although only the motorist actually involved in the accident is guilty of the resultant injury. He is guilty *of* or *for* more than we are, and more harm is his fault; but it does not necessarily follow that he is more guilty or more at fault than the rest of us.

Now there are some character faults that are present to some, though not the same, degree in almost everyone. These flaws sometimes cause enormous amounts of harm. There is some point in saying that all those who share the flaws, even those who have had no opportunity to do mischief by them, are "responsible" when harm results, in the sense that they are morally no better than those whose fault contributed to the harm and are, therefore, properly answerable for the way they are, if only to their own consciences. There is even a point in the exaggeration that ascribes the common fault to everyone without exception, when in fact there are exceptions; for this may serve to indicate that serious and dangerous faults are far more common than is generally believed and may exist in the least suspected places. Since character flaws are dispositions to act or feel in improper ways in circumstances of various kinds, we may never know of a given man that he has the fault in question until circumstances of the appropriate kind arise; and they may never arise.

Can liability of the noncontributorily faulty be morally palatable? Criminal punishment of whole groups of fault-sharers would for a dozen reasons be impracticable. We have no way of confirming statements about what a man with a given character structure would do if the circumstances were different; so if we are determined to avoid punishing the genuinely faultless, we had better wait until the circumstances *are* different. In any case, the larger and more diverse the group of alleged fault-sharers, the less likely it is that they all share—or share to anything like the same degree—the fault in question. If, nevertheless, the fault is properly ascribed distributively to a group of great size, the probability increases that the fault is common also to judge, jury, and prosecutor. Moral uncertainties of this kind are not likely to be present when we have evidence linking the fault of an individual to some harmful upshot. Those luckier ones who share the fault but escape the causal link to harm must, from the point of view of criminal justice, simply be left to profit from their luck. But when we leave political-legal contexts, the case for causation as a necessary condition of liability weakens considerably. The law will neither punish *B* nor force him to compensate *C* for the harm caused by *A*'s fault, when *B* is as prone as *A* to the fault in question; but that is no reason why private individuals should refrain from censuring or snubbing *B* to the same extent as *A*, or why *B* should not hold himself to account.

Contributory group fault: collective and distributive

Sometimes we attribute liability to a whole group because of the contributory fault of each and every member. Group responsibility, so conceived, is simply the sum of all the individual responsibility. Since each individual is coresponsible for the harm in question, no one's responsibility is vicarious. Nevertheless, problems are raised by three kinds of situations: first, where large numbers of people are independently at fault without any concert or communication between them; second, where the harm is caused by a joint undertaking of numerous persons acting cooperatively; and, third, where the harm is to be ascribed to some feature of the common culture consciously endorsed and participated in by every member of the group.

Suppose a man swimming off a public beach that lacks a professional lifeguard shouts for help in a voice audible to a group of one thousand accomplished swimmers lolling on the beach; and yet no one moves to help him, and he is left to drown. The traditional common law imposes no liability, criminal or civil, for the harm in this kind of case. Among the reasons often given are that, if liability were imposed on one, it would, in all consistency, have to be imposed on the whole vast group and that, if a duty to rescue drowning swimmers were imposed on every accomplished swimmer in a position to help, the results would be confusing and chaotic, with hoards of rescuers getting in each other's way and no one quite sure he is not violating the law by not entering the struggle quickly and ardently enough. On the other hand, so the argument goes, if each feels a duty to mitigate the dangerous confusion, there could be an Alphonse-Gaston exchange of courteous omissions on a large and tragic scale. This rationale has always seemed disingenuous to me. I see no reason why legal duties should not correspond here with moral ones: each has a duty to attempt rescue so long as no more than a few others have already begun their efforts. In short, everyone should use his eyes and his common sense and cooperate as best he can. If no one makes any motion at all, it follows that no one has done his best within the limits imposed by the situation, and *all* are subject at least to blame. Since all could have rescued the swimmer, it is true of each of them that, but for *his* failure to attempt rescue in the circumstances that in fact obtained, the harm would not have occurred. It may be awkward to charge all one thousand persons with criminal responsibility, but the difficulties would be no greater than those involved in prosecuting a conspiracy of equal size. As for civil liability, the problems are even less impressive: the plantiff (widow) should simply be allowed to choose her own defendants from among the multitudes who were at fault—those, no doubt, with the "deepest pockets."

The second kind of case exemplifying group fault distributable to each member is that where the members are all privy to a crime or tort as conspirators or accomplices or joint tortfeasors. In complicated crimes, *complicity* is ascribed unavoidably to persons whose degree of participation in the crime is unequal. The common law, therefore, divides guilty felons into four categories, namely, "perpetrators," "abettors," "inciters" (all three of these are "accomplices"), and "criminal protectors," so that one may be guilty of a given crime either as its principal perpetrator (and even perpetration is a matter of degree, abettors counting as "principals in the second degree") or as accessories, that is, inciters or protectors. Thus one can be guilty, as an accessory, even of crimes that one is not competent to perpetrate. A woman, for example, may be found guilty of rape, as an abettor or inciter to the man, who must, of course, be the principal perpetrator of the crime on some other woman.

Suppose *C* and *D* plan a bank robbery, present their plan to a respected friend *A*, receive his encouragement, borrow weapons from *B* for the purpose, hire *E* as getaway driver, and then execute the plan. Pursued by the police, they are forced to leave their escape route and take refuge at the farm of *E*'s kindly uncle *F*. *F* congratulates them, entertains them hospitably, and sends them on their way with his blessing. *F*'s neighbor *G* learns of all that has happened, disapproves, but does nothing. Another neighbor, *H*, learns of it but is bribed into silence. On these facts *A, B, C, D, E,* and *F* are all guilty of the bank robbery—*C* and *D* as perpetrators, *A* and *B* as inciters,[14] *E* as an abettor, and *F* as a protector. *G* is guilty of the misdemeanor called "misprision of felony," and *H* of the misdemeanor called "compounding a felony." On the other hand, if *J*, an old acquaintance of *C* and *D*, sees them about to enter the bank, notices suspicious bulges in their pockets, surmises that they are up to no good, yet does nothing out of simple reluctance to "get involved," he is not legally guilty. Yet he is certainly subject to blame; and, as moralists, we might decide this marginal case differently than the lawyers and brand him a kind of "moral accessory" before the fact, "morally guilty," though to a lesser degree than the others. We can afford to have stricter standards of culpability than the lawyers, since no formal punishment will follow as a result of *our* verdicts and we do not have to worry about procedural complexities.

Part of the problem of determining degrees of responsibility of individuals in joint undertakings, where the responsibility is not vicarious, is assessing the extent of each individual's *contribution* to the undertaking. This involves assessment of various incommensurable dimensions of contribution—degrees of initiative, difficulty or causal crucialness of assigned subtasks, degrees of authority, percentage of derived profit, and so on. Although these matters cannot be settled in any mathematical way, rough and ready answers suggest themselves to common sense, and the legal categories of complicity have proved quite workable. The more difficult problems require estimates of *voluntariness*. Do I carry my own share of "moral guilt" for the Vietnamese abomination as a consequence of my payment of war taxes? Is my position morally analogous to that of *B*, the "inciter" in the bank robbery example? In avoiding protest demonstrations, am I guilty of "cooperating" with evil, perhaps on the model of *J, F, G,* or *H?* The answers to those questions are difficult, I think, not because the (minute) extent of my causal contribution is not easily measurable, but because it is difficult to know how strict should be the standards of voluntariness for cases like this. Since nonpayment of taxes is a crime, the payment of war taxes is less than fully voluntary. To go to prison merely to avoid being associated, however indirectly, with some evil is to adopt the heroic path. The man who "cooperates" with crime under duress is surely in a different position from the man who cooperates, like *H,* as a result of a bribe or, like *J,* out of sloth or cowardice. Yet whether the threat of legal punishment is sufficient duress to excuse "cooperation" with authorities again depends on numerous factors, including the degree of the evil and the probabilities of its alleviation with and without the contemplated resistance. In any case, mere nonresistance does not count as "cooperation" unless various other conditions are fulfilled. Where those conditions are conspicuously unfulfilled, as in Nazi Germany, then nonresistance is entirely involuntary, since its only alternative is pointless self-sacrifice.

The third interesting case of distributive group fault is that which adheres to a group's folkways yet somehow reflects upon every member of the group. Even Dwight Macdonald concedes that there are "folk activities" that a group "takes spontaneously and as a whole . . . which are approved by the popular mores" and which are not merely "things done by sharply differentiated sub-groups."[15] Nazi acts of violence against Jews, Macdonald argued, were not genuine folk activities in this sense. In contrast, the constant and widespread acts of violence "against Negroes throughout the South, culminating in lynchings, may be considered real 'people's actions,' for which the Southern whites bear collective responsibility [because] the brutality . . . is participated in, actively or with passive sympathy, by the entire white community."[16] The postbellum Southern social system, now beginning to crumble, was contrived outside of political institutions and only winked at by the law. Its brutalities were "instrumentalities for keeping the Negro in his place and maintaining the supraordinate position of the white caste."[17] Does it follow from this charge, however, that "Southern whites [*all* Southern whites] bear collective responsibility?" I assume that ninety-nine percent of them, having been shaped by the prevailing mores, wholeheartedly approved of these brutalities. But what of the remaining tiny fraction? If they are to be held responsible, they must be so vicariously, on the ground of their strong (and hardly avoidable) solidarity with the majority. But suppose a few hated their Southern tradition, despised their neighbors, and did not think of themselves as Southerners at all? Then perhaps Macdonald's point can be saved by excluding these totally alienated souls altogether from the white Southern community to which Macdonald ascribes collective responsibility. But total alienation is not likely to be widely found in a community that leaves its exit doors open; and, in a community with as powerful social enforcement of mores as the traditional Southern one, the alienated resident would be in no happier a position than the Negro. Collective responsibility, therefore, might be ascribed to all those whites who were not outcasts, taking respectability and material comfort as evidence that a given person did not qualify for the exemption.

Contributory group fault: collective but not distributive

There are some harms that are ascribable to group faults but not to the fault of every, or even *any,* individual member. Consider the case of the Jesse James train robbery. One armed man holds up an entire car full of passengers. If the passengers had risen up as one man and rushed at the robber, one or two of them, perhaps, would have been shot; but collectively they would have overwhelmed him, disarmed him, and saved their property. Yet they all meekly submitted. How responsible were they for their own losses? Not very. In a situation like this, only *heroes* could be expected to lead the self-sacrificial charge, so no individual in the group was at fault for not resisting. The whole group, however, had it within its power to resist successfully. Shall we say, then, that the group was collectively but not distributively at fault? Can the responsibility of a group be more than the sum of the responsibility of its members? There is surely a point in affirming so. There was, after all, a flaw in the way the group of passengers was organized (or unorganized) that made the robbery possible. And the train robbery situation is a model for a thousand crises in the history of our corporate lives. No individual person can be blamed for not being a hero or a saint (what a strange "fault" that would be!), but a whole people can be blamed for not producing a hero when the times require it, especially when the failure can be charged to some discernible element in the group's "way of life" that militates against heroism.

One would think that, where group fault is nondistributive, group liability must be so too, lest it fall vicariously on individual members who are faultless. But, for all overt unfavorable responses, group liability is inevitably distributive: what harms the group as a whole necessarily harms its members. Hence if the conditions of justifiable collective liability—group solidarity, prior notice, opportunity for control, and so on—are not satisfied, group liability would seem unjustified.

An exception, however, is suggested by the case where an institutional group persists through changes of membership and faultless members must answer for harms caused, or commitments made, by an earlier generation of members. Commitments made in the name of an organized group may persist even after the composition of the group and its "will" change. When, nevertheless, the group reneges on a promise, the fault may be that of no individual member, yet the liability for breach of contract, falling on the group as a whole, will distribute burdens quite unavoidably on faultless members. Consider the philosophy department which debated whether to pass a graduate student on his preliminary examinations. The main argument against doing so was that passing him would commit the department to the supervision of the student's dissertation, and no one who knew this particular student was willing to read his thesis. The affirmative carried when two members volunteered to direct the dissertation themselves. One year later, however, one of these sponsors died, and the other took employment elsewhere. Thus *no member* was willing to supervise this student, and the department as a whole had to renege on its promise. No member felt personally bound by the promises of his departed colleagues, which had been made to the student in no one's name but the department's. No legal action, of course, was possible; but if the department had been *forced* to honor its word, this would have been an excellent example of nondistributive group fault (the departmental reneging) and consequent group liability of a necessarily distributive kind.

There is a different sense of "responsibility," and an important one, in which groups can be responsible collectively and distributively for traits (including faulty traits) in the group structure and history that can be ascribed to no given individual as their cause. Sigmund Freud[18] once raised the question whether individuals are "responsible" for their dreams and then astonishingly answered the question in the affirmative. Freud did not mean, however, that dreams are intentionally *acted out* or *caused* by the dreamer, or that they are, in any sense, the dreamer's *fault,* or that the dreamer is *liable* to censure or punishment or to self-directed remorse or guilt for them. What he did mean was that a person's dreams represent him faithfully in that they reveal in some fundamental way what sort of person he is. Freud was denying that dreams are "the meaningless product of disordered mental activity" or the work of "alien spirits." Rather, they have genuine psychological significance. Hence everyone must "take responsibility" for his dreams and not disown or repudiate them; and this is simply to "own up" to even the unpretty aspects of one's self as truly one's own.

Those who have read such works as Richard Hofstadter's *Paranoid Style in American Politics*[19] can hardly fail to be struck by the similarity between the social historian's revelations about the nation and the psychoanalyst's revelations about the individual. Both dredge up experiences from the past that are held to reveal persisting dispositions, trends, and "styles" of response that might otherwise be unknown to the subject. To deny the reality or significance of the child that still lives in the man, or of the early settlers whose imprint is still upon the nation, is to "deny responsibility" for traits that are truly one's own. When a nation's voices fail to acknowledge its own inherited character, the possibilities of understanding and rational control are just so far diminished, and the consequences for faultless individual citizens (as for the neurotically benighted individual in the other case) can be devastating. But the responsibility I mention here is no kind of agency, causation, fault, or liability; it would less misleadingly, though somewhat awkwardly, be called "representational attributability."

Notes

1. *Leviathan,* ed. Michael Oakeshott (Oxford: Basil Blackwell, 1946), Part I, Ch. 16, 105.

2. *The Concept of Representation* (Berkeley and Los Angeles: University of California Press, 1967), 19.

3. *Ibid.,* 122.

4. *Leviathan,* Part 2, Ch. 18, 113.

5. The limits of "fictitious attribution" (the phrase is from Hobbes) are clearly marked out by A. Phillips Griffiths in "How Can One Person Represent Another?", *Proceedings of the Aristotelian Society,* Supp. 34 (1960), 187–224, and by Pitkin, *op.cit.,* 49–54.

6. W. D. Falk, "Intention, Motive and Responsibility," *Proceedings of the Aristotelian Society,* Supp. 19 (1945), 249.

7. H. M. Lynd, *On Shame and the Search for Identity* (New York: Science Editions, 1961), 23.

8. I have been discussing guilt in the sense of one very special way of being *at fault*. Guilt, in this sense, is usually a necessary condition for guilt in a different sense, namely, that of "criminal liability." The model of guilt in the latter sense is the legal condition brought into existence by an authoritatively pronounced verdict in a criminal court. Guilt in this sense is analogous to the state of civil liability also created by authoritative judicial pronouncement as the end product of a civil suit. To be guilty in the sense of criminally liable is to be properly subject to the imposition of punitive sanctions, just as to be civilly liable is to be properly subject to legal pressure to make pecuniary compensation for harm. To call a man guilty of a crime is either to report that he has been authoritatively pronounced guilty or else to express one's own quite unofficial opinion that the conditions of criminal liability have in fact been satisfied so that an official verdict of "guilty" is or was called for.

Almost always in criminal law the *conditions* of criminal liability (i.e., of "guilt" in one sense) include the requirement that the defendant intentionally acted (or omitted to act) in a way proscribed (or enjoined) by law (i.e., that he was guilty in the other, "at fault" sense of "guilt"). But there is no conceptual necessity that intentional transgression be a condition of guilt (liability). There is no logical contradiction in the rule that permitted German citizens to be found "guilty" of having a Jewish grandparent, or in the rule that makes even bellhops guilty of "possessing" drugs when they carry a hotel guest's bags to his room, or in rules permitting the punishment of "criminal negligence," or in rules creating "strict liability" in criminal law. In Shirley Jackson's famous short story "The Lottery," the "winner" of an annual lottery is customarily stoned to death by his neighbors. The absurdity of calling the randomly selected sacrificial victim "guilty," I submit, is a moral, not a logical or conceptual, absurdity. The condition of criminal liability in this case is not so much being at fault as being unlucky; but, in the sense of "guilt" under consideration, there is no contradiction in saying that a defendant was faultless but guilty nevertheless, providing he satisfied the conditions for liability specified by some rule. The only limit to the possibility of guilt in this sense is the requirement that there be *some conditions or other* for guilt; but the conditions need not include any kind of fault.

9. "Collective Responsibility," *Philosophy,* 23 (1948), 7 (this anthology, p. 22).

10. *Ibid.,* 8 (this anthology, p. 22).

11. L. T. Hobhouse, *Morals in Evolution* (London: Chapman & Hall, 1951), 81.

12. S. B. Chrimes, *English Constitutional History* (London: Oxford University Press, 1953), 77.

13. "Individual, Collective, and Social Responsibility," *Ethics,* 69 (1943), 342.

14. "An inciter . . . is one who, with *mens rea,* aids, counsels, commands, procures, or encourages another to commit a crime, or with *mens rea,* supplies him with the weapons, tools, or information needed for his criminal purpose." Rollin M. Perkins, *Criminal Law* (Brooklyn: The Foundation Press, 1957), 558.

15. *Memoirs of a Revolutionist* (New York: Meridian, 1958), 45.

16. *Loc.cit.* (written in 1945).

17. John Dollard, *Caste and Class in a Southern Town,* as quoted *ibid.,* 45.

18. See *The Collected Papers of Sigmund Freud,* ed. Philip Rieff, BS 189 V, *Therapy and Technique* (New York: Collier Books, 1963), 223–226.

19. (New York: Alfred A. Knopf, 1965.)

5

Morality and Collective Liability

Howard McGary
1986

Discussions of pressing moral issues in the Western World generally are based upon a morality that primarily is concerned with the relationships between individuals. This moral outlook focuses on the rights of individuals and the good society's role in protecting those rights. However, some writers believe there is a moral system that concentrates on the rights of groups and our responsibility to protect group rights.[1]

Critics of the position that we should focus on groups as well as individuals when we attribute moral liability believe that when we do so we adopt a form of tribalism.[2] Their reluctance to focus on groups is due partially to the fact that in the past people were unjustly discriminated against because they were considered to be members of a dangerous, inferior or undesirable group. The Fourteenth Amendment of the U.S. Constitution is interpreted by these critics as endorsing the position that each individual should be judged exclusively on his own merits. In other words, it vests rights in individuals. With similar reasoning, these critics also conclude that concentrating on groups rather than individuals is inappropriate because it will cause the innocent members of groups to suffer and it will reopen the door to the kind of discrimination experienced by racial minorities and other oppressed groups.

Nonetheless, the system of morality that concentrates upon individuals rather than groups is now under seige from those groups who have been frustrated by a long history of oppression and injustice. Group demands and group solidarity on the part of racial minorities and women are, in part, a practical response to a continued discrimination against these groups. Racial minorities, women, and other groups have felt that in order to alleviate their problems as individuals, they also must press claims for their group. Sometimes the opponents of assigning moral concepts to groups associate group solidarity or group identification with separatist movements, be they feminist, racial, or religious, but they are often wrong when they do so because most of the demands of racial minorities and women are not separatist demands. Historically, the goals of these groups have been orientated towards integration into the socioeconomic system rather than separation. But even with this noted, there is still strong opposition against applying moral concepts like blame, praise, and liability to groups as a whole.

I

The aspect of collective liability that has received a great deal of attention can be stated in terms of the following question: can all the members of a group be held morally liable if only some of its members' actions have been faulty? There have been two responses by those who have defended collective liability. One group has argued that, under certain conditions, each member of a group may be held liable even if only some of the group's members' actions have been morally wrong or negligent. They believe that where some just or noble goal will be served by holding all the members of a group morally liable, we are warranted in doing so. According to these critics, we should hold each or most members of the group in question liable even though the fit is not perfect between those members of the group who have wronged others, and those who actually are held to be morally liable. The imperfect fit is excused as an administrative convenience,[3] because attempts to improve the fit would involve drawbacks that would outweigh the good done.

Others have argued that simply being a member of a group can justify liability. In its most severe form proponents of this position conclude from the judgment that S is a member of Group G that S is morally liable for the faulty actions of any member of G. They see the fit as perfect.[4]

Both approaches and conclusions are inadequate. Judgments about the liability of individual members of a group are not logically deducible from judgments about the liability of the group as a whole.[5] It would take additional reasons to warrant such a judgment. It is also unjust to hold a person morally liable on the grounds of administrative convenience if the agent's behavior was not faulty or negligent.

The problem of collective liability, as I see it, is to state and defend the conditions under which moral agents can be held morally liable for "practices" that they themselves did not directly engage in. I shall state and defend these conditions . I should stress that this paper does not address the issue of whether or not, all things considered, restitution should be paid to those who are the victims of unjust practices. My aim is to show that moral liability exists in such cases and that a claim for restitution by the victims can not be rejected simply on the ground that no moral liability exists.

On the account of collective liability I shall develop here, we will focus on "practices" rather than particular faulty individual or group actions. By a practice I shall mean a commonly accepted course of action that may be over time habitual in nature; a course of action that specifies certain forms of behavior as permissable and others as impermissible with rewards and penalties assigned accordingly. An example of an unjust racial practice involving blacks and whites is blockbusting—a practice where a realtor sells a home in an all-white neighborhood to a black family at a price below market value because he knows that this will cause white families to move and allow him to sell their homes to blacks at a handsome profit.

I use the term practice in a way that a number of collective actions are practices, but it should be noted that not every practice is a collective action. This is so because in order for a set of actions to constitute a collective action there must be certain interrelationships among the members of the set and this is not always the case with a practice.

My critics might object to a moral agent being morally liable for a practice on the grounds that one can not be liable for the practice itself since a practice is a type rather than a token.[6] I will agree if their point is that one can be morally liable for something that has no causal effects, but at the same time point out that a person can be morally liable for a practice in virtue of being morally liable for something that does have causal effects, i.e., instituting a practice, refraining from disassociating oneself from a practice, etc.

II

When Joel Feinberg wrote his influential essay, "Collective Responsibility," in 1968,[7] the United States was in the midst of the Civil

Rights Movement and the Vietnam War. Some commentators believed that Americans as a whole should be held morally responsible for war atrocities and that southern whites, as a group, were responsible for the systematic discrimination suffered by blacks. After careful analysis Feinberg concludes that there is no moral justification for collective responsibility as a form of collective liability in such cases.[8]

His discussion of collective responsibility is motivated by the belief that there are various kinds of responsibility; some of which don't entail any kind of official action or liability. He says "to be morally responsible for some thing or action is to be liable not to overt responses, but to a charging against one's record as a man."[9] This leads him to reject collective moral responsibility as a type of collective liability in the two cases above because some white southerners and some Americans can at most be described as responsible in the sense of a stain on their records as persons, but not in the sense of making them liable to overt responses.

He is right that given our present requirements for legal liability it is doubtful that all southern whites could be held legally liable for the negative consequences of racial discrimination in the south, and that all Americans could be held legally liable for disasterous effects of the Vietnam war. However, I disagree with his contention that there is no sense of moral liability that entails overt official responses. Feinberg under-estimates the role that moral norms play in shaping and directing human behavior. Moral norms that form our conventional morality may be followed for a variety of reasons, but I am sure that one of them is that people have come to see from childhood that following these norms is in their best interest.

Feinberg focuses on the differences between legal and moral liability, but there are some important similarities. For example, there are overt responses to violations of moral as well as legal norms; particularly when young people are given moral training. These overt responses are an integral part of their moral training. Even mature adults are subject to quite serious overt responses for violations of norms. We must recognize that not every overt response that has serious consequences on a person's life must be couched in legalistic terms. People are often held liable by withholding favors from them. The withholding of these favors is not ad hoc, it is done in direct response to violations of specific moral norms. Withholding these favors serves to coerce us, as do legal sanctions, to learn and support conventional norms. Being found morally liable is no trivial thing in a morally decent society.

Doing so serves as more than a basis for self-punishment, remorse or pride.

For Feinberg, in order for there to be collective liability in the sense of being open to overt responses there must be (a) group solidarity, (b) prior notice to the liable party, and (c) opportunity for control by the liable party.[10] Feinberg rejects this sense of collective liability in our two controversial cases basically because he believes that condition (a) is not satisfied. Group solidarity exists when all members of a group share interests, feel pride when one of its members does something noteworthy, and feels shame when one of its members acts badly. On the other hand, if we reject Feinberg's account of group solidarity, a group may experience group solidarity although its members have minimal shared interest and feel no pride or shame when members of their group accomplish something noteworthy or act badly.

When a group is "loosely organized" and very large and diversified, not all of Feinberg's requirements for group solidarity are necessary. For example, residents of the state of California can experience group solidarity even though they individually may have little in common and varied interests. The poor Watts ghetto dweller may have little in common with the wealthy person who lives in Beverly Hills, but they can have group solidarity if they both rally around efforts to prevent needed water from being routed to some other state. Feinberg's rejection of collective moral liability rests on drawing a dichotomy between a group with solidarity and a random collection of individuals. Such a dichotomy is misleading. Of course we would reject holding a person morally liable for the faulty actions of a collection of individuals of whom by the luck of circumstances he happened to be a part. But in our two cases above the groups in question are not a random collection of individuals. Members of these groups identify with the group even if they don't support all of the actions of its members. Racial and national identifications are quite strong. In fact, we are not fully conscious of how much we identify with these groups. Strong group identifications have served as a source of self-esteem and as a foundation for cultures. Solidarity, unlike group identification, requires a level of political and social consciousness. As, for example, when a worker begins to define himself as a member of the working class. Just being a worker is not sufficient to have a worker's consciousness. With racial and national identification there is perhaps not the level of political and social consciousness that would allow us to conclude that group solidarity exists, but there is enough group identification to warrant the judgment that the members of the group have chosen to identify with the group for the security and benefits that group membership provides.

We are certainly reluctant to accept the conclusion that all white southerners should be presumed to be liable for the unjust actions of some, but part of this reluctance can be overcome when we move from talking about actions to practices. However, we are still left uneasy about such a conclusion because we believe that people do not have control over such things as their race or sex, while they do have control over whether they will remain a racist or sexist. But people play very different roles in their dealings with one another. There are those who are oppressors and the direct beneficiaries of oppression, those who are nonparticipating beneficiaries of oppression, and those who appear to be innocent bystanders. The last two categories are what prompts Feinberg to conclude that holding southern whites, as a group, collectively liable to overt responses is unjustified. He believes that the contributory fault condition is absent or very weak in the case of some group members. Thus, for him, no such thing as collective responsibility as a type of collective legal liability exists in such cases.

Feinberg is right. It would be unjust to hold a person legally liable for something he did not do because he is a member of a racial group whose actions have been faulty. Even if we add that this person benefitted because of the faulty action or practice, this, itself, would not suffice to show that he is legally liable. Given the present requirements for legal liability. I don't think we can show legal liability for groups as a whole in such cases, but I do think we can show that a form of moral liability that carries with it serious non-legal constraints and sanctions is justified.

III

The theory of collective moral liability that I advocate here assumes that the notion of community is crucial, community in the sense that each member of the society is serving her own interest by freely joining a group to carry on a common struggle for existence. According to my theory, no legal or moral demands should be placed on the individual such that the person who is subjected to them does not remain a free moral agent. My account of collective moral liability makes group members who fail to take certain steps morally liable for the negative consequences that result from their omissions. They have a moral duty to take these steps because it is a necessary part of their chosen strategy to insure that all members of society remain free moral agents, which is an integral part of their reason for joining the moral community in the first place.

Some philosophers have argued that a person who willingly commits an injustice is more blameworthy than a person who merely lets an injustice occur. My purposes here are not to question this admittedly controversial contention, but to grant it and argue that under certain conditions letting an injustice occur, perhaps less faulty than causing an injustice, is faulty enough, in a moral sense, to make a person morally liable.

The following are conditions under which moral agent X can be held morally liable for a faulty practice P:

(1) X knows or should have known about P.
(2) X identifies or has solidarity with those who engage in P or X does not sufficiently disassociate himself from P or X's failure to disassociate from P was not a part of a reasonable strategy to prevent further or greater harm.

When these conditions are satisfied, I hold we have a moral basis for liability. Let us now turn to a clarification and defense of these conditions.

Condition (1)

Condition (1) refers to practices, not the individual or complex actions that occur between individuals. It is satisfied if a person knows that a practice exists even if he or she has not personally been a party to a particular act that is faulty. However, one further clarification is needed.

Often people will use ignorance of a fact or state of affairs as a reason for their not being held accountable. Sometimes such an excuse is valid but there are many other cases where we believe that the ignorance excuse is inadequate. Imagine the case where a tour guide orders the members of his party to drink from a stream which, unbeknown to him, is contaminated. Should the guide not be held responsible for the illness or deaths of members of his party simply because he did not know that the stream was contaminated? We must answer no. He should have known. A part of his duty as a tour guide is to check such things, but we could modify our example in such a way that ignorance could relieve the guide of responsibility. Suppose the guide checked the stream for contaminants but did not test for some highly improbable bacteria that is rarely found in streams. In such a case, it would be wrong to hold him morally liable; he took all responsible precautions. Where reasonable efforts have been made to become knowledgeable, ignorance can warrant the conclusion that the agent is not liable.

In cases of collective moral liability each member of the group will have duties that result from their simply being moral agents or citizens of some state. We can argue about the extent of such duties, but we can safely conclude that they do exist. Therefore, each person has the responsibility to know what his duties are and to know whether he is living up to his obligations. Pleading ignorance is no excuse unless one has made a reasonable effort to become knowledgeable.

Condition (2)

The first part of condition (2) can be satisfied when those involved share some common interest; they need not feel pride or shame when members of the group with which they share a common interest do something noteworthy or act badly. A person can identify or have solidarity with a group even though he or she does not profit in a financial way from faulty practices engaged in or supported by the group. When this is the case, the person is liable because his emotional support for the group that engages in faulty practices enables the group to remain powerful and to continue its unjust practices. Even though the person does not financially profit, he will, at least, profit from the sense of emotional security that is attached to being a member of a powerful group. But this alone does not warrant liability. However, when the powerful group is oppressive and the emotional feelings of security that group members feel contribute to the disadvantage and oppression of members of other groups, it does.

The second disjunct of condition (2) requires disassociation where appropriate. Disassociation can involve publicly denouncing a practice, but only if that is all that one can do, and a refusal to accept any enrichment that occurs as a result of the faulty practice. But usually it will require direct action and a refusal to accept further enrichment. In either case the moral agent is required to do something that separates him from the faulty practice.This may require complete disassociation from the group that he identifies with. Some people will be required to do more than others because of their power and influence, but this is as it should be. In advance we cannot say with great precision what sufficient disassociation entails because different factors are involved from case to case. Some of these factors include risk of harm, time, and opportunity for control; thus, liability will be contingent on these factors.

Before I further explain what disassociation involves, one preliminary remark about the morality of disassociating oneself from an injustice is in order. I do not support the position that all people who disassociate themselves from injustice are doing so from attitudes that are morally commendable. My point simply is that there are cases where disassociation will serve to reduce the injustice and if it does not, it can still be said to be morally commendable because the attitudes that are present are something other than self-righteousness.[11]

A crucial aspect of the disassociation condition is the avenues of action available for disassociation. The avenues of action will be political as well as legal. For example, when chattel slavery was legal in this country, there were laws that closed most of the legal avenues open to those people who opposed slavery, but there were still political avenues available, e.g., abolitionist movements. Some people took those avenues available to them and thus they succeeded in disassociating themselves from the horrible practice of slavery.

The third disjunction of condition (2) is necessary because there might be cases where a person collaborates with a tyrannical power in order not to blow his cover as an agent set on destroying it. In such cases we certainly would not want to hold such persons morally liable. In fact, such persons' actions are morally commendable even though it may prove difficult to distinguish acts of resistance from mere collaboration.

My critics might object that it is physically or psychologically unrealistic to think that a person can be held morally liable because of a failure to disassociate from some unjust practice. Neither objection will suffice. First, the objection that it is physically unrealistic is unsatisfactory because the person is not required to travel great distances or to expend more than a modest sum of money to disassociate from an injustice. Given the present state of mass media and the varied organizations that allow for political participation, it would not be unrealistic to think, in cases involving serious unjust practices against groups, that these injustices could go unnoticed and that there would be no political avenues open to a person who wished to disassociate from them.

The objection that it would be psychologically unrealistic to expect people to disassociate themselves from unjust practices that they did not cause is not valid. If they mean that it would be unrealistic to expect people to be concerned with everyone else's problems, then I think they are correct. People have a difficult enough time keeping a handle on their own problems and the problems of their loved ones. However, this is not what is being required. We are not requiring an individual to be his brother's keeper, but to be aware that he can be held morally liable if he fails to disassociate from an unjust practice caused by a group that he identifies with. It is not my contention that people should widen or disregard their present loyalties, but I do deny that they are relieved of any moral liability, in certain cases, because they would be psychologically more content if they ignored these injustices and their consequences.

My theory differs from Feinberg's and others because it recognizes the importance and role of moral liability in a good society. It also explains why group membership, in certain circumstances, can make one morally liable even though one does not personally cause or explicitly support the faulty practices engaged in by a group of which one is a part. The theory of collective liability that I have advanced is one that recognizes that we live in a world where we can no longer view ourselves as being detached from the actions of groups of which we are a part. We should be aware that efforts to achieve a morally good society for a time may bring about disharmony and social unrest. A morally decent society, in my judgment, is willing to pay these costs.[12]

Notes

1. See L. T. Hobhouse, *Morals in Evolution* (London: Chapman and Hill, 1951) and Peter A. French, *Individual and Collective Responsibility: The Massacre at My Lai* (Cambridge: Schenkman, 1972), esp. pp. 103–118 and 147–165.

2. For example, H. Gomperz, "Individual, Collective, and Social Responsibility," *Ethics* 49 (1939) 329–342.

3. For instance, J. W. Nickel, "Classifications by Race in Compensatory Programs," *Ethics* 84 (1974), 146–150, p. 147.

4. Bernard Boxill supports such a position in "The Morality of Reparation," *Social Theory and Practice* 2 (1972), 113–122.

5. See May Brodbeck, "Methodological Individualism: Definition and Reduction," in Brodbeck's *Readings in the Philosophy of the Social Sciences* (New York: Macmillan, 1968).

6. For a good discussion of the Act-type and Act-token distinction see

Alvin I. Goldman, *A Theory of Human Action* (Englewood Cliffs, N.J.: Prentice Hall, 1970), pp. 63–72.

7. Joel Feinberg, "Collective Responsibility," *The Journal of Philosophy* 65 (1968), 674–688. Revised and reprinted in Feinberg's *Doing and Deserving* (Princeton: Princeton University Press, 1970). All page references will be to *Doing and Deserving*.

8. Ibid., pp. 247–248 (this anthology, p. 71–72).

9. Joel Feinberg, "Problematic Responsibility in Law and Morals," in *Doing and Deserving*, pp. 30–31.

10. *Doing and Deserving*, p. 249 (this anthology, p. 73).

11. For a fuller discussion of this point, see Thomas E. Hill, Jr., "Symbolic Protest and Calculated Silence," *Philosophy and Public Affairs* 9 (1979), 83–102, pp. 99–102.

12. This paper was written with partial support by a Summer Fellowship from the Rutgers University Research Council.

6

Can a Random Collection of Individuals Be Morally Responsible?

Virginia Held
1970

The question I wish to examine, in due course, is whether a random collection of individual persons can ever count as a collectivity or group capable of action for the performance or nonperformance of which the group may be held morally responsible.

For this discussion, I shall mean by a "random collection of individuals" a set of persons distinguishable by some characteristics from the set of all persons, but lacking a decision method for taking action that is distinguishable from such decision methods, if there are any, as are possessed by all persons. Thus passengers on a train or pedestrians on a sidewalk are distinguishable from other persons by their location and destination, in the prosaic sense, but possess thereby no distinguishable method for deciding to act. An organized group or collectivity, on the other hand, is distinguishable not only by certain characteristics that delimit its membership from other persons, but especially by its possession of a decision method for action. 'Action' must here be understood in the wide sense of doing something or causing something to happen or not happen. John R. Lucas defines a *community* as "a body of individuals who have in common a method of deciding disputes," and a *group* as "a social gathering which lacks a decision procedure."[1] My terms for what would be roughly comparable, extensionally, are 'collectivity' (or 'organized group') and 'random collection'.

Before the question I have raised can be dealt with, a number of preliminary assumptions need to be considered. These assumptions concern statements about collectivities and the possible moral responsibility of organized groups.

Some methodological individualists suppose that all statements about the actions of collectivities are "in principle" reducible to statements about the actions of actual human individuals.[2] I assume that a refusal to endeavor such reductions is frequently justifiable on pragmatic grounds, at the very least. We often assert, without difficulty, such empirical statements as "The corporation manufactures *X*," or "State *W* provides higher welfare payments than state *Y*," or "The Democratic Party nominated *Z*." And we often decide, without difficulty, that such statements are true. To require a reduction of such statements to statements about individuals would often be tantamount to abandoning them altogether, and such abandonment would often, I assume, be unacceptable.[3]

A separate argument is required for moral judgments. Even though we may be willing to allow that collectivities can act, the questions whether they can also be held responsible and whether they can be subject to moral judgment, remain. I assume an affirmative answer to both.

Consider the requirements for moral responsibility at the level of an individual. To hold an individual responsible for an action requires that he be aware of the nature of the action, in the sense that he is not doing *A* in the belief that he is doing *B*, and it requires that the judgment "He could have done something else" be valid of the action he has performed.

To hold an individual *morally* responsible for an action requires that he be aware of what I shall call the *moral nature* of the action, which can be understood as either the moral import of the kind of action of which it is an instance or as the moral value of the consequences it may produce. These requirements are not meant to be equivalent to requirements for complete knowledge, either in the case of responsibility of in the case of moral responsibility. But they preclude holding a person responsible for the thoroughly unascertainable aspects of an action he performs. They require that he be aware of the kind of action he is performing, but not that he know everything about either its empirical or its moral aspects.

If, for example, an individual throws an explosive device into an open window, and as a result a child is killed, he may not have been able to foresee this particular consequence, but he could be said to have been aware of the moral nature of his action as an instance of actions that risk causing injury. On the other hand, if an individual flips on a light switch and, by a mechanism of which he could have no knowledge, causes an explosion that kills a child, he could be said to be responsible for flipping on the switch, but not for causing the child's death; he could not be said to be *morally* responsible even for flipping on the light switch, since he could not in this case have been aware of what turned out to be the moral nature of this particular act of flipping on a light switch. He could be said to be morally responsible for the morally neutral act of flipping the switch—if this part of the total action is considered to have moral import—but not for the morally unfortunate action of flipping on the light switch and causing a child's death.

Again, if a person steals a car to go to the aid of a friend, he may be morally responsible for stealing the car if he knows that what he is doing is a case of stealing and not something else. And he may be morally responsible for trying to help a friend, if he is aware that that is what he is doing, even though he may not know whether even he considers the total action right or wrong and even though a more impartial judgment than his that the action *was* right or wrong, taking the relevant moral principles and consequences into account, was not ascertainable at the time of the action.

If these requirements for responsibility and moral responsibility can be met by individual persons, they can, I think, be met by collectives. If the Democratic Party nominates Hubert Humphrey, it is not acting in the belief that it is nominating George McGovern or that it is not nominating anyone; if Dow Chemical Company manufactures napalm, it is aware that the product is not edible gelatin and aware of the kind of activity it is performing. And it may sometimes be as reasonable to assert that a collectivity could have done something else than nominate candidate *X* or manufacture product *Y* as to assert that an individual could have done something else than the action for which he is held responsible.

I assume, further, that we can make moral judgments about the actions of collectivities. The claims that "Alabama should provide higher welfare payments than it does," "Brown University ought to admit more black students," and "the U.S. should not bomb North Vietnam" appear to be meaningful moral claims, and I assume that we are willing to attach the term 'valid' to some moral judgments among competing claims. A *valid* moral judgment about the action of a collectivity requires, among other things, that the collectivity be morally responsible for the action in question.

Some of the assumptions made thus far may be outlined as follows:

(1) Person *M* performed action *A* at time *t*; *M* was aware that he was doing *A; M* was aware of the moral nature of *A*.
(2) *M* could have done *A* or non-*A*.
(3) *M* was morally responsible for doing *A*.

(1) and (2) are requirements for (3).

(4) *A* was right (wrong) or good (bad).
(5) *M* ought (ought not) to have done *A*.

(3) and (4) are requirements for (5).

Other assumptions that might be added for clarification of those listed, but which I shall not employ, are:

(6) The validity of (5) was ascertainable by *M* at *t*.
(7) *M* deserves praise (blame).

(5) and (6) are requirements for (7).

The reductionist position is sometimes thought to have a special force in connection with holding collectives morally responsible, but the same arguments apply against this position as against a reductionist program for descriptive assertions. Suppose someone is considering the justifiability of a personal economic boycott against Dow Chemical for manufacturing napalm or against Westinghouse for price-fixing. He may require judgments of the form "Corporation *Z* should not have done *A*," but he may have no need for further judgments concerning which corporation executives did what in connection with the action. He might happen to be interested in these separate judgments, and other persons, in Congress or in the Anti-Trust Division, might require them for their purposes, but the person considering an economic boycott against a corporation may sometimes justifiably assert "Collectivity *C* should not have done *A*" without acceding to a reductionist demand.

Similarly, someone considering whether or not to join the Democratic Party or go to Brown University or immigrate to the United States may well require what he takes to be valid moral judgments about the actions of the Democratic Party or Brown University or the United States, but he may reject as impossible a reductionist program for such judgments. What Ernest Gellner said of reductionist translations of disposition statements applies as well to moral judgments: "Such translations would . . . be clumsy, long and vague, where the original statement about an institution or feature of the social scene was clear, brief and intelligible."[4]

And if we have no intention of accepting reductionist demands in practice, it is dishonest to concede them "in principle." I propose, then, an honest rejection. What should be conceded to the individualist, however, is that from the judgment "Collectivity *C* ought (ought not) to have done *A*," judgments of the form "Member *M* of *C* ought (ought not) to have done *A*" cannot be derived. From our attribution of an action, and moral responsibility, to a collectivity, it does not follow that the collectivity's members are morally responsible for the action of the collectivity.[5] It is quite possible that other judgments may be supplied indicating that the members are indeed morally responsible or that the members may be morally responsible for the quite different actions of having joined or of retaining membership in the collectivity in question, but judgments about the moral responsibility of its members are not logically derivable from judgments about the moral responsibility of a collectivity. "The Democratic Party is morally responsible for the nomination of Humphrey," and "The United States is morally responsible for sending its planes to bomb North Vietnam," may well be valid judgments, but from such judgments alone one cannot conclude that Democratic Party member *M* or U.S. political-system member *N* is morally responsible for the actions in question.

These somewhat lengthy preliminaries out of the way, we can now turn to the question of whether a random collection of individuals can ever be held morally responsible. I have been dealing so far with "requirements" for moral responsibility rather than with the more precise, and in my view still premature for this context, notions of necessary and sufficient conditions, or good and conclusive reasons. I wish now to consider whether there are requirements that can ever be met for a random collection of individuals to be substituted for *G* in a valid judgment that "*G* is morally responsible for *A* (or non-*A*)," or "*G* ought (ought not) to have done *A* (or non-*A*)."

A first question will be whether a random collection can act. We may consider statements such as "The audience left the theatre," or "The pedestrians blocked the sidewalk," examples of what might be thought to be actions taken by random collections. To the extent that action presupposes intention, there may of course be special problems. But even if we take the position that random collections can act, it is questionable whether they can be held morally responsible in normal circumstances. The action—if it can be called that—taken by a random collection and the collective action taken by an organized group must be distinguished: the former cannot be the outcome of a group decision method, but the latter can. And the requirements for moral responsibility appear to be such that they can be met by random collections only in special circumstances.

It is doubtful whether a random collection can be "aware of the moral nature of its action" or that it "could have done something else" in ways that will satisfy the requirements for moral responsibility, even when the actions of the individual members of the random collection are ones for which those members are individually responsible. But if the action in question is one which could only be taken by the random collection as a group, can a random collection ever be morally responsible for the performance or nonperformance of a collective action?

If we say that, in special circumstances, a random collection can be aware of the moral nature of an act, we do not claim the existence of an inexplicable group awareness over and above the awareness of its individual members, only that we are sometimes entitled to say "Random collection *R* is aware that *p*," even though we cannot carry out a reductionist demand for statements about each individual member. We may know, for instance, that a collection of individuals is composed of normal persons and that the statement "The bystanders were aware that they were standing up" is true even though we may be unable to know which particular persons had this awareness, how many, or exactly who they were.

A parallel point can be made with regard to the claim that the random collection "could have done something else": in special circumstances, we may be entitled to say that it could. But what are these special circumstances?

I shall confine my discussion to the nonperformance of an action, and argue that when the action called for in a given situation is obvious to the reasonable person and when the expected outcome of the action is clearly favorable, a random collection of individuals may be held responsible for not taking a collective action. But when the action called for is not obvious to the reasonable person a random collection may not be held responsible for not performing the action in question, but, in some cases, may be held responsible for not forming itself into an organized group capable of deciding which action to take.

Let us consider the following cases:

(1) Assume that there are seven apparently normal persons in a subway car; none is acquainted with any other; none are sitting together. The second smallest person of the seven rises, pushes the

smallest to the floor, and, in full view and hearing of the remaining five, proceeds to beat and to strangle his victim. If the remaining five persons do nothing for, say, ten minutes, at the end of which time interval the smallest person is dead, would we be able to make a valid judgment that "they ought to have subdued the strangler"? It is possible that no one of the five, acting alone, could have subdued him; it is extremely probable that action by two or more of the group to subdue him would have succeeded, with no serious injury to themselves; the group was not so numerous that, if each member had acted, confusion would have resulted. I think that in such a case we would hold the random collection morally responsible for its failure to act as a group.

There is, of course, a question concerning what we take "the action" to be: is it the act of subduing the strangler, or is it some or all of its "sub-acts," such as holding his arms and legs, etc. Whether or not we can consider such a problem a merely verbal one,[6] which I doubt, the problem would not seem to be inordinately greater for the action of a group than for the action of an individual. If an able-bodied adult were to look on for five minutes while a two-year-old child slashed an infant with a razor blade, he would be held morally responsible for failing to perform the action of taking away the razor blade, although various sub-acts, such as grasping the child's wrist with one of his hands, moving his other hand into position, etc., would have been required to do so.

In both the situations of the passengers observing a strangler and of the child with a razor blade, the action called for in the circumstances specified may be said to have been obvious to the reasonable person. This may be understood, prima facie, in terms of such assumed principles as: "A collection of persons ought to try to prevent one of its members from being beaten and strangled," and "Adults should try to prevent children from seriously injuring infants." If an additional requirement is made that for the action called for to be obvious to the reasonable person, the desirability and probability of its outcome, compared to the outcomes of possible alternatives, must be of a certain level, the requirement can be met in these cases even if this level is set at a high point. And the kinds of action that would have to be taken to prevent the strangling and injuring were in these cases clear.

I would like to interject here that I do not take 'reasonable' to be equivalent to 'rational'. In recent years, the latter term has often been considered equivalent to 'efficiently self-interested' in the impressive and well-developed literature of game theory and decision processes.

'Reasonable', in contrast, has a better chance of retaining an essential moral component, and moralists might do well at the moment to latch onto it, and to hang on.

If, then, the action called for in a given situation is obvious to the reasonable person, it seems that we can sometimes conclude that the judgment "Random collection of individuals *R* is morally responsible for not doing *A*" is valid.

(2) Assume five persons in a train compartment in an old European train; the compartment has a door to the outside. One of the five persons, a doctor, goes for a walk in the corridor, leaving his satchel on his seat. Another passenger, a very large man, begins to have convulsions and, after a few moments, apparently in a frantic search for air, lurches against the door, which opens; he falls out and is killed. The doctor returns, is told by the remaining three persons what has happened, and says, "You should have held him down and administered medicine *x* from my bag." In this case, the desirability and probability of success of the action that the group might have taken, and might only have taken as a group, are again high; a relevant principle, such as "A group ought to try to prevent one of its members from accidentally killing himself," could be assumed without great difficulty; and yet we would not hold the group morally responsible for its failure to perform the action if its members did not, and could not reasonably be expected to, know that the person with convulsions would lurch to the door or that medicine *x* would help him. In this case, the action called for was not obvious to the reasonable person, and hence an essential requirement is missing for the judgment "Random collection of individuals *R* is morally responsible for not doing *A*" to be valid. And the doctor's judgment, accordingly, is not a valid moral judgment, because the validity of "*R* ought to have done *A*" presupposes the validity of "*R* was morally responsible for not doing *A*." (If he had said something of the form "*A* should have been done," this might perhaps have been valid, but I have tried not to include any consideration of such judgments in this paper.)

(3) Assume now three unacquainted pedestrians on an isolated street. A small building collapses; a man inside is trapped; he calls to the three for help. He is bleeding from a lower-leg injury and needs immediate assistance. All four persons know that a tourniquet should be applied to his thigh, but this cannot be done until various beams are removed, and removing any would require the strength of all three. The three observers do not agree on how to proceed. Observer$_1$ argues for action$_1$: moving beam$_1$. Observer$_2$ argues for action$_2$: moving beam$_2$.

Observer$_3$ argues for action$_3$: moving beam$_3$. While they argue, the man slowly bleeds to death.

The situation here depicted was such that any of the proposed actions (plus applying the tourniquet) would have prevented the man from dying. The judgment that "An organized group in these circumstances ought to have done action$_1$ or action$_2$ or action$_3$" can be considered valid. But *which* action to take was not obvious to the reasonable member of the random collection; so, again, an essential requirement for holding a random collection of individuals responsible for the nonperformance of an action was missing.

However, it was obvious to the reasonable person in this case that any one of the three proposed actions would be better than no action. The problem was one of deciding which action to take; that a decision between "action$_1$ or action$_2$ or action$_3$" was called for *was* obvious to the reasonable person. Hence the random collection can be held morally responsible for failing to make a decision on which action to take—for failing, that is, to adopt a decision method.

As previously stated, a distinguishing characteristic of an organized group or collectivity as opposed to a random collection of individuals is that the former has a method for deciding to act: it has officials who can act in its name, or a voting procedure to arrive at its decisions, or customary procedures to guide its actions. The possession of such a decision method, by a collection of individuals, is, we might say, that which transforms a collection of persons into an organized group or collectivity. In the foregoing example, then, we can say that the random collection of pedestrians was morally responsible for failing to turn itself into an organized group capable of taking action requiring a decision. The judgment, then, that "Random collection *R* is morally reponsible for not constituting itself into a group capable of deciding upon an action" is sometimes valid when it is obvious to the reasonable person that action rather than inaction by the collection is called for.

A significant difference between the moral responsibility of a random collection as opposed to the moral responsibility of an organized group is that the former seems to be distributive—that is, if random collection *R* is morally responsible for the failure to do *A*, then every member of *R* is morally responsible for the failure to do *A*, although, perhaps, in significantly different proportions. In contrast, if organized group *G* is morally responsible for the failure to do *A* it does not follow that member *M* of *G* is morally responsible for the failure to do *A*. If a random collection *R* can be represented as a set equivalent, say, to *M* & *N* & *Q*, then, if *R* is morally responsible, we would seem to be able to conclude that *M* is morally responsible & *N* is morally responsible & *Q* is morally responsible. On the other hand, if these same members formed an organized group, the group could not be adequately represented as equivalent simply to *M* & *N* & *Q*, because its depiction would have to include the decision method by which the members act as a group. And the distribution of moral responsibility over such a combination would not seem plausible.

It should be noted that, in saying that the moral responsibility of a random collection is distributive, we may not be saying very much; for if the action is one that could be taken by the random collection only as a group, questions about apportioning responsibility for all the various components of the action, assuming the action can be broken down into its components, remain open.

From the previous analysis it may well follow that in some cases all the individuals in a random collection are responsible for not acting to transform the collection into an organized group, even though none of these individuals is responsible for not taking the action that ought to have been taken by an organized group in these circumstances.

The possible implications of these positions for various political situations may be suggestive. If a reasonable person judges that the overthrow of an existing political system is an action that is obviously called for, he may perhaps consider himself morally responsible for the failure of the random collection of which he is a member to perform this action. If he thinks some action to change an existing political system is obviously called for, but is not clear about which action, he may consider himself morally responsible for the failure of the random collection of which he is a member to perform the quite different action of transforming itself into a group capable of arriving at decisions on such questions. For such decisions, decision methods are required, and there is of course a danger of generating an infinite regress: Can there be responsibility for not deciding upon a method to decide upon a method to decide upon a method . . . to act? But this itself would be a problem occurring in a context, and it might at least be obvious to the reasonable person that a solution should be sought to the question of which decision method would be appropriate for this context. Sometimes, a prescription to let the most knowledgeable decide may recommend itself; sometimes to designate decision-makers by lot may be the most suitable arrangement; sometimes decision by unanimous agreement, or by majority vote, or by some other proportion, may be appropriate, and so on. Answers to questions concerning which decision methods to adopt for which contexts will perhaps seldom be obvious to the reasonable person. But the reasonable person may perhaps then be morally responsible for not acting to transform the random collection of which he is a member into an at least loosely organized group seeking answers to questions concerning the most appropriate and justifiable decision methods for classifiable kinds of contexts. Such a group might be the community of those moral inquirers who are capable of arriving at decisions on moral questions by a process of free inquiry and reasonable discussion.

Notes

1. *The Principles of Politics* (New York: Oxford, 1966), p. 366.

2. See May Brodbeck, "Methodological Individualisms: Definition and Reduction," in Brodbeck, ed., *Readings in the Philosophy of the Social Sciences* (New York: Macmillan, 1968).

3. In stating their frame of reference, Talcott Parsons, Edward A. Shils, and James Olds, representing many others in related fields, write, for instance, that "The *actor* is both a system of action and a point of reference. As a system of action the actor may be either an individual or a collectivity. . . . The *individual-collectivity* distinction is made on the basis of whether the actor in question is a personality system or a social system (a society or subsystem)." *Toward a General Theory of Action* (New York: Harper, 1962), p. 56.

4. Ernest Gellner, "Holism vs. Individualism," in Brodbeck, ed., *op. cit.,* p. 258.

5. See Joel Feinberg, "Collective Responsibility," *Journal of Philosophy,* LXV, 21 (Nov. 7, 1968): 674–688, for the beginning—but only the beginning—of such an argument. See also D. E. Cooper, "Collective Responsibility," *Philosophy,* XLIII, 165 (July 1968): 258–268, for a more developed consideration of it. A traditional rejection of what is called "the barbarous notion of collective or group responsibility" is given by H. D. Lewis in "Collective Responsibility," *Philosophy,* XXIII, 84 (January 1948): 3–18.

6. Joel Feinberg has considered the variability of possible descriptions: "This well-known feature of our language, whereby a man's action can be described as narrowly or broadly as we please, I propose to call the 'accordion effect', because an act, like the folding musical instrument, can be squeezed down to a minimum or else stretched out. . . . We can, if we wish, puff out an action to include an effect, and more often than not our language obliges us by providing a relatively complex action word for the purpose. Instead of saying Smith did *A* (a relatively simple act) and thereby causes *X* in *Y*, we might say

something of the form 'Smith *X*-ed *Y*'; instead of 'Smith opened the door causing Jones to be startled', 'Smith startled Jones'." "Action and Responsibility," in Max Black, ed., *Philosophy in America* (Ithaca, N.Y.: Cornell Univ. Press, 1965), p. 146.

7

The Responsibility of "Random Collections"

Stanley Bates
1971

Virginia Held has written an extremely interesting article investigating the question, "Can a Random Collection of Individuals Be Morally Responsible?"[1] In the course of her article, she discusses (and illuminates) a number of issues concerning responsibility which are not frequently dealt with in the philosophic literature on this topic. I would like to pursue, briefly, the discussion on some of these issues which she has initiated.

One thing that needs to be emphasized is that her use of "random," though clearly explained and though the term is consistently employed, is somewhat idiosyncratic, so that the significance of her claims may be misjudged by a reader who does not attend closely to her usage. "For this discussion, I shall mean by a 'random collection of individuals' a set of persons distinguishable by some characteristics from the set of all persons, but lacking a decision method for taking action that is distinguishable from such decision methods, if there are any, as are possessed by all persons" (p. 471). One immediately notices that a "random" collection of people, in this sense of "random," all share some characteristic in virtue of which they are members of *this* "random" collection. Whether this makes the collection (or set, or group—I will use these terms interchangeably) nonrandom in an ordinary sense of "random" depends on what the characteristic is. Suppose a Martian biologist is told to gather a random sample of the human species for scientific research. Say that he is asked to gather a sample of 100 human beings and to select them at random. He might select a population center at random, perhaps by sticking a pin into a spinning global map of population distribution, go to that center, and take the first 100 people that he sees, or take every tenth person of the first 1,000 that he sees. The members of the set of people whom he selects will all share a certain characteristic, that is, "being one of the first 100 human beings seen by this Martian," or "being one of the group of every tenth of the first 1,000 human beings seen by this Martian." If we, for the moment, accept the rough and ready essentialism that seems to be a part of the metaphysics of the common man, we might call this an extrinsic characteristic of each of these individuals as opposed to their intrinsic characteristics, such as physical features, mental capacities, character traits, etc. Of course, the set of people selected by the Martian might have some intrinsic characteristic or characteristics in common; for example, they might all be blonds (if the Martian lands at a Scandinavian picnic), or they might all be over six feet tall (if he lands at a Tip Toppers meeting), or they might all be homosexuals (if he lands at a Gay Liberation parade). That these sets are not *representative* of the human population does not imply that they have not been randomly selected. Still, there is an assumption that a randomly selected sample of some group, if it is large enough relative to the group of which it is a sample, will be representative of that group. The Martian's selection procedures may not commend themselves to scientific researchers.

If the Martian chooses the first 100 blond people that he sees because they are blond, then he is choosing the sample set in virtue of an intrinsic characteristic. It looks now as though he may have a random sample of blond people but *not* a random sample of human beings. Randomness seems to attach itself not absolutely to the random group, but relatively to what it is a random group of. Further, the collection is random, in an ordinary sense, in virtue of how it is selected—that is, in virtue of the fact that, given the category of which we wish a sample, we select members of that category for our sample because of extrinsic rather than intrinsic characteristics. These points about randomness are relevant, because Held talks about two kinds of "random collections." The first kind, to which she devotes most of her attention, are groups of people brought together in space and time, facing situations which seem morally to call for action by the group. The second kind, which she only refers to briefly, are groups of people who fit her usage of "random collection of individuals" which I quoted above, who are not together in space and time but who, perhaps, are morally responsible for the inaction of the "random collection" of which they are members. I shall return to this topic later, but I might say now that the moral responsibility which is attributable to this second sort of "random collection" may attach to them exactly because of the characteristics which they possess in common which make them, in an ordinary sense, nonrandom collections.

The "random collections" on which Held concentrates in her examples are groups of individuals who have come together at a particular place and time not for any special common purpose, but simply as a result of each person's pursuit of his own ends. They are groups of passengers in a subway train, passengers in railway compartments, and people on an isolated street who happen upon the victim of an accident. Her examples are used to make the main point of her article, which is that, "when the action called for in a given situation is obvious to the reasonable person and when the expected outcome of the action is clearly favorable, a random collection of individuals may be held responsible for not taking a collective action" (p. 94). She adds that, if the action called for is not obvious to a reasonable person, the group is not responsible for not taking the action, though in some cases the group may be responsible for not organizing itself into a group capable of taking the required action. It seems to me that the examples that she gives do, in fact, support her claims. They are cases where my moral intuitions agree with hers—that we would hold a "random collection of individuals" morally responsible for the nonperformance of an action. However, because of the fairly restricted range of these examples, I would like to explore these issues a little further.

One of the features of all of Held's examples is that communication among the members of the "random collection" is possible. The people can talk to each other. This makes possible an action (or the omission of an action—hereafter, omissions are included as actions) for which the group can be held responsible. Another feature of the examples is that they are of situations where the group is confronted with the immediately perceptible distress of another human being, and it is clear that some action is called for, though it is not necessarily clear to a reasonable man in all of the cases exactly which action is called for. She says that, "even if we take the position that random collections can act, it is questionable whether they can be held morally responsible in normal circumstances. The action—if it can be called that—taken by a random collection and the collective action taken by an organized group must be distinguished: the former cannot be the outcome of a group decision method, but the latter can" (p. 94). She then gives her examples which presumably go beyond normal circumstances, and, as I have said, two features in which they differ from normal circumstances are that communication is possible and that some emergency requires action. However, when she suggests that the action of a random collection cannot be the outcome of a group decision method, the claim seems to me to be too strong. Her own proviso was that a "random collection" could possess whatever decision method can be possessed by all people. Now it is quite true that a "random collection" will possess neither established voting procedures, nor officials, nor customary procedures (all of these are instanced as examples of group decision procedures by Held). Nonetheless, unless these are stipulated to exhaust "group decision methods," there are other group decision methods, though they are not formal. Thomas Schelling's book *The Strategy of Conflict* discusses a number of these methods.[2] Very often they involve an implicit bargaining, but, unless we restrict "bargaining" to situations in which only self-interested motives are involved, there seems to be nothing objectionable to this as a rubric for the nonformal kinds of group decision procedures that "random collections" can have. One thing that is necessary for a bargaining procedure to have an outcome is communication between the parties involved (though Schelling discusses some interesting situations in which it can be to the interest of a bargaining party to make further communication impossible), and, as we have seen, this is provided in all of Held's examples. This is important because, at the conclusion of her article, she suggests certain "possible implications" of the points that she has established by her examples. "If a reasonable person judges that the overthrow of an existing political system is an action that is obviously called for, he may perhaps consider himself morally responsible for the failure of the random collection of which he is a member to perform that action" (p. 98). Two things need to be noted about this statement. First, she speaks of "the random collection of which he is a member." This seems odd, since, on her account, each individual would seem to be a member of a practically unlimited number of "random collections," and it is at least unclear as to which of these random collections is failing to overthrow the existing political system, as it is *not* unclear which group of passengers on the subway train failed to come to the aid of an assault victim. This is connected with the second point, namely, that the possibility of communication, hence, of action, has not been established for "the random collection of which he is a member." A person may very well, having perceived the moral necessity for revolution, feel himself to be morally responsible for his own lack of revolutionary activity, but I do not yet see how he could be justified in holding some "random collection" to be collectively responsible for a lack of revolutionary activity. This is not to say that something like this cannot be shown, but I believe that any effort to show it will involve saying a good deal about the so-called random collection.

This leads naturally to the question of the distribution of a group's responsibility. Held accepts a certain notion of collective responsibility (for groups having decision procedures) before she deals with the question asked in the title of her paper, and she rejects certain reductionist claims of "methodological individualism." She then goes on: "What should be conceded to the individualist, however, is that from the judgment 'Collectivity C ought (ought not) to have done A,' judgments of the form 'Member M of C ought (ought not) to have done A' cannot be derived. From our attribution of an action, and moral responsibility, to a collectivity, it does not follow that the collectivity's members are morally responsible for the action of the collectivity" (p. 93). The first of the sentences just quoted is unexceptionable, and if the second is merely meant to epitomize the first, then it too is acceptable. It could, however, seem to leave open the possibility that *none* of the members of a collectivity might be morally responsible for what the collectivity is morally responsible for—and that is not a possibility. What could be true of each member of the collectivity taken separately (that he might not share in the moral responsibility of the collectivity of which he is a member) does not imply that all members of the collectivity might simultaneously lack individual moral responsibility for its actions. Some individuals in the Democratic party are morally responsible for the nomination of Humphrey, and some U.S. political system members are responsible for the bombing of North Vietnam. Nonetheless, Held is quite correct in asserting that these facts are insufficient to establish exactly who is responsible in these cases. She contrasts these cases with those of "random collections." "A significant difference between the moral responsibility of a random collection as opposed to the moral responsibility of an organized group is that the former seems to be distributive—that is, if random collection R is morally responsible for the failure to do A, then every member of R is morally responsible for the failure to do A, although, perhaps, in significantly different proportions" (p. 480). Let us investigate this claim.

There are two kinds of cases to be considered. First, there is the situation in which it is possible for each member of a "random collection" to take some action which a reasonable man would believe to have a high probability of a favorable result. Take a case of ten people, safe in their separate apartments, who all witness an attack by an armed criminal on a woman which takes place outside their apartment building. Let us suppose that each has ready access to a telephone and could call the police, but that this is the only action open to each of them to remedy the situation. (Let us also suppose that a call to the police would probably result in the saving of the life of the woman being attacked.) Each person does *not* make a call to the police. Here it seems clear that every member of this group is morally responsible for the result which he could have prevented at practically no cost to himself. This case is rather different from the cases which Held considers, which are the second kind I want to discuss. These are cases where some joint effort is both possible and necessary for the favorable result. Change the above case to a group of ten people together in one apartment without access to a phone who are witnessing the attack. Suppose further that, though it is obvious that no individual by himself could subdue the attacker, if the group tried to subdue him they would succeed. (This is, roughly, Held's example.) Surely the failure of the group to act is not a sufficient condition to attribute moral responsibility for the lack of action to each and every member of the group. Suppose that one person said, "Four of us can handle him easily and safely, so if three of you will come with me now, we can save the woman." The rest of the group refuse. Suppose he expresses a willingness to go if two others will accompany him, or even if one other person will accompany him, and all the rest still refuse. I submit that no matter what this individual does now, he cannot be held responsible for the failure of the group to act. Of course, one can save the thesis of the distribution of responsibility by saying that the individual mentioned above is *not* a member of the "random collection" that failed to act, that the "collection" in question consists of all those who refused to join in a common action. I must say that such a move seems completely arbitrary and ad hoc to me. He *is* a member of the group, and *he* did his best to save the woman, which is all that morality requires.

Still, there are cases where it does seem to be possible to distribute moral responsibility throughout what Held calls a "random collection," provided that the condition of knowing what he is doing is met by each individual who is a part of the "random collection." I am thinking of the following kind of case. Suppose it is true that the staging of a cockfight depends upon the existence of some minimum-size audience, say 100 people, being willing to attend. It is justifiable to say that every member of the "random collection" correctly designated as "the audience for the cockfight" is morally responsible for the occurrence of the cockfight (as, of course, are the promoters of it) even though it may be possible for every individual member of the audience truly to assert that the cockfight would have occurred even if he had not attended. Well, what if a member of the SPCA bought a ticket in order to leap up at an appropriate moment to try to shame the crowd or to bring the cockfight to a close? I would say that such an attender of the cockfight is not a member of "the audience for the cockfight." Why is this device not arbitrary and ad hoc here? It is not arbitrary because cockfights are staged for the pleasure of their audiences and not in order to provide opportunities for exhortation by members of the SPCA. The SPCA agent does not try to evade moral responsibility by arguing that the cockfight would have occurred even if he had not attended; he avoids moral responsibility because he is able truly to argue that he was doing everything he could to prevent its taking place, and a by-product of this defense is that he can be seen not to be a part of the collective "audience for the cockfight." Another, perhaps clearer, example is that of a lynch mob. If a man wants to avoid sharing in the moral responsibility for the action of such a mob (e.g., a lynching), he cannot do so by arguing that his marginal contribution to the action was zero (i.e., that it would have happened even if he had not been there) but, rather, by arguing that even though he was on the scene he was not a part of the "lynch mob." (Perhaps he is a newspaper reporter getting a story, or a police spy, or someone trying to stop the lynching. We are not concerned here with the question of whether his actions are morally justified, only with the question of whether he shares in the moral responsibility for the lynching.)

Here, we see that, in the cases where moral responsibility can be distributed to every member of a "random collection" it is in virtue of the criterion by which we pick out the members as being members of *that* "random collection" to which we attribute the action for which we are assigning moral responsibility. Interestingly, in both of the examples given above, spatial and temporal contiguity was not enough to decide group membership. When a "random collection" is not defined simply by spatial and temporal contiguity (as collections in Held's examples are), it looks as though the features that define group membership may be the ones in virtue of which moral responsibility is assigned. (These, incidentally, will be the features which make it a nonrandom collection, in the ordinary sense of "random.") Are "white Americans" responsible for the horrible racial situation in this country? If we want a group of which we can say that every member is morally responsible, or bears some moral responsibility, for the situation, I think that we shall have to make our description of this "random collection" more precise. (My infant daughter, though a white American, does not yet seem to be a candidate for this kind of moral responsibility.) Perhaps we should say something like "mature, rational white Americans who know what the racial situation is, and who either take actions to perpetuate or worsen it, or who fail to take actions to alleviate it" bear the moral responsibility for the situation. This, of course, is still a vast group, most of whom would doubtless deny any moral responsibility for America's racial situation. Bad faith is common enough. What is of interest here is that, if this judgment of moral responsibility were correct, then knowing that a person did belong to this "random collection" would be sufficient basis for distributing moral responsibility to him.

The entire issue of collective responsibility needs a great deal of attention. Virginia Held's article is a very useful place to begin examining a number of points associated with this issue.[3]

Notes

1. Virginia Held, "Can a Random Collection of Individuals Be Morally Responsible?" *Journal of Philosophy* 67, no. 14 (July 23, 1970): 471–81. Further references to this article will be made in the body of the text by page numbers in parentheses, referring to the reprint of her paper in this anthology.

2. Thomas C. Schelling, *The Strategy of Conflict* (New York: Oxford University Press, 1963).

3. W. H. Walsh, "Pride, Shame and Responsibility," *Philosophical Quarterly* 20, no. 78 (January 1970): 1–13, is a fine article which deals with a number of related issues and relates them to a broader philosophical context of theories of human nature and society.

II
Applications

8

Why Corporations Are Not Morally Responsible for Anything They Do

Manuel G. Velasquez
1983

Does it really make any sense to say that corporations are "morally responsible" for their wrongful actions? Granted, we often and easily assume that saying this makes perfectly good sense. But a moment's reflection might make us pause before so easily attributing moral responsibility to corporate groups. It is relatively clear what we mean when we say that a human individual is morally responsible for some wrongful act. Simplifying somewhat, we mean, at least, that the individual personally performed or helped to perform the act, that she did so intentionally, and that she is justifiably liable to blame and perhaps punishment. It is not equally clear what we mean when we say that a group of individuals is morally responsible for a wrong—that the Ford Motor Company, for example, is "morally responsible" for causing the deaths of many of those killed in Pinto accidents. Clearly we do not mean that everyone in Ford caused or helped to cause these deaths. Nor do we mean that everyone in Ford should be blamed or punished. Perhaps we mean that the responsibility attaches not to each individual in the group but to "the group as a whole." But what is "the group as a whole" if not every individual in the group?

These are puzzling questions. They are questions that I want to address because of their pivotal importance to the way in which we approach ethical issues in business. On the one hand, some authors assume that only human individuals can properly be held morally responsible and, consequently, think that the proper subject of a business ethic is the individual business person.[1] Other authors assume that moral responsibility should also be attributed to corporate groups, as entities distinct from their members, and, consequently, hold that the corporation must be the (or at least *a*) primary subject of a business ethic.[2] I want to show that this second approach is largely mistaken: I will argue that it makes sense to say that a corporation is morally responsible for a wrongful act only as an elliptical (and somewhat dangerous) way of saying that certain human individuals are morally responsible for that act.

I

To fix our sights let me begin by identifying the kind of responsibility that is at issue here, and let me do this by distinguishing different kinds of responsibility. First, the term *responsible* is sometimes used to mean "trustworthy" or "dependable," as when we say, for example, "Gonzales is a responsible administrator." In this "aretaic" sense, the term denotes a quality of moral character.[3] Second, the term *responsibility* is sometimes used to mean "obligation" or "duty" as in "The social responsibility of business is to serve the public," or "Business has the responsibility of serving the public." In this second sense, the term is usually used to look toward the future, toward what still has to be done. Third, *responsibility* is sometimes used to indicate that an action or its consequences are attributable to a certain agent, as in "Jones is responsible for yesterday's highway accident." In this third sense, it is used to look toward the past, toward something that has already been done.

We can set aside the first, or "aretaic," sense as well as the second, or "forward-looking," sense. My interest here is in the third, the backward-looking sense. But there are several varieties of this backward-looking sense. First, "X is responsible for Y" may mean simply that X is "the" or "a" cause of Y, as in, for example, "The storm was responsible for last night's power failure." Here, responsibility is roughly equivalent to causality and is attributable to purely natural agents. Second, "X is responsible for Y" may mean X must pay for the damages arising from Y, as in, for example, "The parent is responsible for the acts of his child." Here, responsibility is roughly equivalent to compensatory liability and the person who is held responsible for compensating an injured party for the damages arising from an act need not even have performed the act for which he or she is held responsible. We determine compensatory liability on the basis of a variety of considerations, such as social efficiency, distributive justice, ability to pay, and relationship to the agent. Third, "X is responsible for Y" may mean that X intentionally brought Y about, as in "Hitler was responsible for the deaths of millions of Jews." Although this third sense of responsibility incorporates elements of the first two senses, it nonetheless differs from each of them in important ways. Unlike the first sense, the responsible party cannot be a purely natural agent, since intentions can be attributed only to agents that can act on reasons. And unlike the second sense, the responsible party must have brought about or helped to bring about the act for which he or she is held responsible: unlike compensatory liability, this third kind of responsibility does not transfer to other parties.

Now it is this third type of responsibility that concerns me and it is the type to which I will be referring when I use the term *moral responsibility*. This type of responsibility is rendered explicit in the classical (i.e., the nineteenth-century common law) notion of criminal responsibility, which is often taken to be a legal rendition of our common understanding of moral responsibility, but one that is subject to the practicalities of legal enforcement. In its classical form, criminal responsibility requires both an *actus reus* and *mens rea*. That is, the accused will be found criminally responsible for a wrongful act only if (1) he personally brought about the wrongful act (i.e., the act was the conventional or causal result of his own bodily movements) or he personally helped to bring it about or he failed to prevent the act when he could have and should have, and (2) he did so intentionally (i.e., he was in voluntary control of the bodily movements that resulted in the act and he knowingly carried out those bodily movements in order to bring about that act or knowingly refrained from carrying out the bodily movements that could have prevented the act). I am, of course, oversimplifying, since most systems of criminal law incorporate a variety of qualifications pertaining to omissions, crimes of possession, defenses, conspiracies, and so on. But at this juncture, the only point I want to make is that the kind of responsibility for wrongdoing with which I am mainly concerned is the kind that lies at the core of the classical notion of criminal responsibility—the kind that we attribute to an agent only if the agent brought about the wrongful act or helped to bring it about through his own voluntary bodily movements (or omissions) and only if the agent intentionally brought about the act through those movements (or omissions).

The philosophical roots of this notion of responsibility stretch back to scholastic doctrines on "imputability." These doctrines are nicely summarized in Kant's *Metaphysics of Morals,* where he writes:

> An action is called a "deed" insofar as it stands under laws of obligation and, consequently, insofar as the subject is considered in this under the aspect of the freedom of his will. Through such an act, the agent is regarded as the originator of the effect, and this effect together with the action itself can be imputed to him if he is previously acquainted with the law by virtue of which an obligation rests on him. . . . Imputation in its moral meaning is the judgement by which someone is regarded as the originator *(causa libera)* of an action, which is then called a "deed" *(factum)* and stands under laws.[4]

As Kant's summary indicates, to say that an action or an effect is to be morally imputed to an agent is to say that the action or the effect "originated" with that agent and that the agent knew the action was morally right or wrong. In the scholastic doctrine that Kant is summarizing, an action or an effect is said to "originate" in an agent if that agent directly[5] carried out the bodily movements that constituted the action or that had those effects and if he did so intentionally—that is, the movements were his conscious execution of a freely formed intention to perform the action or achieve the effect. This philosophical notion of responsibility as moral imputability coincides with the legal notion of criminal responsibility on all points but one: whereas the philosophical notion requires knowledge of the moral rightness or wrongness of the act, the legal notion of criminal responsibility generally does not require knowledge of the legal rightness or wrongness of the act. This difference, however, can be attributed to the fact that enforcement of a law would be a practical impossibility if ignorance of the law were a generally acceptable defense.

In any case, the core concept of moral responsibility that I am trying to identify is the concept that is present in both the philosophical and the legal notions: moral responsibility is the kind of responsibility that is attributed to an agent only for those actions that *originate* in the agent, insofar as the action derived from the agent's intentions (the *mens rea* requirement) and from the same agent's bodily movements (the *actus reus* requirement). This notion of "origination" is thus tied to a concept of human beings as having a certain kind of mental and bodily unity. An agent originates an action in this sense when (1) he forms a plan of action or intention in his mind and (2) he executes this intention through bodily movements over which he has direct control. The presence of this direct control is normally expressed by speaking of a body as "belonging to" oneself. The body over which I have direct control is the body I refer to as "my" body, and any actions for which I am morally responsible must be brought about by this body.

As a glance in the pages of a dictionary will show, the meaning of this kind of responsibility is conceptually tied to another set of notions: liability to blame and punishment. To say that a person is morally responsible for an act is to say that the person is justly liable to blame and punishment. But neither blame nor punishment are appropriate (i.e., morally justified) when a person is not morally responsible for an act in the sense that I am trying to identify. That is, if an act is not the (causal or conventional) result of my own, direct bodily movements (or omissions) or if it is not an intentional consequence of these movements, then it is not appropriate to blame or punish me for the act.

Although I do not have the space here to explain fully why liability to blame and punishment are conceptually tied to moral responsibility, it is important for my argument that I indicate briefly, at least, why blame and punishment are justified when and only when a person is morally responsible for a wrong. Blame and punishment are conceptually connected to moral responsibility through the medium of familiar moral principles.

First and most well known is the classical utilitarian justification for attaching blame and punishment to intentional wrongdoing (i.e., to wrongs for which one is morally responsible): by blaming and punishing wrongdoers, we deter them and others from doing wrong in the future.[6] It would do little good to attach blame and punishment to unintentional acts, since these are acts over which the agent has no control and therefore cannot be deterred from performing by the prospect of blame or punishment. Nor would our utilitarian principles be satisfied if we were to blame or punish one person for acts brought about by the bodily movements of others. True, we might thereby be led to take greater pains to prevent each other from doing wrong, but the psychological costs of this method of deterrence would be certain to outweigh its benefits (or so utilitarians tell us).

Less familiar are the deontological rationales for attaching blame and punishment to wrongful acts we intentionally bring about through our own bodily movements. One kind of deontological rationale rests on a version of the principle that persons should be treated only as they have freely consented to be treated. On the basis of this principle, blame and punishment are justified insofar as we have consented to them or would consent to them if a choice were possible.[7] To see how such consent is possible, consider that each member of a society may be viewed as having consented to forbear from harming others on the understanding that others will forbear from harming her. But no one would consent to such an arrangement without some assurance that everyone is going to comply with these restraints. Insofar as the members of society see that blame and punishment for wrongdoing are necessary to secure such compliance, they consent to attach blame and punishment to wrongful acts. However, they would consent to attach blame and punishment only to an agent's own, intentionally committed wrongs because rational persons would not consent to an arrangement by which they could not determine by their own, direct movements whether they will be subjected to blame and punishment. Moreover, by blaming and punishing a person only for her intentional acts, society is treating her as she has consented to be treated. For in freely choosing whether or not one will engage in punishable acts, one is freely choosing whether or not one will be punished. And the punishments themselves are of one's own choosing, since one has consented to attach such punishments to such wrongful acts.

A second kind of deontological justification for punishment rests on the natural-law theory that wrongdoing constitutes a disorder that must be set right if justice is to prevail.[8] According to this view, there is a certain set of relationships among rational agents that is just, and departure from these relationships is an injustice. That is, when a wrongdoer departs from these relationships, he acquires an advantage over others that is not his due. Punishment is required to put the wrongdoer back in his proper place by taking something from him that is equal to the unjust advantage he acquired by his wrongdoing. However, a person is to be punished only for wrongs he personally committed, because if one person is punished for the act of another agent, the wrongdoer would not be put back in his place: instead of restoring order, the punishment would introduce additional disorder. Moreover, only intentional acts are to be punished, because only in their intentional acts are rational agents conceived as acting: to punish an agent whose action is unintentional is to punish someone who has not truly acted.

I have only sketched these three kinds of moral rationales for attaching blame and punishment to moral responsibility. All three rationales, I believe, are present in our common understanding of blame and punishment and in our understanding of the way in which liability to blame and punishment are conceptually connected to moral responsibility. What is crucial to notice is that all rationales connect moral responsibility to blame and punishment through the mediation of moral principles that require that blame and punishment be inflicted only upon agents in whom wrongful acts originate; that is, only upon agents who intentionally carried out with their own bodies the direct movements that constituted or brought about the wrongful acts.

These comments should suffice to identify the concept of moral responsibility with which I am mainly concerned in this essay. The kind of moral responsibility I am talking about is the kind that lies at the heart of the classical notion of criminal responsibility and of the classical idea of moral imputability and that serves as the basis for justified blame and punishment through the mediation of several moral principles. It is thus a concept that is embedded in a network of psychological, physiological, and moral concepts.

II

Now let me return to the main question: Does it make any sense to say that corporations are morally responsible for the wrongs they commit in the sense of responsibility that I have just identified? Peter French has laid out the most extended and strongest arguments for the view that moral responsibility can legitimately be attributed to a corporation as an entity logically distinct from its members.[9] The defects of such a view will become obvious if we examine his argument. French argues that corporate organizations can be held morally responsible for their acts because (1) they perform actions that can be attributed only to the corporate organization and not to any of its members and (2) they perform these actions with intentions that can be attributed only to the corporate organization and not to any of its members. Corporate organizations, then, seem to act and they seem to do so intentionally.

French's arguments are significant because they try to show precisely what must be shown if one is to demonstrate that corporations are morally responsible for their acts—namely, that corporations embody the two requirements that are at the heart of the philosophical and legal notions of responsibility: an *actus reus* and *mens rea*. Nonetheless, French is wrong. He is wrong because corporate acts do not originate in the corporation but in the corporation's members.

Consider, first, the requirement of an *actus reus*. Obviously the acts attributed to corporations are not acts that are performed by the corporation as an entity distinct from its members, since corporations do not act except through their members. A corporation may be considered either as a fictitious legal entity to which actions are conventionally attributed or as a real organization comprised of several members whose own actions causally bring about or constitute the corporate act. Considered as a fictitious legal entity, the corporation is related to its members as a legal "principle" is related to those "agents" who are empowered to act on its behalf and whose acts are conventionally attributed to the legal "principle," although the "principle" did not actually perform those acts. Considered as a fictitious legal entity, then, the corporation obviously does not perform any bodily acts itself and it is only by way of a convenient fiction that acts performed by others are conventionally attributed to the corporation.[10] On the other hand, considered as a real organization, the corporation is related to its members as an organized group is related to the individuals who comprise the group. It may thus appear that when a corporate member acts the corporation may be said to have performed the act of the member, much as when a person's bodily limb moves the person is said to have moved his limb. But this similarity is deceptive, because a group, unlike a body, is made up of autonomous individuals. The individuals who make up the organization are autonomous in the sense that each individual can choose not to carry out the direct bodily movements necessary to bring about the corporate act. And this autonomy is due to the fact that the body of each member is under the direct control not of the corporation but of the individual member. But moral responsibility for an act, as we have seen, can be attributed only to that agent who originated the act in his own body, that is, in the movements of a body over which he has direct control. In corporate agency, action does not originate in a body belonging to the corporation to whom the act is attributed, but in bodies belonging to those human beings whose direct movements constituted or brought about the act that is then attributed to the corporation. Consequently, whether considered as a fictional legal entity or as a real organization, corporations do not originate acts in the manner required by attributions of moral responsibility—namely, by directly moving one's own body.

Moreover, in view of the relationship between moral responsibility and liability to blame and punishment that I sketched out above, it is clear that it is inappropriate to attribute moral responsibility to a corporation on the basis of acts performed by its members. If we hold an agent morally responsible for acts that originate in other agents, we will violate the moral principles that connect moral responsibility to blame and punishment. For, as we saw, to say that an agent is morally responsible for a wrongful act is to say, in part, that the agent is justifiably liable to blame and punishment. But the moral principles that thus attach blame and punishment to moral responsibility require that agents be blamed and punished only for those acts that originate in bodies over which they have direct control. Since the acts of a corporation are constituted or brought about wholly by bodily movements that are under the direct control of agents other than itself, it is inappropriate to blame or punish the corporation for those acts.

It is true, as French points out, that some corporate acts cannot be "attributed" to its members in the sense that such acts cannot be *predicated* of its members. When one corporation merges with another, for example, we cannot say of any individual member that he has himself "merged." But this does not imply that the individual member is not morally responsible for such corporate acts. An example may clarify this point. Suppose I deliberately chop down a tree and the tree falls. The fall can be predicated only of the tree (i.e., it is then correct to say, "The tree fell"); it cannot be predicated of me (i.e., it is not correct to say "I fell"). Nevertheless, I am morally responsible for the fall of the tree since I am the one who intentionally brought it about. Similarly, there are a variety of corporate acts that can be predicated only of the corporation (such as mergers, entering into certain contractual arrangements, bringing legal suits, etc.) and that cannot be predicated of the corporation's members. Nevertheless, the corporation's members can be morally responsible for such acts, since they are the ones who bring about all corporate acts. A corporate merger, for example, is an act constituted by or brought about by the bodily movements of certain of the corporation's members. (This does not mean that corporate acts are "reducible" without remainder to acts of individuals: corporate acts require a certain social context and the existence of certain constitutive rules.) Those corporate members who intentionally bring about a corporate act through the medium of their own bodies are as morally responsible for the corporate act as they are for anything else they intentionally bring about. It is a mistake to assume (as French does) that when some act can be predicated only of a corporate group, the corporate group must be the locus of the moral responsibility for that act. Moral responsibility for a corporation's acts lodges with the agents who bring about those acts and not with the corporate entity of which the act is predicated.

French is also wrong on claiming that the intentions we attribute to corporations are the kind on which moral responsibility rests. He is wrong, that is, with respect to the *mens rea* requirement. According to French, corporate "intentions" may be inferred from the corporation's official policies, decision-making procedures, and lines of authority, to which corporate members must adhere and which are typically designed to ensure that the concatenated decisions and actions of these corporate members will achieve certain objectives. French calls this system of policies, procedures, and lines of authority a "CID" (for Corporate Internal Decision) structure that "accomplishes a subordination and synthesis of the intentions and acts of various biological persons into a corporate decision." Although no particular member of the corporation may intend to achieve the objectives mandated or generated by the CID structure, nonetheless the corporation may be said to "intend" to achieve those objectives. And these intentions, according to French, are sufficient to render corporate acts "intentional."

French may be correct in saying that we can infer intentions from a corporation's policies and procedures and that these intentions may be attributed to the corporation and not to its members. But for that very reason, these intentions do not render the corporation's acts intentional. A corporate act, as I have argued, is brought about by the corporation's members, and if these members do not act with a certain intention, then their corporate act cannot be the act of carrying out that intention. But an act is intentional only if it is the carrying out of an intention formed in the mind of the agent whose bodily movements bring about the act. The intentions French attributes to corporations, then, do not mark out corporate acts as intentional because the intentions are attributed to one entity (the corporation) whereas the acts are carried out by another entity (the corporate members).

The underlying reason for corporate policies and procedures being unable to generate intentional action is that the concept of intentional action, as I have suggested, is rooted in the concept of an agent with a certain mental and bodily unity that corporations do not have. Intentional agents are mental insofar as they have minds by which they form plans or intentions; they are bodily insofar as they have bodies whose movements they directly control; and they are a unity insofar as the agent who forms intentions also directly controls the bodily movements by which those intentions are executed. It is in virtue of this fact—this unity—that I am said to originate actions (when the actions are the carrying out of intentions I originally formed) and it is also in virtue of this unity that my actions can be intentional: intentional action in the world requires a unity of mind and physical instrumentality. Corporate agents, as we know them, do not have this kind of unity and consequently their "intentions" do not connect with their actions in the proper way. There is a sense, of course, in which corporations do have minds and bodies: the minds and bodies of their members are at the service of the corporation. But these minds and bodies do not exhibit the proper unity. This does not mean that it is impossible to conceive of a corporate collectivity that does possess the proper kind of unity. Science fiction narratives, in fact, often ask us to imagine what such a collective agent would be like. In science fiction stories, for example, we are sometimes asked to imagine a situation in which bodies are gradually taken over by a single group mind. Here we are being asked to imagine a collectivity that has acquired the proper kind of unity between mind and physical instrumentality.

It is clear, then, that when French and others ask us to look upon the corporation as a collectivity that acts intentionally, they are asking us to conceptualize the corporation as exhibiting a unity of mind and body that a collectivity can possess only if it has a group mind. The genius of French's argument is that it identifies a corporate element—the system of corporate policies and procedures he calls the CID structure—that looks like it might be capable of playing the role of what I have called a group mind. Corporate policies and procedures, however, cannot serve as corporate minds for the simple reason that they are not minds: they do not form intentions, nor do they have direct control over any bodies by which they might carry out these intentions. Because they do not themselves originate intentions and because they do not themselves carry out intentions, corporate policies and procedures cannot be said to originate intentional actions. On the contrary, corporate policies and procedures are themselves wholly the products of the intentional actions of other agents and are carried out only when other agents freely choose to adhere to them.

Let me summarize my main criticisms. Those who, like French, want to attribute moral responsibility to corporations must distinguish two entities, the corporation and the corporation's members, for they want to hold that the corporation, as distinct from its members, can be morally responsible for its acts. However, moral responsibility for an act attaches to the entity that originates the act—i.e., the entity that formed the intention to bring about the act and that carried out that intention by its direct bodily movements. Since the acts of a corporation are brought about not by the direct bodily movements of the corporation (as an entity distinct from its members) but by those of its members, and since the intentions of the corporation (if there are such things) are not the intentions with which those members acted, it follows that the corporation is not the entity that is morally responsible for those acts.[11]

Who, then, is morally responsible for the acts of a corporation? There is no single answer to this question. To the extent that certain members of a corporation each intentionally decide to bring about a corporate act together, those members are each morally responsible for that corporate act. To the extent that a corporate act is the result of policies and procedures that were intentionally designed by certain persons to produce precisely that type of act, those persons are morally responsible for that act. And to the extent that a corporate act is the unintentional result of the concatenated actions of several corporate members, none of whom knew about or intended that outcome, the corporate act may be an act for which no one is morally responsible: it is an unintentional happening.

III

Let me leave French's views now and turn to a second set of arguments that show that corporations as distinct from their members cannot be morally responsible for what they do. This argument will also clarify what we might properly have in mind when we say that a corporation is "morally responsible" for a wrongful act. The argument relies on the way the concept of moral responsibility is conceptually connected to the concepts of blame and punishment. Although I have already indicated how these concepts are connected, I have not yet mentioned that the main reason we are interested in attributing moral responsibility is precisely in order to impose blame and punishment where they are due. This, I take it, is what has motivated many of the authors who have tried to show that corporations may legitimately be held to be morally responsible for wrongful acts. Many of us share, I believe, a legitimate intuition that someone should be blamed and punished for the wrongful corporate acts that we read about in the newspapers. Since the acts are attributed to corporations, we conclude (mistakenly) that "the corporation" should be blamed and punished for the act; and since blame and punishment presuppose moral responsibility, we may assume (again mistakenly) that corporations are the legitimate bearers of moral responsibility. The literature on corporate moral responsibility may thus be seen as an attempt to make sense of these mistaken conclusions and mistaken assumptions. What I will try to show now is that because of the way that moral responsibility is tied to blame and punishment, it makes little literal sense to say that corporations are morally responsible for their wrongful acts.

Obviously, we often say that this or that corporation is morally responsible for a wrongful act and that it should be blamed or punished for the act. Two questions regarding this statement must be addressed here: (1) What is the entity to which we can be referring when we say "the corporation" and (2) What can we mean by saying that that entity (and not another) is morally responsible and should be blamed and punished?

There are, I believe, three main answers to the first question. We sometimes use the term *corporation* to refer to a legal fictitious entity recognized by the law. In this sense the term refers to an entity distinct from the group of human beings that constitutes its members. We sometimes use the term to refer to an organization of human beings, and then it may refer to one of two things. First, it may refer to the set of relationships that obtain among a certain group of human beings. In this sense, "the corporation" refers to the structured set of relationships that allows us to identify a group of human beings and their activities as a corporate organization. Second, when referring to the corporation as an organization we may simply be referring to the group of human beings that constitute the members of the corporation. In this sense, "the corporation" refers to the human beings who make up the corporate organization.

There are, then, three main entities we may be referring to when we use the term *corporation*: (a) the fictitious legal entity, (b) the organization as a structured set of relationships, and (c) the organization as a set of human beings. We may safely set aside the first sense. When people attribute moral responsibility to a corporation and imply that it should be blamed and punished for its wrongdoing, they do not take themselves to be referring to a fictitious entity. That is, they are not referring to that legal entity classically described as "an artificial being, invisible, intangible, and existing only in the contemplation of law."[12] People who hold corporations morally responsible for their acts have in mind real agents that exert physical causality upon the world independently of the law. That is, they are referring to the corporations as an organization either in sense (b) or in sense (c).

Let us turn, then, to the second question: What can one mean by saying that the corporation in sense (b) or in sense (c), and not some other entity, is morally responsible for a wrong and should be blamed or punished? Consider sense (b) first. In attributing moral responsibility for a wrongful act to a corporation in sense (b), one is attributing moral responsibility to a structured set of relationships, and one is implying that this structured set of relationships, and not some other entity, should be blamed and punished for the act. But there are two reasons for thinking that this cannot be what people have in mind when claiming that corporations are morally responsible for a wrongful act. First and most obvious is the fact that it makes little sense to speak of "punishing" relationships. In what sense can relationships feel the shame that is the appropriate response to being blamed and in what sense can relationships experience the suffering or loss that accompanies punishment? When people claim that corporations are morally responsible for some wrongdoing and should be blamed or punished for that act, they are not talking about "punishing" relationships. Second, in saying that a set of organizational structures, and not some other entity, is morally responsible for an act, we imply that only those organizational structures, and not the organization's members, should receive the punishment consequent on that attribution of moral responsibility. (Of course, when we say that a corporation is morally responsible for a wrongdoing, we might want to hold morally responsible the members, in addition to the corporation's structures. But here I am focusing only on the moral responsibility attributed to those structures and on the punishment and blame that should be levied on those structures in virtue of *their* alleged moral corporation. That portion of the blame and punishment to which a corporate structure is liable in virtue of its own (alleged) moral responsibility for a wrong should not fall on the shoulders of the corporation's members.) All that a corporation's members should have to suffer is the blame and punishment consequent on their own moral responsibility; to make them suffer the punishment that should have been levied on the corporate structure would be to punish them twice. But in fact it is not possible to impose blame or punishment upon an organizational structure without having that blame or punishment fall on the shoulders of the corporation's members. It is the members who will feel all the effects and bear all the injuries if the corporation's structures are "fined," if its "public image" is "tarnished," or if these structures are altered or perhaps even dissolved. These members are therefore being unjustly forced to bear the punishment for another entity's moral responsibility (in addition to any punishment they may have to bear for their own moral responsibility for the act). And such unfair shifting of punishment *away* from the morally responsible party is certainly not what one has in mind when one says that corporations are morally responsible for their acts and should therefore be blamed and punished for them.

That leaves us, then, with sense (c): in saying that corporations are morally responsible for wrongful acts, we would have to mean that the group of human beings who constitute the corporation's members are morally responsible for that act and should bear the blame and punishment for the act. But here, again, it is possible to have a number of different things in mind. First, in saying that the group of people who make up the corporation should bear the blame and punishment for wrongful responsible acts, we might mean (1) that the blame and punishment should be imposed only on the "group as a whole" and should not be distributed among any of the particular members who make up the group; (2) that blame and punishment should be distributed to every member of the group; or (3) that blame and punishment should be distributed only to particular members of the group. We can immediately dismiss (1) since it is not possible to punish a "group as a whole" without having those punishments fall on the shoulders of particular members who make up the group. Moreover, these punishments would either fall on the shoulders of *every* member of the group, and then we would have case (2), or they would fall on *some* particular members, and then we would have case (3). So we can dismiss (1) and concentrate on (2) and (3).

It is clear enough, I believe, that when people say that a corporation is morally responsible for a wrongful act and thereby imply that it should be blamed and punished for that act, they cannot properly mean that blame and punishment should be distributed to *every* member of the corporation. For some members of the corporation may have been innocently ignorant of that wrongful act, may have done nothing whatsoever to contribute to the act, and may have been in no position to prevent the act. It would obviously be wrong to impose punishment and blame on such persons for acts of which they were ignorant and with which they had no causal connection. To punish and blame such people (who might include janitors, secretaries, stockholders, etc.) would clearly violate the moral principles on which, as I argued, liability to blame and punishment rests. I take it that when people say that a corporation is morally responsible for a wrongful act and should therefore be blamed and punished, they are not advocating punishment of the innocent (i.e., punishment of those in whom the corporate act in no way originated). We may therefore dismiss (2).

This leaves us, then, with (3). Saying that a corporation is morally responsible for some wrongful act is acceptable only if it is an elliptical way of claiming that there are some people in the corporation who are morally responsible for that act and who should therefore be blamed and punished. Who would these people be? Since it violates our moral principles to impose blame and punishment on those in whom a wrongful act did not originate, we must be elliptically referring to those people in the corporation who intentionally brought the act about through their direct bodily movements or who knowingly contributed to the act (or, in case of omissions, who knowingly failed to carry out the direct bodily movements they could and should have carried out to prevent it). We are often forced to adopt this elliptical way of speaking because, as outsiders, we are usually ignorant of the inner workings of a corporation. Suspecting that some members of a corporation knew that an act they were intentionally carrying out (or helping to carry out, or failing to prevent) was wrong, but not knowing who those members were, we refer to them under the rubric of "the corporation" and say that the corporation is morally responsible for the act. Obviously when we say this we do not mean to indict everyone in the corporation regardless of their complicity. Nor do we mean to indict a merely fictional entity, nor a set of relationships. We are pointing, rather, to the presence within the corporation of people who intentionally brought about the wrongful corporate act. To say that a corporation is morally responsible for some wrongful act, then, is but an elliptical way of saying (if what one is saying makes sense) that some people within the corporation are morally responsible for the act; it is not a way of attributing moral responsibility to some entity or structure called "the corporation" or to the entire corporate membership (except in the special case in which every individual intentionally contributed to the wrongful act). It is thus incorrect to attribute moral responsibility to the corporation as such.

Someone may object that when a company like Ford manufactures a product that injures a number of people, there is a sense in which everyone in the company contributed to the product and thereby contributed to the injuries. Moreover, when law courts compensate victims of such products, all the members of the company end up paying for the compensation (in the form of lowered salaries, decreased earnings, etc.) and all are thus in effect punished for the injurious act. This shows, someone may want to object, that we hold each member in a corporation morally responsible for wrongful corporate acts, whether that member intentionally helped to carry them out or not, and we are quite willing to punish each one merely for being a member of the corporation.

Such an objection, however, would be based on a confusion of different types of responsibility. Nothing that I have said here precludes us from claiming that entire corporate groups may be held "responsible" for a wrongful act in any of the *other* senses of corporation that I identified at the beginning of this essay. But it is important not to confuse attributions of corporation in these other senses with attributions of moral corporation. For example, corporations "as a whole" may legitimately be held *causally* responsible for an act or an effect. It thus makes perfectly good sense to attribute to *every* member of a corporation the *causal* responsibility for producing the products the corporation manufactures. But attributing causal responsibility to a corporate group is clearly not the same as attributing moral responsibility.

Although the issue is more complicated, it also makes perfectly good sense to attribute "compensatory" responsibility for an injury to *every* member of a corporation, even though not every member of the corporation may be morally responsible for the injury. When a party has been injured, of course, we generally rule that the injured party should be compensated by the person who is morally responsible for the injury. But we often abandon this rule when considerations of efficiency, fairness, ability to pay, causal connections, or risk distribution lead us to separate compensatory responsibility from moral responsibility. The law of torts holds, for example, that when an employee injures a third party in the course of the employee's work, the injured party is to be compensated by the employer because the injured party thereby has a greater chance of recovery (since the employer has a "deeper pocket" than the employee) and because the employer can more easily spread the risk for such injuries by purchasing insurance. Here considerations of social efficiency and risk distribution lead us to pin compensatory responsibility for an injury upon an employer, who may not be morally responsible for the injury, and through the employer upon the insurer, who must ultimately compensate the injured party. Charges of this kind, levied upon individuals who bear compensatory responsibility for an injury, obviously should not be counted as forms of punishment or blame (they do not carry with them any opprobrium nor any implication of moral guilt). Such charges are more like taxes levied upon individuals in order to spread among them the costs of our social intercourse in some morally appropriate way. Thus, it is quite appropriate to hold that all members of a corporate group should be made to pay for the damages arising from a corporate act even if not all members are morally responsible for that act. Considerations of efficiency, risk distribution, formal relationships, and ability to pay often lead us to attribute compensatory responsibility to a corporation in a way that affects all its members, even those who are innocent of any wrongdoing. When we thus pin the compensatory responsibility for an act upon a corporation, we are not punishing or blaming its members, nor are we trying to spread among the members of society the cost of injuries arising from our social intercourse. And such distributions of costs should not be confused with implied attributions of moral responsibility.

It is clearly important to keep the various senses of responsibility distinct. It is also important not to run together the meaning the term *moral responsibility* may have when it is applied to human individuals with the meaning it may have when it is applied to corporate organizations. For as used of human beings, the term is embedded in a system of psychological, physiological, and moral notions that distinguish human beings and their modes of acting from corporate groups and the modes of action proper to them. The differences between a human being and a group of human beings are so obvious and enormous that it is quite astonishing to find people wanting to assimilate one to the other. Unfortunately, applying the term *moral responsibility* indiscriminately both to human beings and to corporate groups tends to confuse and hide these morally important (and actually quite gross) differences between them and their modes of acting. Nothing is gained by attempting to lump both human moral responsibility and corporate responsibility under the same term. Doing so merely forces us to look for other ways of drawing the important distinctions that separate the two.

IV

I will end by giving two reasons for thinking it is dangerous to accept the erroneous view that the corporation is a moral agent, that is, an agent that is morally responsible for its actions. First, if we accept the view that moral responsibility for wrongful corporate acts rests with the corporation, we will tend to be satisfied with blaming or punishing only the corporate entity. Instead of pointing our blame and aiming our punishment at the people who carried out the actions that produced these wrongs, we will do nothing but futilely wave our hands before the corporate veil. If we are to deter corporate wrongdoing and be assured that corporate members will comply with our moral and legal norms, our blame and punishment must travel behind the corporate veil to lodge with those who knowingly and intentionally bring about the corporation's acts. Since corporate acts originate in them, they must be blamed and punished for those acts.

Second, and perhaps more important, viewing the corporation as an entity that can "act" and "intend" like a large-scale personality will result in our being tempted to look upon the corporation as a larger-than-human person whose ends and well-being are more important than those of its members. We will be tempted, that is, to look upon the corporation as organic theories of the state looked upon the state: since the corporation is a whole person (with its own group mind) and the member merely a part, the interests of the corporation's members may legitimately be sacrificed to the corporation's interests and the good of the individual may be subordinated to the corporation's good. The extent to which this organic model of the corporation has already started to dominate managerial theory and has led practicing managers to subordinate the individual to the corporation is nicely documented by William Scott and David Hart, who write:

> The word "health" was seldom used in connection with organizations. It has appeared more frequently, in the last fifteen or twenty years, as the analogy of the organization to an organic system has gained widespread acceptance. . . . The organizational imperative [has now become] . . . absolute: Whatever is good for the individual can only come from the modern organization. . . . Therefore, all behavior must enhance the health of such organizations. . . . The overriding concern of managers is to keep their organizations healthy; if their clients are served as a consequence, it is a happy secondary result of the primary managerial concern.[13]

Scott and Hart, of course, note the drift toward an organizational totalitarianism that this organic theory of the corporation implies. My view is that philosophers who subscribe to the theory that the corporation is a moral agent that is morally responsible for its wrongful acts are unwittingly allying themselves with this new form of totalitarianism. As loyalty to the corporation becomes the basic virtue and service to the corporation the basic moral act, the individual will end by being swallowed up by the corporation.

Notes

1. See Manuel Velasquez, *Business Ethics: Concepts and Cases* (Englewood Cliffs, NJ: Prentice-Hall, 1982), p. 17; Michael Keeley, "Organizations as Non-Persons," *Journal of Value Inquiry* 15, no. 2 (1981): 149–55.

2. See Thomas Donaldson, *Corporations and Morality* (Englewood Cliffs, NJ: Prentice-Hall, 1982), pp. 32–34. Donaldson argues that certain types of corporations are "moral agents" (i.e., that they can be held morally responsible for their actions) and then devotes several pages to elaborating a social-contract argument that is supposed to generate a business ethic for these corporate agents. Donaldson is at pains to distinguish his view from what he calls the "moral person view," but in the end his argument attributes to *certain types* of corporations all the significant characteristics of moral personalities. See also David T. Ozar, "The Moral Responsibility of Corporations," in *Ethical Issues in Business: A Philosophical Approach,* ed. Thomas Donaldson and Patricia Werhane (Englewood Cliffs, NJ: Prentice-Hall, 1979), pp. 294–99; Kenneth E. Goodpaster and John B. Matthews, Jr., "Can a Corporation Have a Conscience?" *Harvard Business Review* 60 (1982):132–41.

3. The importance of this usage was pointed out to me by Kenneth E. Goodpaster, who commented on an earlier version of this paper delivered in Columbus, Ohio, at the 1982 meeting of the Western Division of the American Philosophical Association; see Goodpaster and Matthews, op. cit., p.133.

4. Immanuel Kant, *The Metaphysical Elements of Justice,* trans. John Ladd (New York: Bobbs-Merrill Company, 1968), pp. 24, 29.

5. The notion of a "direct" bodily movement is neither mysterious nor obscure. A "direct" bodily movement is simply a bodily movement over which I have the kind of direct control that I have when I deliberately move my arm in a normal manner; this kind of direct control is absent when my arm is paralyzed or "asleep" and I have to move my arm indirectly by pushing or lifting it with another part of my body.

6. See Richard B. Brandt, *Ethical Theory* (Englewood Cliffs, NJ: Prentice-Hall, 1959). Brandt's account of the utilitarian basis of punishment is derived from Jeremy Bentham's *Principles of Morals and Legislation.*

7. For the Kantian roots of this view of punishment, see Jeffrie G. Murphy, "Marxism and Retribution," *Philosophy and Public Affairs* 2 (1973):217–43; and Jeffrie G. Murphy, *Kant: The Philosophy of Right* (London: Macmillan and Co., 1970), pp. 109–12 and 140–44.

8. See Saint Thomas Aquinas, *Summa Theologica,* I-IIae, Q. I, a. I; Q.87, a.3, a.8.; and Saint Augustine, *De Libero Arbitrio,* bk. I, chap. xv, chap. xvi; bk. III, chap. ix.

9. Peter French, "The Corporation as a Moral Person," *American Philosophical Quarterly* 16, no. 3 (July 1979):297–17. Similar arguments appear in Qzar, op. cit.; Goodpaster and Matthews, op. cit.; Thomas Donaldson, "Moral Agency and Corporations," *Philosophy in Context* 10 (1980):51–70; and D. E. Cooper, "Collective Responsibility," *Philosophy* 43 (1968):258–68. See also the articles collected in Peter A. French, ed., *Individual and Collective Responsibility: The Massacre at My Lai* (Cambridge, MA: Schenkman, 1972), especially David Cooper, "Responsibility and the 'System' "; R. S. Downie, "Responsibility and Social Roles"; and Virginia Held, "Moral Responsibility and Collective Action."

10. See Larry May, "Vicarious Agency," a paper delivered at the University of Illinois at Chicago Circle, May 15, 1981, for the Conference on Business and Professional Ethics. May argues that all corporate acts are only "vicariously" attributed to corporations. His argument seems to be based on the assumption that corporations may be conceived only as fictitious legal entities, an assumption I do not share.

11. I will surely be accused at this point of trying to "reduce" corporations to their members. But nothing in my account implies such a reductionist view of the corporation. On the contrary, my view is that a corporation consists of (1) a set of positions ordinarily filled by human beings and (2) a set of relationships that obtain between each of these positions as well as between these positions and other people in society. In addition, it is clear that a corporation cannot exist unless there also exists an accepted set of constitutive rules stipulating that such a set of positions filled by such human beings in such relationships shall count as "a corporation." Thus it is wrong to try to "reduce" a corporation to its members, since corporations not only consist of more than their members, but they also require the existence of a background system of constitutive rules. I also do not hold that the *acts* of a corporation can be "reduced" without remainder to the acts of its members. For a corporate act requires, besides the acts of the members, a certain set of relationships among these acts and the members and between their acts and society, as well as a background system of constitutive rules stipulating that when such corporate members act and when such relationships obtain, their acts shall count as the act of the corporation. Thus a corporate act is an effect brought about by or constituted by the voluntary bodily movements of corporate members (or the omissions of such movements) who are related in a certain way and who act against a background system of constitutive rules. I do, of course, hold that all corporate acts "originate" only in the members of the corporation (in the sense defined above) and, as I will later argue, that the moral responsibility attributed to the corporation does indeed reduce to the moral responsibility of its members. But a reductive view of moral responsibility does not imply a reductive view of corporate acts.

12. Chief Justice Marshall, *Dartmouth College* v. *Woodward,* 4 Wheat 518, 636 (1819).

13. William G. Scott and David K. Hart, *Organizational America* (Boston: Houghton Mifflin Company, 1979), pp. 37, 43, 47.

9

The Corporation as a Moral Person

Peter A. French
1979

I

In one of his *New York Times* columns of not too long ago Tom Wicker's ire was aroused by a Gulf Oil Corporation advertisement that "pointed the finger of blame" for the energy crisis at all elements of our society (and supposedly away from the oil company). Wicker attacked Gulf Oil as the major, if not the sole, perpetrator of that crisis and virtually every other social ill, with the possible exception of venereal disease. It does not matter whether Wicker was serious or sarcastic in making his charges (I suspect he was in deadly earnest). I am interested in the sense ascriptions of moral responsibility make when their subjects are corporations. I hope to provide the foundation of a theory that allows treatment of corporations as members of the moral community, of equal standing with the traditionally acknowledged residents: biological human beings, and hence treats Wicker-type responsibility ascriptions as unexceptionable instances of a perfectly proper sort without having to paraphrase them. In short, corporations can be full-fledged moral persons and have whatever privileges, rights and duties as are, in the normal course of affairs, accorded to moral persons.

II

It is important to distinguish three quite different notions of what constitutes personhood that are entangled in our tradition: the metaphysical, moral and legal concepts. The entanglement is clearly evident in Locke's account of personal identity. He writes that the term "person" is "a *forensic* term, appropriating actions and their merit; and so belongs only to *intelligent agents*, capable of law, and happiness, and misery."[1] He goes on to say that by consciousness and memory persons are capable of extending themselves into the past and thereby become "concerned and *accountable*."[2] Locke is historically correct in citing the law as a primary origin of the term "person." But he is incorrect in maintaining that its legal usage somehow entails its metaphysical sense, agency; and whether or not either sense, but especially the metaphysical, is interdependent on the moral sense, accountability, is surely controversial. Regarding the relationship between metaphysical and moral persons there are two distinct schools of thought. According to one, to be a metaphysical person is to be a moral one; to understand what it is to be accountable one must understand what it is to be an intelligent or a rational agent and vice-versa; while according to the other, being an agent is a necessary but not sufficient condition of being a moral person. Locke holds the interdependence view with which I agree, but he roots both moral and metaphysical persons in the juristic person, which is, I think, wrong-headed. The preponderance of current thinking tends to some version of the necessary pre-condition view, but it does have the virtue of treating the legal person as something apart.

It is of note that many contemporary moral philosophers and economists both take a pre-condition view of the relationship between the metaphysical and moral person and also adopt a particular view of the legal personhood of corporations that effectually excludes corporations *per se* from the class of moral persons. Such philosophers and economists champion the least defensible of a number of possible interpretations of the juristic personhood of corporations, but their doing so allows them to systematically sidestep the question of whether corporations can meet the conditions of metaphysical personhood.[3]

III

John Rawls is, to some extent, guilty of fortifying what I hope to show is an indefensible interpretation of the legal concept and of thereby encouraging an anthropocentric bias that has led to the general belief that corporations just cannot be moral persons. As is well known, Rawls defends his two principles of justice by the use of a thought experiment that incorporates the essential characteristics of what he takes to be a pre-moral, though metaphysical population and then "derives" the moral guidelines for social institutions that they would accept. The persons (or parties) in the "original position" are described by Rawls as being mutually self-interested, rational, as having similar wants, needs, interests and capacities and as being, for all intents and purposes, equal in power (so that no one of them can dominate the others). Their choice of the principles of justice is, as Dennett has pointed out,[4] a rather dramatic rendering of one version of the compelling (though I think unnecessarily complex) philosophical thesis that only out of metaphysical persons can moral ones evolve.

But Rawls is remarkably ambiguous (and admittedly so) regarding who or what may qualify as a metaphysical person. He admits into the category, in one sentence, not only biological human beings but "nations, provinces, business firms, churches, teams, and so on,"[5] then, perhaps because he does not want to tackle the demonstration of the rationality, etc., of those institutions and organizations, or because he is a captive of the traditional prejudice in favor of biological persons, in the next sentence he withdraws entry. "There is, perhaps, a certain logical priority to the case of human individuals: it may be possible to analyze the actions of so-called artificial persons as logical constructions of the actions of human persons . . ."[6] "Perhaps" is, of course, a rather large hedge behind which to hide; but it is, I suppose, of some significance that in *A Theory of Justice* when he is listing the nature of the parties in the "original position" he adds "c. associations (states, churches, or other corporate bodies)."[7] He does not, unhappily, discuss this entry on his list anywhere else in the book. Rawls has hold, I think, of an important intuition: that some associations of human beings should be treated as metaphysical persons capable on his account of becoming moral persons, in and of themselves. He has, however, shrunk from the task of exploring the implications of that intuition and has instead retreated to the comfortable bulwarks of the anthropocentric bias.

IV

Many philosophers, including, I think, Rawls, have rather uncritically relied upon what they incorrectly perceive to be the most defensible juristic treatment of collectivities such as corporations as a paradigm for the treatment of corporations in their moral theories. The concept of corporate legal personhood under any of its popular interpretations is, I want to argue, virtually useless for moral purposes.

Following many writers on jurisprudence, a juristic person may be defined as any entity that is a subject of a right. There are good etymological grounds for such an inclusive neutral definition. The Latin "*persona*" originally referred to *dramatis personae*, and in Roman law the term was adopted to refer to anything that could act on either side of a legal dispute. [It was not until Boethius' definition of a person: "*Persona est naturae rationabilis individua substantia* (a person is the individual subsistence of a rational nature)" that metaphysical traits were ascribed to persons.] In effect, in Roman legal tradition persons are creations, artifacts, of the law itself, i.e., of the legislature that enacts the law, and are not considered to have, or only have incidentally, existence of any kind outside of the legal sphere. The law, on the Roman interpretation, is systematically ignorant of the biological status of its subjects.

The Roman notion applied to corporations is popularly known as the Fiction Theory. Hallis characterizes that theory as maintaining that "the personality of a corporate body is a pure fiction and owes its existence to a creative act of the state."[8] Rawls' view of corporate persons could not, however, be motivated by adherence to the Fiction Theory for two reasons. The theory does not demand a dichotomy between real and artificial persons. All juristic persons, on the theory, are creations of the law. The theory does not view the law as recognizing or verifying some pre-legally existing persons; it argues that the law creates its own subjects. Secondly, the theory, in its pure form at least, does not regard any juristic persons as composites. All things which are legislatively created as subjects of rights are nonreducible or, if you will, primitive individual legal persons. (It is of some note that the Fiction Theory is enshrined in English law in regard to corporate bodies by no less an authority than Sir Edward Coke who wrote that corporations "rest only in intendment and consideration of the law."[9])

The Fiction Theory's major rival in American jurisprudence and the view that does seem to inform Rawls' account is what I shall call "the Legal Aggregate Theory of the Corporation." It holds that the names of corporate bodies are only umbrellas that cover (but do not shield) certain biological persons. The Aggregate Theory treats biological status as having legal priority and corporate existence as a contrivance for purposes of summary reference. (Generally, it may be worth mention, Aggregate Theorists tend to ignore employees and identify corporations with directors, executives and stockholders. The model on which they stake their claim is no doubt that of the primitive partnership.) I have shown elsewhere[10] that to treat a corporation as an aggregate for any purposes is to fail to recognize the key logical differences between corporations and mobs. The Aggregate Theory, then, despite the fact that it has been quite popular in legislatures, courtrooms, and on streetcorners simply ignores key logical, socio-economic and historical facts of corporate existence. [It might prove of some value in clarifying the dispute between Fiction and Aggregate theorists to mention a rather famous case in the English law. (The case is cited by Hallis.) It is that of *Continental Tyre and Rubber Co., Ltd.* vs *Daimler Co. Ltd.* Very sketchily, the Continental Tyre company was incorporated in England and carried on its business there. Its business was the selling of tires made in Germany, and all of its directors were German subjects in residence in Germany, and all but one of its shares were held by German subjects. The case arose during the First World War, and it turned on the issue of whether the company was an English subject by virtue of its being incorporated under the English law and independent of its directors and stockholders, and could hence bring suit in an English court against an English subject while a state of war existed. The majority opinion of The Court of Appeals (5–1) was that the corporation was an entity created by statute and hence was "a different person altogether from the subscribers to the memorandum or the shareholders on the register."[11] Hallis aptly summarizes the judgment of the court when he writes that "The Continental Tyre and Rubber Co., Ltd., was an English company with a personality at law distinct from the personalities of its members and could therefore sue in the English Courts as a British Subject."[12] The House of Lords, however, supporting the Aggregate Theory and no doubt motivated by the demands of the War, overturned the Court of Appeals. Lord Buckley wrote "The artificial legal entity has no independent power of motion. It is moved by the corporator. . . . He is German in fact although British in form."[13] This view has seen many incarnations since on both sides of the Atlantic. I take Rawls' burying of his intuition in the logical priority of human beings as a recent echoing of the words of Lord Parker who in the Continental Tyre case wrote for the majority in the House of Lords: ". . . the character in which the property is held and the character in which the capacity to act is enjoyed and acts are done are not *in pari materia*. The latter character is a quality of the company itself, and conditions its capacities and its acts and is attributable only to human beings . . ."][14]

In Germanic legal tradition resides the third major rival interpretation of corporate juristic personhood. Due primarily to the advocacy of Otto von Gierke, the so-called Reality Theory recognizes corporations to be pre-legal existing sociological persons. Underlying the theory is the view that law cannot create its subjects, it only determines which societal facts are in conformity with its requirements. At most, law endorses the pre-legal existence of persons for its own purposes. Gierke regards the corporation as an offspring of certain social actions having then a *de facto* personality, which the law only declares to be a juridical fact.[15] The Reality Theory's primary virtue is that it does not ignore the non-legal roots of the corporation while it, as does the Fiction Theory, acknowledges the non-identity of the corporation and the aggregate of its directors, stockholders, executives and employees. The primary difference between the Fiction and Reality Theories, that one treats the corporate person as *de jure* and the other as *de facto*, however, turns out to be of no real importance in regard to the issue of the moral personhood of a corporation. Admittedly the Reality Theory encapsulates a view at least superficially more amenable to arguing for discrete corporate moral personhood than does the Fiction Theory just because it does acknowledge *de facto* personhood, but theorists on both sides will admit that they are providing interpretations of only the formula "juristic person = the subject of rights," and as long as we stick to legal history, no interpretation of that formula need concern itself with metaphysical personhood or agency. The *de facto* personhood of the Reality Theory is that of a sociological entity only, of which no claim is or need be made regarding agency or rationality etc. One could, without contradiction, hold the Reality Theory and deny the metaphysical or moral personhood of corporations. What is needed is a Reality Theory that identifies a *de facto* metaphysical person not just a sociological entity.

Underlying all of these interpretations of corporate legal personhood is a distinction, embedded in the law itself, that renders them unhelpful for our purposes. Being a subject of rights is often contrasted in the law with being an "administrator of rights." Any number of entities and associations can and have been the subjects of legal rights. Legislatures have given rights to unborn human beings, they have reserved rights for human beings long after their death, and in some recent cases they have invested rights in generations of the future.[16] Of course such subjects of rights, though they are legal persons, cannot dispose of their rights, cannot administer them, because to administer a right one must be an agent, i.e., able to act in certain ways. It may be only an historical accident that most legal cases are cases in which "the subject of right *X*" and "the administrator of right *X*" are co-referential. It is nowhere required by law, under any of the three above theories or elsewhere, that it be so. Yet, it is possession of the attributes of an administrator of rights and not those of a subject of rights that are among the generally regarded conditions of moral personhood. It is a fundamental mistake to regard the fact of juristic corporate personhood as having settled the question of the moral personhood of a corporation one way or the other.

V

Two helpful lessons however, are learned from an investigation of the legal personhood of corporations: (1) biological existence is not essentially associated with the concept of a person (only the fallacious Aggregate Theory depends upon reduction to biological referents) and (2) a paradigm for the form of an inclusive neutral definition of a moral person is provided: "a subject of a right." I shall define a moral person as the referent of any proper name or description that can be a non-eliminatable subject of what I shall call (and presently discuss) a responsibility ascription of the second type. The non-eliminatable nature of the subject should be stressed because responsibility and other moral predicates are neutral as regards person and person-sum predication.[17] Though we might say that The Ox-Bow mob should be held responsible for the death of three men, a mob is an example of what I have elsewhere called an aggregate collectivity with no identity over and above that of the sum of the identities of its component membership, and hence to use "The Ox-Bow mob" as the subject of such ascriptions is to make summary reference to each member of the mob. For that reason mobs do not qualify as metaphysical or moral persons.

VI

There are at least two significantly different types of responsibility ascriptions that should be distinguished in ordinary usage (not counting the lauditory recommendation, "He is a responsible lad.") The first-type pins responsibility on someone or something, the who-dun-it or what-dun-it sense. Austin has pointed out that it is usually used when an event or action is thought by the speaker to be untoward. (Perhaps we are more interested in the failures rather than the successes that punctuate our lives.)

The second-type of responsibility ascription, parasitic upon the first, involves the notion of accountability. ''Having a responsibility'' is interwoven with the notion ''Having a liability to answer,'' and having such a liability or obligation seems to imply (as Anscombe has noted[18]) the existence of some sort of authority relationship either between people or between people and a deity or in some weaker versions between people and social norms. The kernel of insight that I find intuitively compelling, is that for someone to legitimately hold someone else responsible for some event there must exist or have existed a responsibility relationship between them such that in regard to the event in question the latter was answerable to the former. In other words, ''*X* is responsible for *y*,'' as a second-type ascription, is properly uttered by someone *Z* if *X* in respect to *y* is or was accountable to *Z*. Responsibility relationships are created in a multitude of ways, e.g., through promises, contracts, compacts, hirings, assignments, appointments, by agreeing to enter a Rawlsian original position, etc. The right to hold responsible is often delegatable to third parties; though in the case of moral responsibility no delegation occurs because no person is excluded from the relationship: moral responsibility relationships hold reciprocally and without prior agreements among all moral persons. No special arrangement needs to be established between parties for anyone to hold someone morally responsible for his acts or, what amounts to the same thing, every person is a party to a responsibility relationship with all other persons as regards the doing or refraining from doing of certain acts: those that take descriptions that use moral notions.

Because our interest is in the criteria of moral personhood and not the content of morality we need not pursue this idea further. What I have maintained is that moral responsibility, although it is neither contractual nor optional, is not a class apart but an extension of ordinary, garden-variety, responsibility. What is needed in regard to the present subject then is an account of the requirements for entry into any responsibility relationship, and we have already seen that the notion of the juristic person does not provide a sufficient account. For example, the deceased in a probate case cannot be held responsible in the relevant way by anyone, even though the deceased is a juristic person, a subject of rights.

VII

A responsibility ascription of the second type amounts to the assertion of a conjunctive proposition, the first conjunct of which identifies the subject's actions with or as the cause of an event (usually an untoward one) and the second conjunct asserts that the action in question was intended by the subject or that the event was the direct result of an intentional act of the subject. In addition to what it asserts it implies that the subject is accountable to the speaker (in the case at hand) because of the subject's relationship to the speaker (who the speaker is or what the speaker is, a member of the "moral community," a surrogate for that aggregate). The primary focus of responsibility ascriptions of the second type is on the subject's intentions rather than, though not to the exclusion of, occasions. Austin wrote: "In considering responsibility, few things are considered more important than to establish whether a man *intended* to do A, or whether he did A intentionally."[19] To be the subject of a responsibility ascription of the second type, to be a party in responsibility relationships, hence to be a moral person, the subject must be at minimum, what I shall call a Davidsonian agent.[20] If corporations are moral persons, they will be non-eliminatable Davidsonian agents.

VIII

For a corporation to be treated as a Davidsonian agent it must be the case that some things that happen, some events, are describable in a way that makes certain sentences true, sentences that say that some of the things a corporation does were intended by the corporation itself. That is not accomplished if attributing intentions to a corporation is only a shorthand way of attributing intentions to the biological persons who comprise e.g. its board of directors. If that were to turn out to be the case then on metaphysical if not logical grounds there would be no way to distinguish between corporations and mobs. I shall argue, however, that a *C*orporation's *I*nternal *D*ecision Structure (its CID Structure) is the requisite redescription device that licenses the predication of corporate intentionality.

Intentionality, though a causal notion, is an intentional one and so it does not mark out a class of actions or events. Attributions of intentionality in regard to any event are referentially opaque with respect to other descriptions of that event, or, in other words, the fact that, given one description, an action was intentional does not entail that on every other description of the action it was intentional. A great deal depends upon what aspect of an event is being described. We can correctly say, e.g., "Hamlet intentionally kills the person hiding in Gertrude's room (one of Davidson's examples), but Hamlet does not intentionally kill Polonius," although "Polonius" and "the person hiding in Gertrude's room" are co-referential. The event may be properly described as "Hamlet killed Polonius" and also as "Hamlet intentionally killed the person hiding in Gertrude's room (behind the arras)," but not as "Hamlet intentionally killed Polonius," for that was not Hamlet's intention. (He, in fact, thought he was killing the King.) The referential opacity of intentionality attributions, I shall presently argue, is congenial to the driving of a wedge between the descriptions of certain events as individual intentional actions and as corporate intentional actions.

Certain events, that is, actions, are describable as simply the bodily movements of human beings and sometimes those same events are redescribable in terms of their upshots, as bringing about something, e.g. (from Austin[21]) feeding penguins *by* throwing them peanuts ("by" is the most common way we connect different descriptions of the same event[22]), and sometimes those events can be redescribed as the effects of some prior cause; then they are described as done for reasons, done in order to bring about something, e.g., feeding the penguins peanuts in order to kill them. Usually what we single out as that prior cause is some desire or felt need combined with the belief that the object of the desire will be achieved by the action undertaken. (This, I think, is what Aristotle meant when he maintained that acting requires desire.) Saying "someone (*X*) did *y* intentionally" is to describe an event (*y*) as the upshot of *X*'s having had a reason for doing it which was the cause of his doing it.

It is obvious that a corporation's doing something involves or includes human beings doing things and that the human beings who occupy various positions in a corporation usually can be described as having reasons for *their* behavior. In virtue of those descriptions they may be properly held responsible for their behavior, *ceteris paribus*. What needs to be shown is that there is sense in saying that corporations and not just the people who work in them, have reasons for doing what they do. Typically, we will be told that it is the directors, or the managers, etc., that really have the corporate reasons and desires, etc., and that although corporate actions may not be reducible without remainder, corporate intentions are always reducible to human intentions.

IX

Every corporation has an internal decision structure. CID Structures have two elements of interest to us here: (1) an organizational or responsibility flow chart that delineates stations and levels within the corporate power structure and (2) corporate decision recognition rule(s) (usually embedded in something called "corporation policy"). The CID Structure is the personnel organization for the exercise of the corporation's power with respect to its ventures, and as such its primary function is to draw experience from various levels of the corporation into a decision-making and ratification process. When operative and properly activated, the CID Structure accomplishes a subordination and synthesis of the intentions and acts of various biological persons into a corporate decision. When viewed in another way, as already suggested, the CID Structure licenses the descriptive transformation of events, seen under another aspect as the acts of biological persons (those who occupy various stations on the organizational chart), to corporate acts by exposing the corporate character of those events. A functioning CID Structure *incorporates* acts of biological persons. For illustrative purposes, suppose we imagine that an event E has at least two aspects, that is, can be described in two non-identical ways. One of those aspects is "Executive *X*'s doing *y*" and one is "Corporation *C*'s doing *z*." The corporate act and the individual act may have different properties; indeed they have different causal ancestors though they are causally inseparable. (The causal inseparability of these acts I hope to show is a product of the CID Structure, *X*'s doing *y* is not the cause of *C*'s doing *z* nor is *C*'s doing *z* the cause of *X*'s doing *y* although if *X*'s doing *y* causes event *F* then *C*'s doing *z* causes *F* and *vice versa*.)

Although I doubt he is aware of the metaphysical reading that can be given to this process. J. K. Galbraith rather neatly captures what I have in mind when he writes in his recent popular book on the history of economics: "From [the] interpersonal exercise of power, the interaction . . . of the participants, comes the *personality* of the corporation."[23] I take Galbraith here to be quite literally correct, but it is important to spell out how a CID Structure works this "miracle."

In philosophy in recent years we have grown accustomed to the use of games as models for understanding institutional behavior. We all have some understanding of how rules in games make certain descriptions of events possible that would not be so if those rules were nonexistent. The CID Structure of a corporation is a kind of constitutive rule (or rules) analogous to the game rules with which we are familiar. The organization chart of a corporation distinguishes "players" and clarifies their rank and the interwoven lines of responsibility within the corporation. An organizational chart tells us, for example, that anyone holding the title "Executive Vice President for Finance Administration" stands in a certain relationship to anyone holding the title "Director of Internal Audit" and to anyone holding the title "Treasurer," etc. In effect it expresses, or maps, the interdependent and dependent relationships, line and staff, that are involved in determinations of corporate decisions and actions. The organizational chart provides what might be called the grammar of corporate decision-making. What I shall call internal recognition rules provide its logic.

By "recognition rule(s)" I mean what Hart, in another context, calls "conclusive affirmative indication"[24] that a decision on an act has been made or performed for corporate reasons. Recognition rules are of two sorts. Partially embedded in the organizational chart are procedural recognitors: we see that decisions are to be reached collectively at certain levels and that they are to be ratified at higher levels (or at inner circles, if one prefers that Galbraithean model). A corporate decision is recognized internally, however, not only by the procedure of its making, but by the policy it instantiates. Hence every corporation creates an image (not to be confused with its public image) or a general policy, what G. C. Buzby of the Chilton Company has called the "basic belief of the corporation,"[25] that must inform its decisions for them to be properly described as being those of that corporation. "The moment policy is side-stepped or violated, it is no longer the policy of that company."[26]

Peter Drucker has seen the importance of the basic policy recognitors in the CID Structure (though he treats matters rather differently from the way I am recommending.) Drucker writes:

> Because the corporation is an institution it must have a basic policy. For it must subordinate individual ambitions and decisions to the *needs* of the corporation's welfare and survival. That means that it must have a set of principles and a rule of conduct which limit and direct individual actions and behavior . . .[27]

X

Suppose, for illustrative purposes, we activate a CID Structure in a corporation, Wicker's favorite, the Gulf Oil Corporation. Imagine that three executives *X, Y* and *Z* have the task of deciding whether or not Gulf Oil will join a world uranium cartel. *X, Y* and *Z* have before them an Everest of papers that have been prepared by lower echelon executives. Some of the papers will be purely factual reports, some will be contingency plans, some will be formulations of positions developed by various departments, some will outline financial considerations, some will be legal opinions and so on. In so far as these will all have been processed through Gulf's CID Structure system, the personal reasons, if any, individual executives may have had when writing their reports and recommendations in a specific way will have been diluted by the subordination of individual inputs to peer group input even before *X, Y* and *Z* review the matter. *X, Y* and *Z* take a vote. Their taking of a vote is authorized procedure in the Gulf CID Structure, which is to say that under these circumstances the vote of *X, Y* and *Z* can be redescribed as the corporation's making a decision: that is, the event "*XYZ* voting" may be redescribed to expose an aspect otherwise unrevealed, that is quite different from its other aspects e.g., from *X*'s voting in the affirmative. Redescriptive exposure of a procedurally corporate aspect of an event, however, is not to be confused with a description of an event that makes true a sentence that says that the corporation did something intentionally. But the CID Structure, as already suggested, also provides the grounds in its other type of recognitor for such an attribution of corporate intentionality. Simply, when the corporate act is consistent with, an instantiation or an implementation of established corporate policy, then it is proper to describe it as having been done for corporate reasons, as having been caused by a corporate desire coupled with a corporate belief and so, in other words, as corporate intentional.

An event may, under one of its aspects, be described as the conjunctive act "*X* did *a* (or as *X* intentionally did *a*) & Y did *a* (or as *Y* intentionally did *a*) & *Z* did *a* (or as *Z* intentionally did *a*)" (where *a* = voted in the affirmative on the question of Gulf Oil joining the cartel). Given the Gulf CID Structure, formulated in this instance as the conjunction of rules: when the occupants of positions *A, B* and *C* on the organizational chart unanimously vote to do something and if doing that something is consistent with, an instantiation or an implementation of general corporate policy and *ceteris paribus,* then the corporation has decided to do it for corporate reasons, the event is redescribable as "the Gulf Oil Corporation did *j* for corporate reasons *f*" (where *j* is "decided to join the cartel" and *f* is any reason (desire + belief) consistent with basic policy of Gulf Oil, e.g., increasing profits) or simply as "Gulf Oil Corporation intentionally did *j*." This is a rather technical way of saying that in these circumstances the executives voting is, given its CID Structure, also the corporation deciding to do something, and that regardless of the personal reasons the executives have for voting as they do and even if their reasons are inconsistent with established corporate policy or even if one of them has no reason at all for voting as he does, the corporation still has reasons for joining the cartel; that is, joining is consistent with the inviolate corporate general policies as encrusted in the precedent of previous corporate actions and its statements of purpose as recorded in its certificate of incorporation, annual reports, etc. The corporation's only method of achieving its desires or goals is the activation of the personnel who occupy its various positions. However, if *X* voted affirmatively purely for reasons of personal monetary gain (suppose he had been bribed to do so) that does not alter the fact that the corporate reason for joining the cartel was to minimize competition and hence pay higher dividends to its shareholders. Corporations have reasons because they have interests in doing those things that are likely to result in realization of their established corporate goals regardless of the transient self-interest of directors, managers, etc. If there is a difference between corporate goals and desires and those of human beings it is probably that the corporate ones are relatively stable and not very wide ranging, but that is only because corporations can do relatively fewer things than human beings, being confined in action predominately to a limited socio-economic sphere. The attribution of corporate intentionality is opaque with respect to other possible descriptions of the event in question. It is, of course, in a corporation's interest that its component membership view the corporate purposes as instrumental in the achievement of their own goals. (Financial reward is the most common way this is achieved.)

It will be objected that a corporation's policies reflect only the current goals of its directors. But that is certainly not logically necessary nor is it in practice true for most large corporations. Usually, of course, the original incorporators will have organized to further their individual interests and/or to meet goals which they shared. But even in infancy the melding of disparate interests and purposes gives rise to a corporate long range point of view that is distinct from the intents and purposes of the collection of incorporators viewed individually. Also, corporate basic purposes and policies, as already mentioned, tend to be relatively stable when compared to those of individuals and not couched in the kind of language that would be appropriate to individual purposes. Furthermore, as histories of corporations will show, when policies are amended or altered it is usually only peripheral issues that are involved. Radical policy alteration constitutes a new corporation, a point that is captured in the incorporation laws of such states as Delaware. ("Any power which is not enumerated in the charter and the general law or which cannot be inferred from these two sources is *ultra vires* of the corporation.") Obviously underlying the objection is an uneasiness about the fact that corporate intent is dependent upon policy and purpose that is but an artifact of the socio-psychology of a group of biological persons. Corporate intent seems somehow to be a tarnished illegitimate offspring of human intent. But this objection is another form of the anthropocentric bias. By concentrating on possible descriptions of events and by acknowledging only that the possibility of describing something as an agent depends upon whether or not it can be properly described as having done something (the description of some aspect of an event) for a reason, we avoid the temptation to look for extensional criteria that would necessitate reduction to human referents.

The CID Structure licenses redescriptions of events as corporate and attributions of corporate intentionality while it does not obscure the private acts of executives, directors etc. Although *X* voted to support the joining of the cartel because he was bribed to do so, *X* did not join the cartel, Gulf Oil Corporation joined the cartel. Consequently, we may say that *X* did something for which he should be held morally responsible, yet whether or not Gulf Oil Corporation should be held morally responsible for joining the cartel is a question that turns on issues that may be unrelated to *X*'s having accepted a bribe.

Of course Gulf Oil Corporation cannot join the cartel unless *X* or somebody who occupies position *A* on the organizational chart votes in the affirmative. What that shows, however, is that corporations are collectivities. That should not, however, rule out the possibility of their having metaphysical status, as being Davidsonian agents, and being thereby full-fledged moral persons.

This much seems to me clear: we can describe many events in terms of certain physical movements of human beings and we also can sometimes describe those events as done for reasons by those human beings, but further we can sometimes describe those events as corporate and still further as done for corporate reasons that are qualitatively different from whatever personal reasons, if any, component members may have for doing what they do.

Corporate agency resides in the possibility of CID Structure licensed redescription of events as corporate intentional. That may still appear to be downright mysterious, although I do not think it is, for human agency as I have suggested, resides in the possibility of description as well.

Although further elaboration is needed, I hope I have said enough to make plausible the view that we have good reasons to acknowledge the non-eliminatable agency of corporations. I have maintained that Davidsonian agency is a necessary and sufficient condition of moral personhood. I cannot further argue that position here (I have done so elsewhere). On the basis of the foregoing analysis, however, I think that grounds have been provided for holding corporations *per se* to account for what they do, for treating them as metaphysical persons *qua* moral persons.[28]

Notes

1. John Locke. *An Essay Concerning Human Understanding* (1960), Bk. II, Ch. XXVII.
2. *Ibid.*
3. For a particularly flagrant example see: Michael Jensen and William Meckling, "Theory of the Firm: Managerial Behavior, Agency Costs and Ownership Structure," *Journal of Financial Economics,* vol. 3 (1976), pp. 305–360. On p. 311 they write, "The private corporation or firm is simply one form of legal fiction which serves as a nexus for contracting relationships . . ."
4. Daniel Dennett, "Conditions of Personhood" in *The Identities of Persons* ed. by A. O. Rorty (Berkeley, 1976), pp. 175–196.
5. John Rawls, "Justice as Reciprocity," in *John Stuart Mill, Utilitarianism,* ed. by Samuel Gorovitz (Indianapolis, 1971), pp. 244–245.
6. *Ibid.*
7. John Rawls, *A Theory of Justice* (Cambridge, 1971), p. 146.
8. Frederick Hallis, *Corporate Personality* (Oxford, 1930), p. xlii.
9. 10 *Co. Rep.* 253, see Hallis, p. xlii.
10. "Types of Collectivities and Blame," *The Personalist,* vol. 56 (1975), pp. 160–169, and in the first chapter of my *Collective and Corporate Responsibility* (NY, 1984).
11. "Continental Tyre and Rubber Co., Ltd. vs. Daimler Co., Ltd." (1915), K. B., p. 893.
12. Hallis, p. xlix.
13. "Continental Tyre and Rubber Co., Ltd. vs. Daimler Co., Ltd." (1915), K. B., p. 918.
14. (1916), 2 A. C., p. 340.

15. See in particular Otto von Gierke, *Die Genossenschoftstheorie* (Berlin, 1887).

16. And, of course, in earlier times animals have been given legal rights.

17. See Gerald Massey, "Tom, Dick, and Harry, and All The King's Men," *American Philosophical Quarterly,* vol. 13 (1976), pp. 89–108.

18. G. E. M. Anscombe, "Modern Moral Philosophy," *Philosophy,* vol. 33 (1958), pp. 1–19.

19. J. L.Austin, "Three Ways of Spilling Ink" in *Philosophical Papers* (Oxford, 1970), p. 273.

20. See for example Donald Davidson, "Agency," in *Agent, Action, and Reason,* ed. by Binkley, Bronaugh, and Marras (Toronto, 1971).

21. Austin, p. 275.

22. See Joel Feinberg, *Doing and Deserving* (Princeton, 1970), p. 134f.

23. John Kenneth Galbraith, *The Age of Uncertainty* (Boston, 1971), p. 261.

24. H. L. A. Hart, *The Concept of Law* (Oxford, 1961), Ch. VI.

25. G. C. Buzby, "Policies—A Guide to What A Company Stands For," *Management Record,* vol. 24 (1962), p. 5ff.

26. *Ibid.*

27. Peter Drucker, *Concept of Corporation* (New York, 1964/1972), pp. 36–37.

28. This chapter owes much to discussions and comments made by J. L. Mackie, Donald Davidson and Howard K. Wettstein. An earlier version was read at a conference on "Ethics and Economics" at the University of Delaware. I also acknowledge the funding of the University of Minnesota Graduate School that supports the project of which this is a part.

10

Ethical Responsibilities of Engineers in Large Organizations: The Pinto Case

Richard T. De George
1981

The myth that ethics has no place in engineering has been attacked, and at least in some corners of the engineering profession has been put to rest.[1] Another myth, however, is emerging to take its place—the myth of the engineer as moral hero. A litany of engineering saints is slowly taking form. The saints of the field are whistle blowers, especially those who have sacrificed all for their moral convictions. The zeal of some preachers, however, has gone too far, piling moral responsibility upon moral responsibility on the shoulders of the engineer. This emphasis, I believe, is misplaced. Though engineers are members of a profession that holds public safety paramount,[2] we cannot reasonably expect engineers to be willing to sacrifice their jobs each day for principle and to have a whistle ever by their sides ready to blow if their firm strays from what they perceive to be the morally right course of action. If this is too much to ask, however, what then is the actual ethical responsibility of engineers in a large organization?

I shall approach this question through a discussion of what has become known as the Pinto case, i.e., the trial that took place in Winamac, Indiana, and that was decided by a jury on March 16, 1980.

In August 1978 near Goshen, Indiana, three girls died of burns in a 1973 Pinto that was rammed in traffic by a van. The rear-end collapsed "like an accordian,"[3] and the gas tank erupted in flames. It was not the first such accident with the Pinto. The Pinto was introduced in 1971 and its gas tank housing was not changed until the 1977 model. Between 1971 and 1978 about fifty suits were brought against Ford in connection with rear-end accidents in the Pinto.

What made the Winamac case different from the fifty others was the fact that the State prosecutor charged Ford with three (originally four, but one was dropped) counts of reckless homicide, a *criminal* offense, under a 1977 Indiana law that made it possible to bring such criminal charges against a corporation. The penalty, if found guilty, was a maximum fine of $10,000 for each count, for a total of $30,000. The case was closely watched, since it was the first time in recent history that a corporation was charged with this criminal offense. Ford spent almost a million dollars in its defense.

With the advantage of hindsight I believe the case raised the right issue at the wrong time.

The prosecution had to show that Ford was reckless in placing the gas tank where and how it did. In order to show this the prosecution had to prove that Ford consciously disregarded harm it might cause and the disregard, according to the statutory definition of "reckless," had to involve "substantial deviation from acceptable standards of conduct."[4]

The prosecution produced seven witnesses who testified that the Pinto was moving at speeds judged to be between 15 and 35 mph when it was hit. Harly Copp, once a high ranking Ford engineer, claimed that the Pinto did not have a balanced design and that for cost reasons the gas tank could withstand only a 20 mph impact without leaking and exploding. The prosecutor, Michael Cosentino, tried to introduce evidence that Ford knew the defects of the gas tank, that its executives knew that a $6.65 part would have made the car considerably safer, and that they decided against the change in order to increase their profits.

Federal safety standards for gas tanks were not introduced until 1977. Once introduced, the National Highway Traffic Safety Administration (NHTSA) claimed a safety defect existed in the gas tanks of Pintos produced from 1971 to 1976. It ordered that Ford recall 1.9 million Pintos. Ford contested the order. Then, without ever admitting that the fuel tank was unsafe, it "voluntarily" ordered a recall. It claimed the recall was not for safety but for "reputational" reasons.[5] Agreeing to a recall in June, its first proposed modifications failed the safety standards tests, and it added a second protective shield to meet safety standards. It did not send out recall notices until August 22. The accident in question took place on August 10. The prosecutor claimed that Ford knew its fuel tank was dangerous as early as 1971 and that it did not make any changes until the 1977 model. It also knew in June of 1978 that its fuel tank did not meet federal safety standards; yet it did nothing to warn owners of this fact. Hence, the prosecution contended, Ford was guilty of reckless homicide.

The defense was led by James F. Neal who had achieved national prominence in the Watergate hearings. He produced testimony from two witnesses who were crucial to the case. They were hospital attendants who had spoken with the driver of the Pinto at the hospital before she died. They claimed she had stated that she had just had her car filled with gas. She had been in a hurry and had left the gas station without replacing the cap on her gas tank. It fell off the top of her car as she drove down the highway. She noticed this and stopped to turn around to pick it up. While stopped, her car was hit by the van. The testimony indicated that the car was stopped. If the car was hit by a van going 50 mph, then the rupture of the gas tank was to be expected. If the cap was off the fuel tank, leakage would be more than otherwise. No small vehicle was made to withstand such impact. Hence, Ford claimed, there was no recklessness involved. Neal went on to produce films of tests that indicated that the amount of damage the Pinto suffered meant that the impact must have been caused by the van's going at least 50 mph. He further argued that the Pinto gas tank was at least as safe as the gas tanks on the 1973 American Motors Gremlin, the Chevrolet Vega, the Dodge Colt, and the Toyota Corolla, all of which suffered comparable damage when hit from the rear at 50 mph. Since no federal safety standards were in effect in 1973, Ford was not reckless if its safety standards were comparable to those of similar cars made by competitors; that standard represented the state of the art at that time, and it would be inappropriate to apply 1977 standards to a 1973 car.[6]

The jury deliberated for four days and finally came up with a verdict of not guilty. When the verdict was announced at a meeting of the Ford Board of Directors then taking place, the members broke out in a cheer.[7]

These are the facts of the case. I do not wish to second-guess the jury. Based on my reading of the case, I think they arrived at a proper decision, given the evidence. Nor do I wish to comment adversely on the judge's ruling that prevented the prosecution from introducing about 40% of his case because the evidence referred to 1971 and 1972 models of the Pinto and not the 1973 model.[8]

The issue of Ford's being guilty of acting recklessly can, I think, be made plausible, as I shall indicate shortly. But the successful strategy argued by the defense in this case hinged on the Pinto in question being hit by a van at 50 mph. At that speed, the defense successfully argued, the gas tank of any subcompact would rupture. Hence that accident did not show that the Pinto was less safe than other subcompacts or that Ford acted recklessly. To show that would require an accident that took place at no more than 20 mph.

The contents of the Ford documents that Prosecutor Cosentino was not allowed to present in court were published in the *Chicago Tribune* on October 13, 1979. If they are accurate, they tend to show grounds for the charge of recklessness.

Ford had produced a safe gas tank mounted over the rear axle in its 1969 Capri in Europe. It tested that tank in the Capri. In its over-the-axle position, it withstood impacts of up to 30 mph. Mounted behind the axle, it was punctured by projecting bolts when hit from the rear at 20 mph. A $6.65 part would help make the tank safer. In its 1971 Pinto, Ford chose to place the gas tank behind the rear axle without the extra part. A Ford memo indicates that in this position the Pinto has more trunk space, and that production costs would be less than in the over-the-axle position. These considerations won out.[9]

The Pinto was first tested it seems in 1971, after the 1971 model was produced, for rear-end crash tolerance. It was found that the tank ruptured when hit from the rear at 20 mph. This should have been no surprise, since the Capri tank in that position had ruptured at 20 mph. A memo recommends that rather than making any changes Ford should wait until 1976 when the government was expected to introduce fuel tank standards. By delaying making any change, Ford could save $20.9 million, since the change would average about $10 per car.[10]

In the Winamac case Ford claimed correctly that there were no federal safety standards in 1973. But it defended itself against recklessness by claiming its car was comparable to other subcompacts at that time. All the defense showed, however, was that all the subcompacts were unsafe when hit at 50 mph. Since the other subcompacts were not forced to recall their cars in 1978, there is *prima facie* evidence that Ford's Pinto gas tank mounting was substandard. The Ford documents tend to show Ford knew the danger it was inflicting on Ford owners; yet it did nothing, for profit reasons. How short-sighted those reasons were is demonstrated by the fact that the Pinto thus far in litigation and recalls alone has cost Ford $50 million. Some forty suits are still to be settled. And these figures do not take into account the loss of sales due to bad publicity.

Given these facts, what are we to say about the Ford engineers? Where were they when all this was going on, and what is their responsibility for the Pinto? The answer, I suggest, is that they were where they were supposed to be, doing what they were supposed to be doing. They were performing tests, designing the Pinto, making reports. But do they have no moral responsibility for the products they design? What after all is the moral responsibility of engineers in a large corporation? By way of reply, let me emphasize that no engineer can morally do what is immoral. If commanded to do what he should not morally do, he must resist and refuse. But in the Ford Pinto situation no engineer was told to produce a gas tank that would explode and kill people. The engineers were not instructed to make an unsafe car. They were morally responsible for knowing the state of the art, including that connected with placing and mounting gas tanks. We can assume that the Ford engineers were cognizant of the state of the art in producing the model they did. When tests were made in 1970 and 1971, and a memo was written stating that a $6.65 modification could make the gas tank safer,[11] that was an engineering assessment. Whichever engineer proposed the modification and initiated the memo acted ethically in doing so. The next step, the administrative decision not to make the modification was, with hindsight, a poor one in almost every way. It ended up costing Ford a great deal more not to put in the part than it would have cost to put it in. Ford still claims today that its gas tank was as safe as the accepted standards of the industry at that time.[12] It must say so, otherwise the suits pending against it will skyrocket. That it was not as safe seems borne out by the fact that only the Pinto of all the subcompacts failed to pass the 30 mph rear impact NHTSA test.

But the question of wrongdoing or of malicious intent or of recklessness is not so easily solved. Suppose the ordinary person were told when buying a Pinto that if he paid an extra $6.65 he could increase the safety of the vehicle so that it could withstand a 30 mph rear-end impact rather than a 20 mph impact, and that the odds of suffering a rear-end impact of between 20 and 30 mph was 1 in 250,000. Would we call him or her reckless if he or she declined to pay the extra $6.65? I am not sure how to answer that question. Was it reckless of Ford to wish to save the $6.65 per car and increase the risk for the consumer? Here I am inclined to be clearer in my own mind. If I choose to take a risk to save $6.65, it is my risk and my $6.65. But if Ford saves the

$6.65 and I take the risk, then I clearly lose. Does Ford have the right to do that without informing me, if the going standard of safety of subcompacts is safety in a rear-end collision up to 30 mph? I think not. I admit, however, that the case is not clear-cut, even if we add that during 1976 and 1977 Pintos suffered 13 firey fatal rear-end collisions, more than double that of other U.S. comparable cars. The VW Rabbit and Toyota Corolla suffered none.[13]

Yet, if we are to morally fault anyone for the decision not to add the part, we would censure not the Ford engineers but the Ford executives, because it was not an engineering but an executive decision.

My reason for taking this view is that an engineer cannot be expected and cannot have the responsibility to second-guess managerial decisions. He is responsible for bringing the facts to the attention of those who need them to make decisions. But the input of engineers is only one of many factors that go to make up managerial decisions. During the trial, the defense called as a witness Francis Olsen, the assistant chief engineer in charge of design at Ford, who testified that he bought a 1973 Pinto for his eighteen-year-old daughter, kept it a year, and then traded it in for a 1974 Pinto which he kept two years.[14] His testimony and his actions were presented as an indication that the Ford engineers had confidence in the Pinto's safety. At least this one had enough confidence in it to give it to his daughter. Some engineers at Ford may have felt that the car could have been safer. But this is true of almost every automobile. Engineers in large firms have an ethical responsibility to do their jobs as best they can, to report their observations about safety and improvement of safety to management. But they do not have the obligation to insist that their perceptions or their standards be accepted. They are not paid to do that, they are not expected to do that, and they have no moral or ethical obligation to do that.

In addition to doing their jobs, engineers can plausibly be said to have an obligation of loyalty to their employers, and firms have a right to a certain amount of confidentiality concerning their internal operations. At the same time engineers are required by their professional ethical codes to hold the safety of the public paramount. Where these obligations conflict, the need for and justification of whistle blowing arises.[15] If we admit the obligations on both sides, I would suggest as a rule of thumb that engineers and other workers in a large corporation are morally *permitted* to go public with information about the safety of a product if the following conditions are met:

1) if the harm that will be done by the product to the public is serious and considerable;

2) if they make their concerns known to their superiors; and
3) if, getting no satisfaction from their immediate superiors, they exhaust the channels available within the corporation, including going to the board of directors.

If they still get no action, I believe they are morally *permitted* to make public their views; but they are not morally *obliged* to do so. Harly Copp, a former Ford executive and engineer, in fact did criticize the Pinto from the start and testified for the prosecution against Ford at the Winamac trial.[16] He left the company and voiced his criticism. The criticism was taken up by Ralph Nader and others. In the long run it led to the Winamac trial and probably helped in a number of other suits filed against Ford. Though I admire Mr. Copp for his actions, assuming they were done from moral motives, I do not think such action was morally required, nor do I think the other engineers at Ford were morally deficient in not doing likewise.

For an engineer to have a moral *obligation* to bring his case for safety to the public, I think two other conditions have to be fulfilled, in addition to the three mentioned above.[17]

4) He must have documented evidence that would convince a reasonable, impartial observer that his view of the situation is correct and the company policy wrong.

Such evidence is obviously very difficult to obtain and produce. Such evidence, however, takes an engineer's concern out of the realm of the subjective and precludes that concern from being simply one person's opinion based on a limited point of view. Unless such evidence is available, there is little likelihood that the concerned engineer's view will win the day simply by public exposure. If the testimony of Francis Olsen is accurate, then even among the engineers at Ford there was disagreement about the safety of the Pinto.

5) There must be strong evidence that making the information public will in fact prevent the threatened serious harm.

This means both that before going public the engineer should know what source (government, newspaper, columnist, TV reporter) will make use of his evidence and how it will be handled. He should also have good reason to believe that it will result in the kind of change or result that he believes is morally appropriate. None of this was the case in the Pinto situation. After much public discussion, five model years, and failure to pass national safety standards tests, Ford plausibly defends its original claim that the gas tank was acceptably safe. If there is little likelihood of his success, there is no moral obligation for the engineer to go public. For the harm he or she personally incurs is not offset by the good such action achieves.[18]

My first substantive conclusion is that Ford engineers had no moral *obligation* to do more than they did in this case.

My second claim is that though engineers in large organizations should have a say in setting safety standards and producing cost-benefit analyses, they need not have the last word. My reasons are two. First, while the degree of risk, e.g., in a car, is an engineering problem, the acceptability of risk is not. Second, an engineering cost-benefit analysis does not include all the factors appropriate in making a policy decision, either on the corporate or the social level. Safety is one factor in an engineering design. Yet clearly it is only one factor. A Mercedes-Benz 280 is presumably safer than a Ford Pinto. But the difference in price is considerable. To make a Pinto as safe as a Mercedes it would probably have to cost a comparable amount. In making cars as in making many other objects some balance has to be reached between safety and cost. The final decision on where to draw the balance is not only an engineering decision. It is also a managerial decision, and probably even more appropriately a social decision.

The difficulty of setting standards raises two pertinent issues. The first concerns federal safety standards. The second concerns cost-benefit analyses. The state of the art of engineering technology determines a floor below which no manufacturer should ethically go. Whether the Pinto fell below that floor, we have already seen, is a controverted question. If the cost of achieving greater safety is considerable—and I do not think $6.65 is considerable—there is a built-in temptation for a producer to skimp more than he should and more than he might like. The best way to remove that temptation is for there to be a national set of standards. Engineers can determine what the state of the art is, what is possible, and what the cost of producing safety is. A panel of informed people, not necessarily engineers, should decide what is acceptable risk and hence what acceptable minimum standards are. Both the minimum standards and the standards attained by a given car should be a matter of record that goes with each car. A safer car may well cost more. But unless a customer knows how much safety he is buying for his money, he may not know which car he wants to buy.

This information, I believe, is information a car buyer is entitled to have.

In 1978, after the publicity that Ford received with the Pinto and the controversy surrounding it, the sales of Pintos fell dramatically. This was an indication that consumers preferred a safer car for comparable money, and they went to the competition. The state of Oregon took all its Pintos out of its fleet and sold them off. To the surprise of one dealer involved in selling turned-in Pintos, they went for between $1000 and $1800.[19] The conclusion we correctly draw is that there was a market for a car with a dubious safety record even though the price was much lower than for safer cars and lower than Ford's manufacturing price.

The second issue is the way cost-benefit analyses are produced and used. I have already mentioned one cost-benefit analysis used by Ford, namely the projection that by not adding a part and by placing the gas tank in the rear the company could save $20.9 million. The projection, I noted, was grossly mistaken for it did not consider litigation, recalls, and bad publicity which have already cost Ford over $50 million. A second type of cost-benefit analysis sometimes estimates the number and costs of suits that will have to be paid, adds to it fines, and deducts that total amount from the total saved by a particular practice. If the figure is positive, it is more profitable not to make a safety change than to make it.

A third type of cost-benefit analysis, which Ford and other auto companies produce, estimates the cost and benefits of specific changes in their automobiles. One study, for instance, deals with the cost-benefit analysis relating to fuel leakage associated with static rollover. The unit cost of the part is $11. If that is included in 12.5 million cars, the total cost is $137 million. That part will prevent 180 burn deaths, 180 serious burn injuries and 2100 burned vehicles. Assigning a cost of $200,000 per death, $67,000 per major injury, and $700 per vehicle, the benefit is $49.5 million. The cost-benefit ratio is slightly over 3–1.[20]

If this analysis is compared with a similar cost-benefit analysis for a rear-end collision, it is possible to see how much safety is achieved per dollar spent. This use is legitimate and helpful. But the procedure is open to very serious criticism if used not in a comparative but in an absolute manner.

The analysis ignores many factors, such as the human suffering of the victim and of his or her family. It equates human life to $200,000, which is based on average lost future wages. Any figure here is questionable, except for comparative purposes, in which case as long as the same figure is used it does not change the information as to relative benefit per dollar. The ratio, however, has no *absolute* meaning, and no decision can properly be based on the fact that the resulting ratio of cost to benefit in the above example is 3 to 1. Even more important, how can this figure or ratio be compared with the cost of styling? Should the $11 per unit to reduce death and injury from roll-over be weighed against a comparable $11 in rear-end collision or $11 in changed styling? Who decides how much more to put into safety and how much more to put into styling? What is the rationale for the decision?

In the past consumers have not been given an opportunity to vote on the matter. The automobile industry has decided what will sell and what will not, and has decided how much to put on safety. American car dealers have not typically put much emphasis on safety features in selling their cars. The assumption that American drivers are more interested in styling than safety is a decision that has been made for them, not by them. Engineers can and do play an important role in making cost-benefit analyses. They are better equipped than anyone else to figure risks and cost. But they are not better equipped to figure the acceptability of risk, or the amount that people should be willing to pay to eliminate such risk. Neither, however, are the managers of automobile corporations. The amount of acceptable risk is a public decision that can and should be made by representatives of the public or by the public itself.

Since cost-benefit analyses of the types I have mentioned are typical of those used in the auto industry, and since they are inadequate ways of judging the safety a car should have, given the state of the art, it is clear that the automobile companies should not have the last word or the exclusive word in how much safety to provide. There must be national standards set and enforced. The National Highway Traffic Administration was established in 1966 to set standards. Thus far only two major standards have been established and implemented: the 1972 side impact standard and the 1977 gasoline tank safety standard. Rather than dictate standards, however, in which process it is subject to lobbying, it can mandate minimum standards and also require auto manufacturers to inform the public about the safety quotient of each car, just as it now requires each car to specify the miles per gallon it is capable of achieving. Such an approach would put the onus for basic safety on the manufacturers, but it would also make additional safety a feature of consumer interest and competition.

Engineers in large corporations have an important role to play. That role, however, is not usually to set policy or to decide on the acceptability of risk. Their knowledge and expertise are important both to the companies for which they work and to the public. But they are not morally responsible for policies and decisions beyond their competence and control. Does this view, however, let engineers off the moral hook too easily?

To return briefly to the Pinto story once more, Ford wanted a subcompact to fend off the competition of Japanese imports. The orders came down to produce a car of 2,000 pounds or less that would costs $2000 or less in time for the 1971 model. This allowed only 25 months instead of the usual 43 months for design and production of a new car.[21] The engineers were squeezed from the start. Perhaps this is why they did not test the gas tank for rear-end collision impact until the car was produced.

Should the engineers have refused the order to produce the car in 25 months? Should they have resigned, or leaked the story to the newspapers? Should they have refused to speed up their usual routine? Should they have complained to their professional society that they were being asked to do the impossible—if it were to be done right? I am not in a position to say what they should have done. But with the advantage of hindsight, I suggest we should ask not only what they should have done. We should especially ask what changes can be made to prevent engineers from being squeezed in this way in the future.

Engineering ethics should not take as its goal the producing of moral heroes. Rather it should consider what forces operate to encourage engineers to act as they feel they should not; what structural or other features of a large corporation squeeze them until their consciences hurt? Those features should then be examined, evaluated, and changes proposed and made. Lobbying by engineering organizations would be appropriate, and legislation should be passed if necessary. In general I tend to favor voluntary means where possible. But where that is utopian, then legislation is a necessary alternative.

The need for whistle blowing in a firm indicates that a change is necessary. How can we preclude the necessity for blowing the whistle?

The Winamac Pinto case suggests some external and internal modifications. It was the first case to be tried under a 1977 Indiana law making it possible to try corporations as well as individuals for the criminal offenses of reckless homicide. In bringing the charges against Ford, Prosecutor Michael Cosentino acted courageously, even if it turned out to have been a poor case for such a precedent-setting trial. But the law concerning reckless homicide, for instance, which was the charge in question, had not been rewritten with the corporation in mind. The penalty, since corporations cannot go to jail, was the maximum fine of $10,000 per count—hardly a significant amount when contrasted with the 1977 income of Ford International which was $11.1 billion in revenues and $750 million in profits. What Mr. Cosentino did *not* do was file charges against individuals in the Ford Company who were responsible for the decisions he claimed were reckless. Had highly placed officials been charged, the message would have gotten through to management across the country that individuals cannot hide behind corporate shields in their decisions if they are indeed reckless, put too low a price on life and human suffering, and sacrifice it too cheaply for profits.

A bill was recently proposed in Congress requiring managers to disclose the existence of life-threatening defects to the appropriate Federal agency.[22] Failure to do so and attempts to conceal defects could result in fines of $50,000 or imprisonment for a minimum of two years, or both. The fine in corporate terms is negligible. But imprisonment for members of management is not.

Some argue that increased litigation for product liability is the way to get results in safety. Heavy damages yield quicker changes than criminal proceedings. Ford agreed to the Pinto recall shortly after a California jury awarded damages of $127.8 million after a youth was burned over 95% of his body. Later the sum was reduced, on appeal, to $6.3 million.[23] But criminal proceedings make the litigation easier, which is why Ford spent $1,000,000 in its defense to avoid paying $30,000 in fines.[24] The possibility of going to jail for one's actions, however, should have a salutary effect. If someone, the president of a company in default of anyone else, were to be charged in criminal suit, presidents would soon know whom they can and should hold responsible below them. One of the difficulties in a large corporation is knowing who is responsible for particular decisions. If the president were held responsible, outside pressure would build to reorganize the corporation so that responsibility was assigned and assumed.

If a corporation wishes to be moral or if society or engineers wish to apply pressure for organizational changes such that the corporation acts morally and responds to the moral conscience of engineers and others within the organization, then changes must be made. Unless those at the top set a moral tone, unless they insist on moral conduct, unless they punish immoral conduct and reward moral conduct, the corporation will function without considering the morality of questions and of corporate actions. It may by accident rather than by intent avoid immoral actions, though in the long run this is unlikely.

Ford's management was interested only in meeting federal standards and having these as low as possible. Individual federal standards should be both developed and enforced. Federal fines for violations should not be token but comparable to damages paid in civil suits and should be paid to all those suffering damage from violations.[25]

Independent engineers or engineering societies—if the latter are not co-opted by auto manufacturers—can play a significant role in supplying information on the state of the art and the level of technical feasibility available. They can also develop the safety index I suggested earlier, which would represent the relative and comparative safety of an automobile. Competition has worked successfully in many areas. Why not in the area of safety? Engineers who work for auto manufacturers will then have to make and report the results of standard tests such as the ability to withstand rear-end impact. If such information is required data for a safety index to be affixed to the windshield of each new car, engineers will not be squeezed by management in the area of safety.

The means by which engineers with ethical concerns can get a fair hearing without endangering their jobs or blowing the whistle must be made part of a corporation's organizational structure. An outside board member with primary responsibility for investigating and responding to such ethical concerns might be legally required. When this is joined with the legislation pending in Congress which I mentioned, the dynamics for ethics in the organization will be significantly improved. Another way of achieving a similar end is by providing an inspector general for all corporations with an annual net income of over $1 billion. An independent committee of an engineering association might be formed to investigate charges made by engineers concerning the safety of a product on which they are working;[26] a company that did not allow an appropriate investigation of employee charges would become subject to cover-up proceedings. Those in the engineering industry can suggest and work to implement other ideas. I have elsewhere outlined a set of ten such changes for the ethical corporation.[27]

In addition to asking how an engineer should respond to moral quandaries and dilemmas, and rather than asking how to educate or train engineers to be moral heroes, those in engineering ethics should ask how large organizations can be changed so that they do not squeeze engineers in moral dilemmas, place them in the position of facing moral quandaries, and make them feel that they must blow the whistle.

The time has come to go beyond sensitizing students to moral issues and solving and resolving the old, standard cases. The next and very important questions to be asked as we discuss each case is how organizational structures can be changed so that no engineer will ever again have to face *that* case.

Many of the issues of engineering ethics within a corporate setting concern the ethics of organizational structure, questions of public policy, and so questions that frequently are amenable to solution only on a scale larger than the individual—on the scale of organization and law. The ethical responsibilities of the engineer in a large organization have as much to do with the organization as with the engineer. They can be most fruitfully approached by considering from a moral point of view not only the individual engineer but the framework within which he or she works. We not only need moral people. Even more importantly we need moral structures and organizations. Only by paying more attention to these can we adequately resolve the questions of the ethical responsibility of engineers in large organizations.

Notes

1. The body of literature on engineering ethics is now substantive and impressive. See, *A Selected Annotated Bibliography of Professional Ethics and Social Responsibility in Engineering,* compiled by Robert F. Ladenson, James Choromokos, Ernest d'Anjou, Martin Pimsler, and Howard Rosen (Chicago: Center for the Study of Ethics in the Professions, Illinois Institute of Technology, 1980). A useful two-volume collection of readings and cases is also available: Robert J. Baum and Albert Flores, *Ethical Problems in Engineering,* 2nd edition (Troy, N.Y.: Rensselaer Polytechnic Institute, Center for the Study of the Human Dimensions of Science and Technology, 1980). See also Robert J. Baum's *Ethics and Engineering Curricula* (Hastings-on-Hudson, N.Y.: Hastings Center, 1980).

2. See, for example, the first canon of the 1974 Engineers Council for Professional Development Code, the first canon of the National Council of Engineering Examiners Code, and the draft (by A. Oldenquist and E. Slowter) of a "Code of Ethics for the Engineering Profession" (all reprinted in Baum and Flores, *Ethical Problems in Engineering*.

3. Details of the incident presented in this paper are based on testimony at the trial. Accounts of the trial as well as background reports were carried by both the *New York Times* and the *Chicago Tribune*.

4. *New York Times,* February 17, 1980, IV, p. 9.

5. *New York Times,* February 21, 1980, p. A6. *Fortune,* September 11, 1978, p. 42.

6. *New York Times,* March 14, 1980, p. 1.

7. *Time,* March 24, 1980, p. 24.

8. *New York Times,* January 16, 1980, p. 16; February 7, 1980, p. 16.

9. *Chicago Tribune,* October 13, 1979, p. 1, and Section 2, p. 12.

10. *Chicago Tribune,* October 13, 1979, p. 1; *New York Times,* October 14, 1979, p. 26.

11. *New York Times,* February 4, 1980, p. 12.

12. *New York Times,* June 10, 1978, p. 1; *Chicago Tribune,* October 13, 1979, p. 1, and Section 2, p. 12. The continuous claim has been that the Pinto poses "No serious hazards."

13. *New York Times,* October 26, 1978, p. 103.

14. *New York Times,* February 20, 1980, p. A16.

15. For a discussion of the conflict, see, Sissela Bok, "Whistleblowing and Professional Responsibility," *New York University Educational Quarterly,* pp. 2–10. For detailed case studies see, Ralph Nader, Peter J. Petkas, and Kate Blackwell, *Whistle Blowing* (New York: Grossman Publishers, 1972); Charles Peters and Taylor Branch, *Blowing the Whistle: Dissent in the Public Interest* (New York: Praeger Publishers, 1972); and Robert M. Anderson, Robert Perrucci, Dan E. Schendel and Leon E. Trachtman, *Divided Loyalties: Whistle-Blowing at BART* (West Lafayette, Indiana: Purdue University, 1980).

16. *New York Times,* February 4, 1980, p. 12.

17. The position I present here is developed more fully in my book *Business Ethics* (New York: Macmillan, forthcoming in fall 1981). It differs somewhat from the dominant view expressed in the existing literature in that I consider whistle blowing an extreme measure that is morally obligatory only if the stringent conditions set forth are satisfied. Cf. Kenneth D. Walters, "Your Employees' Right to Blow the Whistle," *Harvard Business Review,* July–August, 1975.

18. On the dangers incurred by whistle blowers, see Gene James, "Whistle-Blowing: Its Nature and Justification," *Philosophy in Context,* 10 (1980), pp. 99–117, which examines the legal context of whistle blowing; Peter Raven-Hansen, "Dos and Don'ts for Whistleblowers: Planning for Trouble," *Technology Review,* May 1980, pp. 34–44, which suggests how to blow the whistle; Helen Dudar, "The Price of Blowing the Whistle," *The New York Times Magazine,* 30 October, 1977, which examines the results for whistleblowers; David W. Ewing, "Canning Directions," *Harpers,* August, 1979, pp. 17–22, which indicates "how the government rids itself of troublemakers" and how legislation protecting whistleblowers can be circumvented; and Report by the U.S. General Accounting Office, "The Office of the Special Counsel Can Improve Its Management of Whistleblower Cases," December 30, 1980 (FPCD-81-10).

19. *New York Times,* April 21, 1978, IV, p. 1, 18.

20. See Mark Dowie, "Pinto Madness," *Mother Jones,* September/October, 1977, pp. 24–28.

21. *Chicago Tribune,* October 13, 1979, Section 2, p. 12.

22. *New York Times,* March 16, 1980, IV, p. 20.

23. *New York Times,* February 8, 1978, p. 8.

24. *New York Times,* February 17, 1980, IV, p. 9; January 6, 1980, p. 24; *Time,* March 24, 1980, p. 24.

25. *The Wall Street Journal,* August 7, 1980, p. 7, reported that the Ford Motor Company "agreed to pay a total of $22,500 to the families of three Indiana teen-age girls killed in the crash of a Ford Pinto nearly two years ago. . . . A Ford spokesman said the settlement was made without any admission of liability. He speculated that the relatively small settlement may have been influenced by certain Indiana laws which severely restrict the amount of damages victims or their families can recover in civil cases alleging wrongful death."

26. A number of engineers have been arguing for a more active role by engineering societies in backing up individual engineers in their attempts to act responsibly. See, Edwin Layton, *Revolt of the Engineers* (Cleveland: Case Western Reserve, 1971); Stephen H. Unger, "Engineering Societies and the Responsible Engineer," *Annals of the New York Academy of Sciences,* 196 (1973), pp. 433–37 (reprinted in Baum and Flores, *Ethical Problems in Engineering,* pp. 56–59; and Robert Perrucci and Joel Gerstl, *Profession Without Community: Engineers in American Society* (New York: Random House, 1969).

27. Richard T. De George, "Responding to the Mandate for Social Responsibility," *Guidelines for Business When Societal Demands Conflict* (Washington, D.C.: Council for Better Business Bureaus, 1978), pp. 60–80.

11

Collective Responsibility and the Nursing Profession

James L. Muyskens
1982

Members of the nursing profession, for a variety of reasons including the nature of the profession but also economic exploitation and sexism,[1] have been "caught in the middle." On the one hand, for example, the nurse is hired to carry out the directives of the physician and to support the policy of the hospital administration. The system cannot function as presently constituted without such co-operation and support in carrying out the decisions and policies of those higher up in the hierarchy. Yet, on the other hand, the nurse is legally and morally accountable for her or his judgments exercised and actions taken. "Neither physician's prescriptions nor the employing agency's policies relieve the nurse of ethical or legal accountability for actions taken and judgments made."[2]

A common predicament of nurses is expressed in the April issue of *Nursing 78* by a nurse at a West Coast university hospital. She says:

> Our biggest problem right now is that our nursing leadership at the administrative level is completely impotent. They have no voting rights on any committee that has direct control over the hospital and/or nursing. Worse, the acting director and her associate have no idea of taking any power into their own hands, where it rightfully belongs. They ask permission to improve staffing ratios, by increasing or closing beds, and when they're turned down, say to us 'Sorry girls! Work doubles' . . .[3]

The overwork and understaffing not only make working conditions less than desirable for the nurse, they clearly endanger patients. When, for example, one registered nurse and an aide must try to care for thirty to thirty-six patients who have just undergone surgery, the situation is very dangerous and health care cannot be delivered in accordance with acceptable standards.

We can all sympathize with the nurse who wrote the following:

> I am supposed to be responsible for the control and safety of techniques used in the operating theatre. I have spent many hours teaching the technicians and the aides the routines necessary for maintaining aseptic conditions during surgery. They have learned to prepare materials and to maintain an adequate supply for all needs. They have learned to handle supplies with good technique.
>
> I find it is extremely difficult to have these appropriate routines carried out constantly by employees with little theoretical background or understanding. The surgeons are frequently breaking techniques and respond in a belligerent manner when breaks in technique are brought to their attention. I find a reminder of techniques often brings a determined response to ignore the reminder and proceed with surgery. For a male surgeon to be questioned by a female nurse is a serious breach of respect to them.
>
> One day a surgeon wore the same gown for two successive operations even though there were other gowns available. I quietly called this to his attention, but I had no authority which really allowed me to control his behavior for the good of the patient. In this situation even the hospital administrator was of no help to me.[4]

This nurse is responsible for the control and safety of techniques used in the operating rooms. The conditions over which she is responsible have fallen below acceptable standards. Although she has done her best, the assigned task has not been accomplished. The patients who have a right to expect, and have paid for, a safe and aseptic operating room have been let down.

Nursing is the largest group of health care professionals within the vast health care delivery system—a system that, despite some dramatic achievements, is increasingly under attack as dehumanizing, exploitative, and cost-ineffective. Despite the seeming powerlessness of any individual nurse, taken collectively nursing more than any other health care profession is a necessary component in the emergence of the present health care delivery system. The present system could not have developed without nursing. If all nurses were to walk out tomorrow, the system would collapse. This cannot be said for any other group of health care professions including physicians. Hence, if the health care delivery system is substandard (as I believe it is), the nurse is not merely a victim of the system (along with the rest of us), but she or he is also an accomplice. As an accomplice she shares responsibility for the system's deficiencies. The nurse's plight is by no means unique. The paradoxical plight of the nurse of being both powerless and powerful, responsible yet not responsible, is a plight in which we almost all find ourselves in some aspects of our lives.

One way to try to make sense of these paradoxical situations—the way to be explored in this essay—is to introduce the notion of collective responsibility. Two dramatic and widely discussed illustrations of this are the prosecution's case against certain middle-level Nazis after World War II and the defense's case for First Lieutenant William Calley charged with murder at My Lai.

In the prosecution case, blame for the actions of certain individual members of the collective is ascribed to all members. Karl Jaspers expressed this view when he said: "Every German is made to share the blame for the crimes committed in the name of the Reich . . . inasmuch as we let such a regime arise among us."[5] In condemning every German, Jaspers is not merely blaming each German for his active or passive tolerance of the Nazis. He is saying that "the world of German ideas," "German thought," and "national tradition" are to blame. Collective responsibility is used as a net from which no member of the collective can escape.

In the defense case, the individual whose behavior has fallen below the acceptable standard is shielded from the full weight of blame, because the weight is shifted to the collective. It is the collective, the system, that must bear the brunt of the burden rather than the individual. In the Calley case it was claimed that Americans as a group failed to perform as they could have been expected.

In a recent survey of nurses' attitudes[6] this defense strategy was tacitly used. It was reported that, although nurses saw themselves as performing well given the work conditions, they "felt they ought somehow to deliver even when the system won't let them." The writers of the report indicate that this blame is misplaced ("not deserved"). Although performing below the acceptable standard, they were not to be blamed because as individuals each was doing the best possible for her in the situation. The system itself was to be blamed.

If the blame appropriately ascribed in a situation is no greater than the sum of all the ascriptions of blame to the individuals, we do not have a case of collective responsibility except in a weak (distributive) sense. By collective responsibility in the strong (non-distributive) sense—as the term is to be used in this essay—we mean that the responsibility of the group is not equivalent to that of the individuals. That is, the whole is not equal to the sum of its parts.

It is incontrovertible that we do ascribe responsibility to collectives in this strong sense. To use an example of D. E. Cooper[7], if we say that the local tennis club is responsible for its closure we don't necessarily or usually mean that the officers of the club or any particular members are responsible for its closure. If you were to question the speaker he may be unwilling to blame any particular individuals or the officers of the club. It is not that any person failed to do what was expected of him. Yet something was missing. "It was just a bad club as a whole."[8] From the claim that the local tennis club is responsible for its closure no statements about particular individuals follow. "This is so," as Cooper says, "because the existence of a collective is compatible with a varying membership. No determinate set of individuals is necessary for the existence of a collective."[9]

As R. S. Downie has argued, ". . . to provide an adequate description of the actions, purposes, and responsibilities of a certain range of collectives, such as governments, armies, colleges, incorporated business firms, etc., we must make use of concepts which logically cannot be analyzed in individualistic terms."[10] The reductionists who deny this have the principle of parsimony on their side, but little else. Although the reductionist says the ascriptions of collective responsibility could be reduced to statements about individuals, he does not do it. These reductionistic attempts suffer from the same problems and deserve the same fate as the discredited reductionist programs in theory of knowledge and philosophy of science.

The question to ask then is what set of conditions must obtain in order properly to ascribe non-distributive, collective blame or responsibility. The conditions advanced by Cooper in his essay "Responsibility and the 'System'" are sufficiently accurate and refined for purposes of this essay. These conditions are:

1. Members of a group perform undesirable acts.
2. Their performing these acts is partly explained by their acting in accordance with the "way of life" of the group (i.e. the rules, mores, customs, etc. of the group).
3. These characteristics of the group's "way of life" are below standards we might reasonably expect the group to meet.
4. It is not necessarily the case that members of the group, in performing the acts, are falling below standards we can reasonably expect individuals to meet.[11]

A few comments about these conditions are in order. Clearly we do not *hold* an individual or group responsible—that is, following its etymology: having liability to answer to a *charge*—if undesirable acts have not been performed. When no undesirable acts occur, the question of blame or responsibility in the sense of liability does not arise. Hence we see the need for condition 1.

The second condition is not strictly necessary. It does seem, as Virginia Held has argued,[12] that when special conditions obtain even a random collection of individuals can be held responsible (a claim denied by condition 2). However, for present purposes—consideration of collective responsibility of members of a profession—this stronger claim need not be defended. The most plausible cases for ascribing collective responsibility are those cases in which the group has distinctive characteristics, has a sense of solidarity and cohesion (for example, feels "vicarious pride and shame"[13]) and members identify themselves as members of the group (for example, "Who are you?" I am a nurse.") and some of these group feelings or characteristics are appealed to in explaining the acts in question. For example, if the citizens of Syldavia can be characterized as being rather hostile and distrustful of foreigners, and their customs, laws, and policies reflect this, then, when (say) some border guards—in overzealously carrying out the Syldavian policy—kill some visiting dignitaries, we blame not only the border guards but also the Syldavians. In contrast, if these border guards steal from the visiting dignitaries but in accounting for this behavior we would not be inclined to appeal to any larger group feelings or characteristics, we definitely would not wish to ascribe collective blame.

We have seen above in the variety of cases discussed that it is when a collective fails to live up to what can reasonably be expected of it—i.e., it falls below an acceptable standard—that it can incur collective blame. Hence we see the need for condition 3.

Condition 4 is necessary because the standards applied to groups may be different from those applied to individuals. For example, we may feel that the nurse (in the case cited above) who was charged with responsibility for the control and safety of techniques used in the operating rooms adequately met her obligations. She did not fall below standards we can reasonably expect an individual to meet. After all, as Joel Feinberg has argued, "no individual person can be blamed for not being a hero or a saint." Yet, as Feinberg goes on to say, "a whole people can be blamed for not producing a hero when the times require it, especially when the failure can be charged to some discernible element in the group's 'way of life' that militates against heroism.''[14] Although Feinberg was not talking about this case or collective responsibility of the nursing profession (he was talking about a Jesse James train robbery case), his remarks are especially apt for this case and many other situations within the nursing profession.

One can readily see that conditions outlined for properly ascribing non-distributive collective responsibility obtain in many situations within professions. Professions more than most other collectives are bound together by common aspirations, values, methodologies and training. In too many cases, they also have similar socio-economic backgrounds and are of the same sex and ethnic group. As we have seen, the more cohesive the group, the less problematic the ascription of collective responsibility. The fact that professions such as nursing promulgate codes of ethics or standards of behavior toward which they expect members to strive, provides a clear criterion for judging whether the actual practices of the profession fall below standards to which we can reasonably hold the group.

In addition to meeting these formal criteria for ascribing collective responsibility, there are several other reasons unique to professions for ascribing collective responsibility in certain situations.

A. There are several ways by which one becomes responsible. One can be *saddled* with it by circumstances, one can have responsibility *assigned* to one, or one can deliberately *assume* responsibility.[15] Typically a profession is chosen. In choosing the profession, one *assumes* the responsibility concomitant with being a professional. One chooses to adopt the values, methodology, and "way of life" of the profession. Such choice is much less prominent with most other basic group affiliations. One does not choose family membership, region of birth, usually not citizenship, and often not military service. Once in the profession, of course, as one goes about his job he will also sometimes be saddled with responsibility by circumstances and be assigned responsibility. But these assignments are all within the context of choice to assume professional responsibility. This choice to assume professional responsibility provides the backdrop for all his professional activities. Hence, as a professional, more than most other group affiliations, one sees oneself as a member of the group and has—with eyes open—chosen the identification.

B. Nurses (as is, of course, also the case in several other professions) have been vested by the state with the power to regulate and control nursing practice. This collective power or right—given exclusively to the profession—has concomitant with it a collective responsibility or duty to see to it that acceptable standards are maintained. Since it is possible that each individual nurse including officers of the American Nursing Association is meeting acceptable standards in her or his own assignments and yet the group's "way of life" must be characterized as below an acceptable standard, appeal to collective responsibility is one of the tools the public has at its disposal to try to insure adequate nursing and general health care. Obviously in these cases (when no individual has failed to meet her or his legal obligation) the public does not have recourse to lawsuits against individuals.

C. Supposedly as a means to protect the public, the licensing statutes of the states allow only those who have passed certain requirements set down by the state to practice nursing. One result of this is that the profession which is by law also self-regulatory becomes a protected monopoly. If a person is going to receive nursing care, this care must be provided by a member of the profession. If nursing care is to be upgraded, it must be from within with at most prodding from without. Quite clearly one of the most effective tools for such prodding is that of demonstrating collective responsibility, a responsibility that goes beyond the sum of each individual's responsibility.

From the discussion thus far, it is evident that the appeal to collective responsibility when some substandard behavior or undesirable acts have occurred is a two-edged sword. It can be used to show that, despite undesirable performances or actions or conditions in a collective, a particular member of the collective is not individually responsible. However, it can also be used to show that, despite the fact that the behavior of individuals does not fall below standards we can reasonably require individuals to meet (given that we cannot *demand* that an individual be a hero), the group's conduct is below standards we can reasonably expect the group to meet. One of the reasons the weapon of collective responsibility looks suspect in the widely discussed World War II prosecution and Vietnam conflict defense cases is that only one edge of the sword is used while the other edge is conveniently ignored.

If conditions for properly ascribing collective responsibility are satisfied, to the extent that the individual is exonerated, the group is indicted. To the degree the individual *qua* individual is indicted, the group is exonerated. Either way the individual group member bears responsibility. For any member of a collective but especially (for reasons cited above) a professional, it is not enough just to know that one has done all that could be expected of him or her strictly as an individual. The arm of responsibility for a professional has a longer reach than that of the individual.

Specific situations within the nursing profession illustrate the two edges of the sword of collective responsibility. These situations should be seen within the context of the rapid evolution of the nursing profession in recent years. In recent years there has been considerable effort both within and outside the profession (e.g. the medical profession) to upgrade the requirements for licensure. These efforts have borne results. The scope of the professional nurse has expanded greatly as exemplified by medical assistant programs and the use of nurses as paramedical practitioners to relieve the shortage of medical doctors in certain areas. The history of the struggle first to adopt a code of ethics for American nurses and then to revise it reflects this evolution. Tentative codes were presented in the 20's, 30's and 40's. These efforts were met by opposition from those who feared the professionalization of nursing. A striking instance of this is the advice given by a physician to one of the earliest advocates of a code of ethics for American nurses: "Be good women but do not have a code of ethics."[16] It was not until 1950 that a code of ethics was adopted.

The code has been changed several times since then, the most recent being in 1976. Two of the most interesting changes from our vantage point have been the following: Earlier versions stated that the nurse had an obligation to carry out physician's orders. The 1968 and 1976 versions of the code stress instead the nurse's obligation to the patient (called client in the 1976 version). The physician just mentioned who advised against having a code may have foreseen this development! Whereas earlier versions of the code point to an obligation to sustain confidence in associates, this has been replaced by the obligation to protect the patient from incompetent, unethical, or illegal practice from any quarter.[17]

With this background one can see why it is especially interesting to look at the nursing profession when speaking of collective responsibility in the professions. The fundamental issue in the on-going struggle to upgrade the profession—reflected in the code changes—has been that of accountability, the willingness to make decisions and accept responsibility for these decisions. The crucial question in the attempt to upgrade the profession is that of the interface of individual and collective responsibility.

The author of an article in the *Quarterly Record of the Massachusetts General Hospital Nurses Alumnae Association* wrote about "blame avoidance" behavior in nurses. As explained, blame avoidance behavior is exhibited when the nurse says such things as "I did this because the supervisor told me to do it," or "the doctor ordered it," or "the hospital rules demanded it." The author maintains that accountability requires that the nurse can say, "I did this because in my best judgment it is what the patient needed."[18] Setting aside the many good qualities common to nurses, blame avoidance behavior does seem to be one of the more prevalent, endemic faults of the nursing profession. As we have seen, a concerted effort by many within the profession has made inroads on this "way of life" of the profession.

These efforts have been made without explicit appeal to the concept of collective responsibility. As a result, judgment in cases of blame avoidance and other unacceptable or undesirable behavior has tended either to be too harsh or too lenient. That is, either (A) one judges that the individual nurse caught in the middle and in difficult circumstances has done all one can reasonably expect her to do. After all, we can not expect or demand that she be a hero or a saint. Hence, the nurse is exonerated. Yet the unacceptable practice or condition continues unabated. Or (B) one focuses on professional responsibility and the fact that, if some individuals do not stand up against substandard practices—no matter what the odds of thereby improving the situation and no matter at what price to the individual—these practices likely will not be stopped. From this perspective the individual nurse who fails to do all within her power—including actions that will likely cost her her position—to insure the best care possible for patients in her care is judged to be a moral coward.

For example, in the case of the nurse charged with responsibility for maintaining a safe and aseptic operating room, without appeal to the concept of collective responsibility we are likely to say either: i) that she has done all we can require of her—(She has asked the surgeon to comply. She does not have the authority or status to demand compliance to proper procedures. The lack of compliance quite properly was followed by a report to the hospital administration); or ii) that she has not done all we can require of her—(She cannot allow dangerous violations of operating room aseptic standards to take place. In doing so, she is failing to carry out her assignment and is allowing the patient's life to be placed in jeopardy. She should not be cowed by the surgeon's arrogance and sexism. Even at the risk of losing her job, she cannot allow the operation to take place in these conditions).

The problem is that i) is too lenient a judgment and ii) is too harsh. We cannot require the nurse *qua* individual to do more than she has done. But the nurse *qua* nurse shares blame with her colleagues in such cases despite the much greater blame which must be placed on the surgeon violating reasonable requirements. The lack of aggressive advocacy for the patient's welfare, the willingness to be dominated by the (usually male) physician or surgeon—unfortunate even if understandable "ways of life" of the nursing profession—which partially explain this nurse's behavior are below the standard we can rightfully expect the group authorized to provide nursing services to meet. Appeal to collective responsibility yields a judgment neither too harsh nor too lenient.

This judgment conforms to the moral intuitions of the nurses surveyed who were mentioned earlier. Despite a feeling that as individuals they were doing all that could reasonably be required of them in their circumstances, they still felt dissatisfied with their performance. As nurses they felt blame for falling short of the mark set for the profession.

This dissatisfaction, when seen in the light of collective responsibility, can be turned to positive use. The nurse who has done all she is required to do as an individual need not suffer debilitating guilt. Guilt, in such cases, is misplaced. Her individual actions do not warrant guilt. And, in contrast to non-distributive collective responsibility, there is no non-distributive collective guilt. "Guilt," as Feinberg has said, "consists in the intentional transgression of a prohibition." ". . . there can be no such thing as vicarious guilt."[19] However, although rightfully free of guilt, she cannot be complacent. She is a member of a group that stands judged (i.e. is liable) and must, with her colleagues, take appropriate steps to alleviate the undesirable conditions. It is not enough for a professional to do all that is required of her or him as an individual. Having freely accepted the privileges and benefits of the profession, one's responsibility in the areas of professional competence are greater than would be those of an equally skilled and knowledgeable individual who was not a member of the profession.

In order to meet this larger responsibility, as the American Nursing Association has recognized, "there should be an established mechanism for the reporting and handling of incompetent, unethical, or illegal practice within the employment setting so that such reporting can go through official channels and be done without fear of reprisal. The nurse should be knowledgeable about the mechanism and be prepared to utilize it if necessary."[20]

Paradoxically if such machinery which collective responsibility requires were put in place, individual accountability would increase and the need to appeal to collective responsibility would decrease. If reporting incompetent, unethical, or illegal conduct could be done effectively through official channels and done without fear of reprisal, such reporting—which under more dangerous and less effective circumstances is not required—would be morally required of the individual. Hence, it may be that a profession should strive to organize itself and regulate itself to such a degree that the conditions for proper ascription of collective responsibility do not arise. But this is not the situation within the nursing profession at the present. Therefore, I conclude that the notion of collective responsibility is a timely weapon of considerable force for those who are working toward upgrading the nursing profession and the health care delivery system.

Notes

1. Cf. Jo Ann Ashley, *Hospitals, Paternalism, and the Role of the Nurse* (New York: Teachers College Press, 1976) for a discussion of economic exploitation and sexism which have plagued the nursing profession.
2. "Code for Nurses with Interpretive Statements" (Kansas City, Mo.: American Nurses' Association, 1976), p. 10.
3. Marjorie A. Godfrey, "Job Satisfaction—Or Should That Be Dissatisfaction? How Nurses Feel About Nursing," Part I, *Nursing 78* (April 1978), pp. 101–02.
4. Barbara L. Tate, ed., *The Nurse's Dilemma* (New York: American Journal of Nursing Company, 1977), pp. 47–48.
5. Quoted by D. E. Cooper, "Responsibility and the 'System,'" in Peter French, ed., *Individual and Collective Responsibility* (Cambridge, Mass.: Schenkmen Publishing Co., 1972), p. 86.
6. Godfrey, *ibid.,* Part II, *Nursing 78* (May 1978), p. 110.
7. D. E. Cooper, "Collective Responsibility," *Philosophy,* vol. XLIII, no. 165 (July 1968), pp. 38–40. Page numbers refer to the reprint of his essay in this anthology.
8. *Ibid.,* p. 40.
9. *Ibid.,* p. 38.
10. R. S. Downie, "Responsibility and Social Roles," in French, *op. cit.,* p. 69.
11. "Responsibility and the 'System,'" in French, *op. cit.,* pp. 90–91.
12. Virginia Held, "Can a Random Collection of Individuals Be Morally Responsible?" *The Journal of Philosophy,* vol. LXVII, no. 14 (July 23, 1970), pp. 89–100. Page numbers refer to the reprint of her article in this anthology.
13. Joel Feinberg, "Collective Responsibility," *The Journal of Philosophy,* vol. LXV, no. 21 (Nov. 7, 1968), p. 63. Page numbers refer to the reprint of his article in this anthology.

14. *Ibid.*, p. 73.

15. Kurt Baier, "Guilt and Responsibility," in French, *op. cit.*, p. 209. Page numbers refer to the reprint of his essay in this anthology.

16. Lavinia L. Dock, *A History of Nursing*, vol. III (New York: G. P. Putnam's Sons, 1912), p. 129.

17. Cf. Kathleen M. Sward, "An Historical Perspective," in *Perspectives on the Code for Nurses* (Kansas City, Mo.: American Nurses' Association, 1978) for a discussion of these and other changes in the versions of the code.

18. Quoted by Barbara Durand, "A Nursing Practice Perspective," in *Perspectives on the Code for Nurses* (Kansas City, Mo.: American Nurses' Association, 1978), p. 19.

19. Feinberg, *ibid.*, p. 60.

20. Sward, *ibid.*, p. 8.

12

Conduct and Responsibility in War

Richard Wasserstrom
1980

I

A common way to think about normative issues of war is to concentrate upon the question of how persons ought to behave in time of war. For the question of what is permissible and impermissible in war seems both answerable and important in a way in which other moral questions about war are not. Persons who approach war this way are, therefore, inclined to focus their attention upon the laws of war—upon, that is, the rules that deal with matters such as the use of poison gas and the treatment of prisoners of war—and to view the fundamental moral issue as one of the degree to which there has been compliance with the laws of war. Implicit in this way of thinking of things is the idea that if war is fought in accordance with the laws of war then behavior in time of war is, on the whole, morally unproblematic. Concomitantly, if in war persons engage in acts that violate the laws of war, that is morally wrong, and such persons, typically soldiers, are properly held accountable for misbehavior of a most serious sort.

This way of thinking about things was certainly common in the United States during the Vietnam War. Many commentators upon, and even many critics of, the war tended to direct their attention to the question of whether the United States forces were violating any of the laws of war in the way they were fighting. If they were, that was an identifiable wrong and one that needed correction; if they were not, there were no significant *moral* issues to discuss. Similarly, many persons thought it ludicrous to consider whether the military and civilian leaders should be held accountable or thought culpable for any aspect of the Vietnam War, but they had no comparable incredulity when considering the behavior of soldiers in combat.

There is much about this general point of view that is puzzling, unsatisfactory, and even paradoxical. In what follows I consider several of the most troublesome features and consequences of this concentration upon how war should be fought and upon the centrality of the laws of war as the focus of inquiry.

II

The case that many persons think is the easiest case in which to justify judgments of culpability and decisions of punishment is that of the soldier in combat who violates the laws of war. I think it is a far less easy case than is typically supposed. For one thing, if persons are to be held to answer for their behavior in time of war, it is surely important that they be held to answer under a scheme of substantive law that is not fundamentally unfair. This requires that they should not be held liable for actions that are indistinguishable in the significant, relevant respects from actions that are not proscribed. Thus, if it is correct that the bombing of cities cannot be distinguished in a convincing way from other ways of killing civilians, it is hard to justify the punishment of persons who do the latter while persons who do the former go unpunished (and even sometimes receive medals). For another thing, it is important that there be defensible *mens rea* requirements that a soldier be shown to have satisfied before liability for behavior can properly be thought to attach.[1] The dominant conception of the laws of war makes it very difficult, as I shall try to show, to formulate and apply a defensible set of *mens rea* requirements to the typical combat soldier.

One prominent issue, typically present in any situation of combat, is that of the problem of superior orders. An army is, by definition, a rigidly hierarchical structure in which activities are undertaken as a result of commands and orders proceeding in a uniform direction from the top to the bottom. As a result, the person who finally executes the action that directly constitutes a putative violation of the laws of war is usually the combat soldier who receives, but does not himself give, military orders and commands. The question, therefore, is whether individuals in that place in the hierarchy can claim that they are excused from whatever liability might otherwise exist because what they did was done pursuant to orders from above.

The existing laws of war, to the extent to which they address principles of individual responsibility, illustrate some of the difficulties in resolving this issue. The issue was addressed in a quite confusing way at Nuremberg.[2]

The Charter of the International Military Tribunal was the document prepared in 1945 by France, Great Britain, Russia, and the United States that stated the principles that were to be employed by the Tribunal in the war crimes trials that were to be held. The Charter took what might be characterized as a very hard line in respect to the problem of superior orders.

> The fact that the defendant acted pursuant to order of his government or of a superior shall not free him from responsibility, but may be considered in mitigation of punishment if the Tribunal determined that justice so required.[3]

The Tribunal, when it came to apply the provisions of the Charter to the particular cases before it and to state its reasons for its decisions in its written Judgment, modified (without indicating it was doing so) the position of the Charter by only accepting in part the Charter's rejection of the plea of superior orders as a complete defense or excuse. The Tribunal did this by introducing some sort of a defense of duress—but what sort is not clear. What the Tribunal said was this:

> It was . . . submitted on behalf of most of these defendants that in doing what they did they were acting under the orders of Hitler, and therefore cannot be held responsible for the acts committed by them in carrying out these orders. . . .
>
> The provisions of . . . Article [Eight] are in conformity with the law of all nations. That a soldier was ordered to kill or torture in violation of the international law of war has never been recognized as a defense to such acts of brutality, though, as the Charter here provides, the order may be urged in mitigation of the punishment. The true test, which is found in varying degrees in the criminal law of most nations, is not the existence of the order, but whether moral choice was in fact possible.[4]

It is difficult, I think, to imagine a more obscure way of characterizing the nature of the defense that the Tribunal was prepared to allow, but what is clear is that the Tribunal accepted superior orders as an excuse (provided "moral choice" was not possible) whereas in the Charter they were at best a mitigating circumstance.

A problem exists because the idea of *moral choice* and its absence is not a clear one. One notion which probably underlies the Tribunal's concern and which makes good sense is this. The mere fact that an actor had been ordered to do something does not by itself excuse the actor from responsibility for his actions. This is as it should be because, at a minimum, we must know something about both the stipulated consequences for disobedience and the likely consequences of disobedience before we can decide whether someone who acts in obedience to orders should be excused for his obedience. This is what the talk about the existence of "moral choice" comes to. Suppose, for instance, that there is a general standing order that soldiers are to kill rather than capture all enemy prisoners. At the very least, we would not want to excuse completely a soldier who complied with that order and who shot all his prisoners until we knew a good deal more about such things as the announced penalty for disobeying that order, the probable penalty for disobedience, the typical soldier's reasonable beliefs about the penalty, and this soldier's belief as to what the penalty was. If, for example, the announced, probable, and understood penalty for disobedience was summary execution the case would be a very different one from that where the penalty was demotion in rank. Where the penalty for disobedience is very great, and believed to be such, then one rationale for permitting the defense—for saying moral choice was not possible—is that of excuse; in such circumstances a person will be very strongly inclined, almost inevitably inclined, to act so as to avoid the very severe penalty. In such circumstances, there is at least some pull in the direction of regarding the action in compliance with the order as one that the actor could not help but perform.

A somewhat different rationale would not focus upon the causal difficulty of choosing to disobey in such circumstances so much as upon the poignancy of the dilemma in which the actor finds himself. It is not that he cannot help but seek to avoid the penalty; it is rather that human beings, when caught in such circumstances, ought not be blamed for opting so as to save their lives even at the cost of causing the deaths of others. Persons, on this view, are not to be blamed, even when they act wrongly, for failing to behave heroically, or with a high degree of altruism by bringing consequences of such a severely detrimental character upon themselves.

In either case, the defense of superior orders would be a defense provided the accused could show that the choice involved either had this forced quality to it or was an unduly hard one to require individuals to make in a certain way.

But to say that a soldier in combat is only excused from liability where the consequences of disobedience were perceived by him to be very severe does not, I think, do full justice to the plight of the ordinary combat soldier. For what this account leaves out is the context within which he will surely have been trained and within which he will find himself once in combat. His training will consist very largely in a process designed to inculcate within him habits of obedience to command. And this is, I think, an inevitable part of military training because an army functions successfully only if habitual, unquestioning obedience is as a rule forthcoming on the part of the ordinary soldier. Thus, even if a portion (and it will often be a very small portion) of basic training is devoted to a discussion of the laws of war, even if a soldier is instructed that he ought not obey any order that is manifestly prohibited by the laws of war, the dominant thrust of his training will have consisted of efforts directed toward transforming him into a person who will obey without question and without hesitation. Thus, it may not be sufficient to excuse him when moral choice was not present; he ought, perhaps, to be excused whenever he does what he is told to do because this is what he will have been trained and even conditioned to do.

But, suppose that a soldier's training is not this monolithic in respect to obedience to orders. Suppose instead that a genuine and serious attempt is made to inculcate only habits of limited obedience. Suppose soldiers are earnestly encouraged to believe that while obedience to orders is important it is not all that is important; and suppose in particular, that soldiers are convincingly taught that an order that is clearly or obviously illegal, one that requires the soldier to do what it is clearly wrong to do, ought not to be obeyed. Even if there were such a system of training there is still a powerful argument that obedience to orders ought to be a defense in many cases. The argument turns upon the character of the existing laws of war and concomitantly, upon the soldier's capacity to assess what is and is not a violation of the laws of war. There are two related characteristics of the system of the laws of war that are of particular significance. In the first place, although war crimes are typically thought to be the most clearly defined of the three sorts of activities in respect to war for which persons may be held responsible, they, themselves, are often extremely vague and imprecise. Thus, to revert once again to Article 23(e) of the Annex to the Hague Convention of 1907, which prohibits the use of weapons calculated to cause unnecessary suffering, it seems to me to place an ordinary soldier in an extremely difficult position to require him to decide when he is using a weapon calculated to cause unnecessary suffering. In a more systematic way, moreover, the doctrine of military necessity (conceived of as even a partial, general justifying condition) makes it virtually impossible for the soldier to determine from his limited perspective whether an ostensible war crime in fact comes under this exemption. It is, in short, often a fiction that the soldier in the field is in any position to ascertain to which situations the laws of war apply and to which they do not.

In the second place, the problem of knowledge is compounded by the fact that the laws of war are not a rational, coherent scheme of rules and principles. Were there an intelligible rationale to the laws of war, recourse to this rationale might assist the soldier in his attempt to determine which of his actions were war crimes and which were not. For the reasons already indicated, it does not appear that such a rationale can be derived from the existing laws. As a result, unless the soldier happens to get ordered to do one of those few, unambiguously proscribed acts, like firing a projectile filled with glass, there is no readily applicable general principle to which he can appeal for guidance. As the laws of war are presently constituted, he cannot, for instance, appeal in any simple, straightforward way to the idea that either the intentional or knowing killing of noncombatants is necessarily a prohibited act—as it is not, for instance, when the army of which he is a part shells or bombs occupied, urban areas.

So far I have discussed primarily the problem of the soldier who is ordered to do an action that may be a war crime. I have tried to explain why, in such cases, there are serious problems of duress and knowledge that ought to be dealt with before criminal liability is fairly imposed. But still, it might be urged, all of this leaves unaffected cases of the gratuitous commission of war crimes—cases where there were no direct superior orders and where soldiers on their own behaved in ways that were clearly proscribed by the laws of war, and known by them to be such. My Lai, arguably, was one such case; no one ordered the soldiers involved to line up the unarmed women, children, and elderly people and machinegun them. The laws of war do make it plain that such behavior is forbidden. What is to be said about this kind of case?

I think there is no question but that there is genuine culpability in such cases. However, the culpability even here is diminished, perhaps, by a variety of factors typically present. At the very least we can, I believe, understand why the ordinary soldier sometimes regards this sort of behavior as reasonable and appropriate, even though it is not.

To begin with, all that I have said about the uncertainty and irrationality of the laws of war applies regardless of whether the soldiers in question did what they did because they were ordered to do it or for some other reason. What is more, the typical combat situation is hardly conducive to a reflective consideration of the application of the laws of war to particular situations.

In addition, contemporary ideas about warfare have certain consequences of their own. In combat it is certainly more plausible than it would be in any other context to regard everyone who is not clearly on your side as your enemy. Because so many things are permissible in war that are not permissible elsewhere, and because even more things are practiced which would never be practiced elsewhere, it certainly makes it reasonable to be extremely suspicious of anyone who is not unquestionably your friend or who is not utterly and completely helpless. If the threat to your life as a foot soldier can so easily and permissibly come from so many sources against which you are defenseless (e.g., airplanes), apparent cruelty and wanton barbarism often turn out to be nothing more than moderately pursued self-defense. Such is one consequence, one might say, of the logic of contemporary war.

Closely related to what has just been said is the fact that modern war can be extraordinarily corruptive of the capacity to behave morally. If the distinctions between what is obligatory, what is permissible, and what is prohibited appear to rest on no intelligible grounds or persuasive principles, if one is encouraged in war to neglect as morally uninteresting many of those distinctions which in any other context are of utmost moral importance, and if one has no reasonable assurance (as one cannot in time of war) that others will behave with a careful regard for the moral point of view, then it is not surprising if persons lose interest in and concern for even the minimum demands of morality. They are somewhat excusable, even when they do terrible things, because war has, in some important ways, the very strong tendency to make a kind of psychopathic view of matters appear reasonable. Thus, I find quite unconvincing the claim, mentioned earlier, that the laws of war are important and valuable because they ". . . diminish the corrosive effect of mortal combat on the participants."[5] The distinction between military and nonmilitary killings, in which the former are justifiable and the latter not, is neither a clear nor morally very central one. The laws of war do not embody and reflect in a coherent way fundamental moral distinctions or truths. As a result, the distinctions soldiers grasp in conforming their behavior to the laws of war will not by themselves do very much to keep the soldiers moral during war or to return the soldiers to civil society with a well-grounded sense for the requirements of the moral life.

Once again, the dominant conception of the laws of war and its view of how modern war limits the nature and applicability of these laws have a good deal to do with this state of affairs, because it is the laws of war that define what is and is not permissible for soldiers to do in time of war. If there were a different, more rigorous conception of the nature of war crimes, if the laws of war corresponded more convincingly and fully with fundamental moral principles, it would surely be easier and more appropriate than it is at present to expect or require behavior consistent with them on the part of combatants. But that, as I have suggested, would require a substantial reexamination of the context within which the laws of war are formulated. It would require that many of the most familiar and effective ways by which wars are fought today be abandoned because of their unjustifiable effect upon noncombatants. It would require at a minimum that the conception of a very nature of modern warfare be altered drastically in the direction of a more limited kind of combat fought largely if not exclusively between armies.

III

When we turn to the leaders—both civilian and military—we come to those persons to whom many principles of responsibility most obviously and plausibly apply, and to whom culpability most fairly and appropriately appears to attach. For these are the persons who are least subject to formal military discipline, they have substantially more discretion in respect to their own behavior; they are the ones who give orders and formulate battle plans and objectives; they are in a position more accurately to assess the consequences of their action; they are removed from combat and can, therefore, reflect and deliberate. To the degree to which various *mens rea* requirements ought to depend upon the presence of just these conditions, these requirements are satisfied here in a way in which they are seldom satisfied in the case of combat soldiers.

This truth is, of course, reflected in the principles and the practices of Nuremberg. It was the leaders—both civilian and military—whose culpability seemed easiest to establish and most difficult to deny. In terms of what was done at Nuremberg, as well as what was said, it was leaders and not ordinary soldiers who were held primarily responsible for the commission of crimes against peace and crimes against humanity.

I do not, however, mean to suggest that there are no problems with the standards and principles of responsibility that were applied at Nuremberg to the various leaders. To take just one example, the already described vague and elastic properties of the substantive laws of war create some of the same difficulties for leaders that they do for all other persons. And there are, as I shall indicate later, major issues that center upon any particular leader's knowledge of and causal connection with the actual commission of war crimes by others under his supervision, direction, or control. Nonetheless, the problems of culpability in respect to leaders often are too greatly exaggerated. What is more, other issues of a puzzling, more extraneous sort are often introduced. That is certainly one of the things that happened when the question was raised of the culpability of the military and civilian leaders of the United States for the conduct of the war in Vietnam.

I am not referring to the argument that it would have been impractical, nationally divisive, or generally unwise to try to hold the leaders of the United States criminally responsible for their respective roles in the Vietnam War. Nor am I referring to the practical difficulty of getting the formal, legal institutions of a country to take seriously the question of the culpability of high-ranking members of the civilian and military establishment. Instead, I am referring to the rather widely held view that they did not at all satisfy the conditions of either legal or moral culpability. At least, that is the way the topic was sometimes discussed—when it was even taken seriously enough to be discussed at all.

One rather common argument for the view that there are no genuine issues of culpability in respect to the leaders—although it was far more often held implicitly rather than stated explicitly—was that there is a special *mens rea* requirement that must be satisfied before leaders (but not combat soldiers) can properly be thought culpable or held accountable. One version of this argument was presented by Townsend Hoopes in an article entitled, "The Nuremberg Suggestion." It states both the claim I wish to examine and the general sense of incredulity that greeted proposals by opponents of the Vietnam War that the Nuremberg framework applied in a straightforward way to American leaders.

> The tragic story of Vietnam is not, in truth, a tale of malevolent men bent upon conquest for personal gain or imperial glory. It is the story of an entire generation of leaders (and an entire generation of followers) so conditioned by the tensions of the Cold War years that they were unable to perceive in 1965 (and later) that the communist adversary was no longer a monolith, but rather a fragmented ideology and apparat. . . .
>
> Lyndon Johnson, though disturbingly volatile, was not in his worst moments an evil man in the Hitlerian sense. And his principal advisers were, almost uniformly, those considered when they took office to be among the ablest, the best, the most humane and liberal men that could be found for public trust. No one doubted their honest, high-minded pursuit of the best interests of their country, and indeed of the whole non-communist world, as they perceived those interests. Moreover, the war they waged was conducted entirely within the framework of the Constitution, with the express or tacit consent of a majority of the Congress and the country until at least the autumn of 1967, and without any press censorship. . . .
>
> . . . [S]hould we . . . establish a war crimes tribunal . . . and try President Nixon and Dr. Kissinger as "war criminals?" The absurd questions answer themselves.
>
> . . . [A]bove all [we must avoid] the destructive and childish pleasure of branding as deliberate criminals duly elected and appointed leaders who, whatever their human failings, are struggling in good conscience to uphold the Constitution and to serve the broad national interests according to their lights.[6]

Several features of the argument are puzzling; the one I wish to concentrate upon is the insistence that there was something about the state of mind of the leaders of the United States which made it obvious that their conduct in respect to Vietnam was not culpable.

We might, I think, be tempted to reject the argument out of hand on the ground that it confuses two notions that the criminal law tries very hard to keep straight, namely, motive and intention. That is to say, one way to regard what Hoopes has to say is to see it as depending upon the claim that a person whose motives are good is not properly held legally, and perhaps even morally, culpable for his or her acts. On this view, it is wrong to characterize or regard as criminal the behavior of leaders whose motives in waging war were not evil ones and who sought to pursue the national interest as they understood it. The good motives make all the difference; Hitler was different: his motives in waging war were malevolent because he sought personal gain and imperial glory. He was evil. Those who were punished at Nuremberg were properly punished there for the doing of those proscribed acts which they did with despicable motives for acting.

Now it is plain, I think, that in any simple form this is not an accurate account of the way in which the criminal law views the relevance of one's motives for acting, nor is it such an obviously attractive view for the criminal law to take of things. We might, for example, think that a person who robs a poor widow of her life savings in order to have a wild week in Monaco is worse than a person who robs the same widow in order to give the money to the cancer fund. We might even think it appropriate that the punishment of the two persons should be different. But we would reject, I take it, the claim that a person ought not be held liable at all merely because his motive in robbing the widow was, in the abstract, a commendable one. And the same is true in more overtly political contexts. A black militant who selflessly risked her life in order to help other black militants escape from prison would be deemed fully culpable by the criminal law even if she sincerely believed (even reasonably so) that they had been unjustly convicted and confined there. What would be said in the law is that we are not interested primarily in the motive or in the purpose in acting. What we want to know is whether the actor intended to do the act in question; whether he intended to take another's money by force, whether she intended to aid in an escape from jail. If so, then the crimes were committed. Similarly, for Nuremberg to be applicable, it would be sufficient within this set of culpability requirements for the leaders to have intended (in this sense) to have done those actions that are in fact prohibited by Article Six of the Charter; it would not be of central importance to inquire into their motives for acting.

But this is not, perhaps, to put an end to the matter. Someone might reply that the distinction between intention and motive is not always a clear one. Nor, someone might add, is it obvious that motive ought to be as irrelevant to issues of serious culpability as the criminal law appears at times to make it. Moreover, it might still be claimed, there does seem to be something to be said for the original argument that the American leaders were different from the leaders of the Nazi regime in ways that are of moral, if not legal, significance.

Thus, there is, I think, a somewhat more sophisticated defense that might be made of Hoopes's position, although it, too, ultimately does not succeed. To begin with, it might be argued that at least some of the crimes established at Nuremberg did mean to include motive (in the sense I have been using it) as a part of the definition of the offense. Thus, it could be maintained that the waging of aggressive war means not simply the initiation of war (whatever the motive or purpose) but rather the initiation of war provided there is a certain objective or end in view, namely, to achieve personal gain or the imperial accession of territory. Even more to the point, given the way the laws of war encompass the notion of military necessity, the separation of motive and intention seems less easy than appeared at first; perhaps the idea of military necessity implies something about the view of things taken by the actor. Up to a point, suggestions such as these seem to me plausible and I want to consider them further. However, it is also important to observe that there is nothing about the Nuremberg principles and the judgment of the Tribunal that supports in an unqualified way an interpretation of this sort. While it may be true that the German motives for doing some of the things that were done were especially despicable, it is certainly a mistake to identify the Nuremberg rationale for culpability with a condemnation of wrongful behavior only if it was accompanied by motives such as theirs.

Still, as I have said, there may be something to this point of view. Perhaps the truth to be extracted is that culpability is and ought to be limited to those actions that the actor knows to be wrong. This is not quite the same as insisting upon the presence of a malevolent motive. Rather it is to emphasize that serious liability ought not attach unless the actor had a certain conception of what he was doing—unless he knew or should have known that what he was doing was wrong.[7] And this is a principle that we do—at least to some degree—embrace in the operation of our own municipal legal system.

However, it is ambiguous to put it this way, too. The principle that the actor must know that what he is doing is wrong can be the principle that the actor must know that what he is doing is legally wrong—that it is forbidden by the legal system. Or, it can be the very different principle that the actor must know that what he is doing is morally wrong—that he is doing what one who is concerned to be moral ought surely not do.

In our own legal system it is certainly sufficient, although not necessary, if the actor knows, or ought to know,[8] that what he or she is doing is legally wrong. It is regarded as wholly appropriate to impose criminal liability upon an actor who intended to do an action that he knew to be proscribed by the law, and in such a case the actor is not absolved of liability by his belief that it was morally right, or not morally wrong, to do the action.[9]

It is also surely the case that the conception with which the Nuremberg Tribunal worked was one in which intending to do an illegal act was sufficient to justify liability, irrespective of the knowledge on the actor's part that the action was illegal. For the Tribunal was concerned to establish that the actions of the accused were violations of international law and in some cases known to be such by them. The Tribunal took appreciable pains to demonstrate the preexisting illegality of the acts denominated as crimes against peace and crimes of war. It did so, arguably, because it deemed it wholly sufficient to justify the imposition of criminal liability that these acts were in fact illegal. To be sure, the Tribunal may also have been concerned to establish that the defendants either knew or should have known of the illegality of their acts. It may even have been confident that the defendants were fully aware of the gross immorality of their conduct. But none of this was made an essential condition for liability. The point is that the Tribunal was quite unconcerned to establish the way things might have looked from within the defendant's point of view. It did not see as central the views of the accused about either the illegality or immorality of their actions.

It is possible to fall back to still another position: that in respect to the kinds of crimes dealt with at Nuremberg, persons ought only to be held accountable if they knew or ought to have known that they were violating the relevant laws and had bad motives for doing so. At this stage it is not clear how one ought to reply. This is not the requirement that was applied at Nuremberg. It is, indeed, quite possible that some of the leaders convicted at Nuremberg did not have bad motives at all, for example, Speer. Perhaps the claim is that if this is so, such persons ought not to have been punished. This would certainly not be a question that could easily or briefly be answered. What is plain is that the case for such a new, more stringent *mens rea* requirement has yet to be made out. Until it is, it is hard to see why the motives of United States leaders ought to have been taken to be a decisively relevant aspect of the question of their culpability for war crimes in Vietnam.

If we reject the idea that bad motives are an essential requirement for responsibility, we are left with the question of what is the appropriate test for the responsibility of leaders. Anyone thinking about this topic is led sooner or later to the Yamashita case.[10] For it does deal with the two significant factors of knowledge and causality.

General Yamashita was the Commanding General of the Japanese Army in the Philippine Islands during the latter part of the Second World War. He was brought to trial before a United States military commission in 1945 on the charge that, while commander, he violated the laws of war by failing to discharge his duty to control the soldiers under his command, thereby permitting them to commit acts in violation of the laws of war against both civilians and prisoners of war. He was convicted by the commission and sentenced to death. The case found its way to the United States Supreme Court for final review. One central issue was that of for what acts and omissions General Yamashita had in fact been found culpable.

A majority of the Court, speaking through Chief Justice Stone, upheld the conviction and sentence on the theory that the standard applied to General Yamashita was an appropriate one and one specified by the laws of war. That standard made a commander culpable for failing to take measures within his control to prevent violations of the laws of war by his subordinates. The majority declined to reexamine the factual determination made by the commission that there had been measures within his control that General Yamashita had failed to take.

Justices Murphy and Rutledge dissented and joined in each other's opinions. The opinion of Justice Murphy focused upon the degree to which there was insufficient evidence in the record to establish that there was anything General Yamashita could have done that he failed to do to prevent his troops from committing the atrocities they committed. In his view, General Yamashita was held to a standard of virtual strict liability under which he was held liable for having been the commander of troops who engaged in widespread violations of the laws of war. As Justice Murphy saw it, there was no charge or proof that General Yamashita had committed, ordered, or condoned any violations of the laws of war by his troops. Nor was there any evidence that he was negligent in failing to do more than he did, or that he could have done anything more. The commission, he argued, founded its conviction wholly upon the assumption that the violations must have resulted from General Yamashita's inefficiency, and hence negligence, as a commander.

As the discussions of the Yamashita case engendered by the Vietnam War brought out, there are two rather different ways in which the case can be thought relevant. One approach is to concentrate upon the situation in which General Yamashita found himself, to focus upon the apparent harshness of holding him responsible for the behavior of his troops in the circumstances of that case. The other approach is to emphasize the criteria for culpability elaborated in the majority opinion without worrying about whether those criteria were in fact fairly applied to General Yamashita.

There is something to be said for the former, quite draconian approach, but not, I think, a great deal. If it is the case that General Yamashita was unaware of the brutalities committed by his troops, was not even responsible for having encouraged them to behave as they did, and was in no position to have prevented them from so behaving, then it is tempting, surely, to conclude that he was unjustly held criminally liable for their conduct. As a result, we might also be led to conclude that it would have been equally unjust to hold American leaders responsible if they were in a similar position in respect to the commission of war crimes in Vietnam.

However, it is not quite as easy as that. For we can surely find intelligible the claim that it would have been inappropriate in the context of Vietnam to engage in a scrupulous reexamination of the fairness of the treatment by the United States of the German and Japanese leaders after the Second World War. The point is not that precedents ought or must be mindlessly applied without regard to the fairness of the rule. Rather, the point is that, having ourselves applied rules and principles to others in a certain way, the institutions of the United States were then in a poor position to determine that those same rules and principles were really unfair and therefore not to be applied to United States leaders.

One can, I think, acknowledge the force of this argument without being wholly convinced by it. If General Yamashita was treated as badly as he appears to have been, that might have been a good reason for trying to make certain that no one else ever was treated in a similar fashion in the future—even those from the country responsible for his mistreatment.

But to reject this application of the Yamashita case is not to dismiss the problem with which the case dealt. For there is still the question of the appropriate test for the culpability of leaders for war crimes committed by forces in the field.

It is reasonably clear that under any plausible theory it would have been appropriate to hold the military and civilian leaders of the United States responsible for those acts which they ordered United States and South Vietnamese troops to perform and which they knew to be violations of the laws of war. Thus, the live issues concern, rather, their culpability in less clear cases. The chief issues were and are these: (1) Is it sufficient if the leaders simply adopted or knowingly permitted the adoption of policies and objectives the realization of which were likely to lead to the commission of war crimes? Under this test, if an emphasis upon "body counts" led to the killing rather than the capture of enemy soldiers who wished to surrender, then the leaders who knowingly encouraged or permitted this emphasis would have been properly held liable for the ensuing war crimes. (2) Is it necessary, as an addition to (1), that the leaders should have known that such a policy was likely to have such consequences? That is to say, is it necessary to ask whether the leaders should have known that an emphasis upon body counts would have this effect? Or, (3) is the test more stringent, still? Must there have been an inquiry into the actual state of mind of the leaders to see whether they in fact knew that such a policy was likely to have such consequences?

Similar questions can be asked about policies or programs, the implementation of which may in fact have constituted the commission of war crimes. Thus, if the use of antipersonnel bombs is a war crime, is it sufficient that the leaders directed or knew of the use of this weapon? Or is it necessary to establish that they ought to have known that the use of such a weapon was a war crime? Or is it necessary to establish that they in fact knew that the use of such a weapon was a war crime?

As I have indicated, actual knowledge in either of these kinds of cases has not usually been required, and was certainly not required in respect to the leaders prosecuted after the Second World War. On the other hand, strict liability is hardly a more attractive notion for war crimes than it is in our own legal system. The appropriate test in this regard appears, therefore, to be what the leaders ought to have known or foreseen about the policies and programs under their authorship, direction, or control. It is upon this question, and not the question of their motives, that attention ought to have focused far more intensely than it was during and after the Vietnam War.

Notes

1. This is a particular instance of the more general point that blameworthiness or culpability be linked not just with a wrongful act or wrongdoing, but with relevant mental states going to the actor's intentions, knowledge, purposes, and the like.

2. Although I tend to draw upon the proceedings at Nuremberg per se, I mean in some of my references to Nuremberg to include all of the war crimes trials that took place after the Second World War.

3. The Charter of the International Military Tribunal, Article Eight.

4. Judgment of the International Military Tribunal, Trial of the Major War Criminals I, pp. 223–24.

5. Telford Taylor, *Nuremburg and Vietnam* (NY: Quadrangle, 1970), p. 40.

6. Hoopes, "The Nuremberg Suggestion," in Falk, Kolko, and Lifton, eds. *Crimes of War* (NY: Random House, 1971), pp. 235–37.

7. Aspects of this issue are discussed in my "Punishment," *Philosophy and Social Issues* (IN: Notre Dame, 1980), pp. 119–20.

8. There are clearly differences between the requirement that the actor *know* and the requirement that the actor *ought to know*. For the present I wish to ignore the differences, but I return to them at the very end.

9. It might, of course, have been the right thing to do, even if it was against the law. This is the question discussed in "The Obligation to Obey the Law," in *Philosophy and Social Issues, op. cit.*

10. In re Yamashita, 327 U.S. 1 (1945).

13

Guilt and Responsibility

Kurt Baier
1972

Who Was to Blame?

An enemy village, according to intelligence reports "the base camp of the experienced, tough, and long-lived 48th Viet Cong Local Force Battalion"[1] which at that time in the morning was expected to be virtually empty of non-combatants, had been made the target of one of the regular search-and-destroy missions. However, contrary to expectations, the attackers met with no resistance.[2] The people they encountered were not enemy soldiers but old men, women, children, and babies. None of them was armed, all of them perfectly cooperative. Those that had survived the preparatory bombardment and blind firing by the advancing troops were systematically rounded up, herded together, and then summarily shot.

How, one wants to know, could this happen? Who was responsible for this? Who was to blame? Is it those who did the actual shooting, Lieutenant William Calley and Sergeant David Meadlo? Is it Calley and Captain Ernest Medina who gave the order to "get rid of them"? Or does the blame lie with those staff officers who conceived of the "free-fire zones" and "search-and-destroy missions" whose very aim seems to have been the destruction of all living things, including non-combatants and domestic animals? Or those who led us into this war? Is it all of us, in America and elsewhere, who support this war? Or is it all of us, irrespective of whether we are for or against it, even if we actively oppose it? Is anyone free from guilt? Or is the whole idea of pinning responsibility on someone a mistake? Is only God to blame, as was suggested by Wilbur Hamman, one of the psychiatrists called by Calley's counsel?

Calley's Guilt

In his trial Calley was formally charged with violating Article 118 of the Uniform Code of Military Justice, relating to murder. The formal charges were that at My Lai he murdered, with premeditation, not less than 107 people, including an unspecified number of women and children and one specified two-year-old. Some have argued that Calley must or should have known that his conduct was criminal. "A reasonable man, for instance, ought to know that murdering children who are only standing around is a crime even if no one has taken the trouble to explain that fact to him."[3] As an officer, he must or should have been familiar with the major provisions of the Army's Uniform Code of Military Justice and Law of Land Warfare. As an officer he also should have known the relevant portions of international law relating to war crimes, such as the Hague Convention of Land Warfare of 1907, the Nuremberg Principles laid down in 1946 in connection with the Nuremberg Trials, and the Geneva Conventions on the Laws of War of 1949.[4]

Thus, the Law of Land Warfare, Paragraph 2, headed *Purposes of the Law of War,* reads:

> . . . the law of land warfare . . . is inspired by the desire to diminish the evils of war by:
>
> a. Protecting both combatants and non-combatants from unnecessary suffering;
>
> b. Safeguarding certain fundamental human rights of persons who fall into the hands of the enemy, particularly prisoners of war, the wounded and sick, and civilians . . .

And paragraph 3, headed Basic Principles, reads as follows:

> a. Prohibitory Effect. The law of war places limits on the exercise of a belligerent's power in the interests mentioned in paragraph 2 and requires that belligerents refrain from employing any kind or degree of violence which is not actually necessary for military purposes and that they conduct hostilities with regard for the principles of humanity and chivalry.
>
> The prohibitory effect of the law of war is not minimized by "military necessity" which has been defined as that principle which justifies those

> measures *not forbidden by international law* [my italics] which are indispensable for securing the complete submission of the enemy as soon as possible. Military necessity has been generally rejected as a defense for acts forbidden by the customary and conventional laws of war inasmuch as the latter have been developed and framed with consideration for the concept of military necessity.

Article 3 of The Geneva Conventions on the Laws of War states:

> . . . (1) Persons taking no active part in the hostilities, including members of armed forces who have laid down their arms and those placed *hors de combat* by sickness, wounds, *detention* [my italics], or any other cause, shall in all circumstances be treated humanely, without any adverse distinction founded on race, color, religion, faith, . . . To this end, the following acts are and shall remain prohibited at any time and in any place whatsoever with respect to the above-mentioned persons:
>
> (a) violence to life and person, in particular murder of all kinds, mutilation, cruel treatment, and torture. . . .

Calley's conduct, at least in the two mass shootings, constituted what the reasonable man should know were moral wrongs. They also constituted a violation of the "fundamental human rights of persons who fall into the hands of the enemy, particularly . . . civilians," as required by Article 2 of the U.S. Law of Land Warfare and by Article 3 of the Geneva Conventions on the Laws of War. Therefore, being forbidden equally by U.S. and international law, such conduct could not be justified even by military necessity. In any case, there was no such necessity.

Calley, however, was also required to obey lawful superior orders. He claimed that the briefings by Captain Medina given officers and troops on the eve of the attack on My Lai were to destroy all living things, including women, children, and domestic animals. Though denied by Medina, some other soldiers claimed to have interpreted the briefing in this way. Whatever Medina's actual words, the briefing was given at a time when Intelligence reports suggested that the village was the base of a V.C. company and had been evacuated by civilians. The incorrectness of this information became obvious soon after the occupation of My Lai, and an officer should have been able to take this into account in his interpretation of the instructions. However, Calley also claimed that during the operation Medina issued the specific order "to get rid" of the people he had rounded up—"to waste them." Medina denied giving this order, but it is not improbable that Calley interpreted his words in this way. We shall therefore assume that Calley believed, and indeed had adequate reason to believe, that he was given the order to kill all living things including the civilians in the village. What bearing does that have on whether he was guilty as charged?

The Law of Land Warfare, section 509, headed *Defense of Superior Orders,* has this to say:

> a. The fact that the law of war has been violated pursuant to an order of a superior authority, whether military or civil, does not deprive the act in question of its character as a war crime nor does it constitute a defense in the trial of an accused individual, unless he did not know and could not reasonably have been expected to know that the act was unlawful. In all cases where the order is held not to constitute a defense to an allegation of war crime, the fact that the individual was acting pursuant to orders may be considered in mitigation of punishment.
>
> b. In considering the question of whether a superior order constitutes a valid defense, the court shall take into consideration the fact that obedience to lawful military orders is the duty of every member of the armed forces; that the latter cannot be expected, in conditions of war discipline, to weigh scrupulously the legal merits of the order received; that certain rules of warfare may be controversial; or that an act otherwise amounting to a war crime may be done in obedience to orders conceived as a measure of reprisal. *At the same time it must be borne in mind that members of the armed forces are bound to obey only lawful orders.* [my italics]

Counsel for Calley, in his opening address, spoke of the "resentment and anger . . . engendered in the minds and hearts of the survivors by the means and methods used by the enemy. The use of mines, booby traps, sniper fire, and ambushes aided by civilians of all ages and sexes had taken its toll."[5] Thus it seemed he wished to construe Calley's acts as "Reprisals." On this subject the Army Field Manual on the Law of Land Warfare says:

> . . . Reprisals against the persons or property of prisoners of war, including the wounded and sick, and protected civilians, are forbidden. Collective penalties and punishment of prisoners of war and protected civilians are likewise prohibited. . . . Reprisals are never adopted merely for revenge, but only as an unavoidable last resort to induce the enemy to desist from unlawful practices. They should never be employed by individual soldiers except by direct orders of a commander, and the latter should give such orders only after careful inquiry into the alleged offense.

According to military regulations, then, an order such as the one given to Calley was unlawful and therefore not binding on him. Even if Medina gave that order, this would not exonerate Calley. An order to do something unlawful cannot make doing it lawful; even an authorized superior cannot obligate one to obey it.

Still, Calley could advance two other excuses. He might claim that although he knew the order to be unlawful, he considered it too dangerous to risk "such disobedience in the face of the enemy." In other words, though he did not think that what he did was justified, he could claim that he could not have been expected to take the risk involved in doing what was right. In the circumstances this would be a very weak excuse indeed, for several others (e.g. Conti and Dursi) refused the very same orders in the face of the enemy. Calley, who was not even near Medina when he claimed to have received the order, cannot therefore have had any genuine apprehension about what would happen to him if he disobeyed.

The other excuse would be to say that he regarded Medina's order as legal and binding because he did not see anything seriously wrong in killing large numbers of Vietnamese non-combatants, including children and babies, since that was a necessary part of what was, after all, described as a "search and destroy" mission. Concerning this excuse Colonel Kennedy, the judge in the Calley trial, instructed the jury as follows:

> A determination that an order is illegal does not, of itself, assign criminal responsibility to the person following the order for acts done in compliance with it. Soldiers are taught to follow orders and special attention is given to obedience of orders on the battlefield. Military effectiveness depends on obedience to orders. On the other hand, the obedience of a soldier is not the obedience of an automaton. A soldier is a reasoning agent, obliged to respond, not as a machine, but as a person. The law takes these factors into account in assessing criminal responsibility for acts done in compliance with illegal orders. The acts of a subordinate done in compliance with an unlawful order given him by his superior are excused and impose no criminal liability upon him unless the superior's order is one which a man of ordinary sense and understanding would, under the circumstances, know to be unlawful, or if the order in question is actually known to the accused to be unlawful.[6]

Thus, to be guilty as charged, Calley must be "criminally responsible." He is criminally responsible if Medina did not give the order in question, if Calley believed that the order was unlawful, or if a reasonable man in the circumstances would have known it. It did not become clear beyond reasonable doubt that Medina did not give the order in question or that Calley did not have adequate reason to think that he was under such orders, or, for that matter, that Calley believed these orders were unlawful.

But is it fair to say that Calley was "criminally responsible" simply on the grounds that a "man of ordinary sense and understanding" would have known that the order was unlawful? Surely a person should be declared criminally responsible only if he *should* have known that such an order was unlawful. But from the fact that a man of ordinary sense and understanding *would* have known, it does not follow that every type of person *should* have known. If Calley was not a person of that type—and much of the psychiatric evidence produced during the trial cast doubt on whether he was—then it would be necessary to show, in addition, either that it was Calley's fault (not someone else's) that he was not such a person, or that he should have known better, even though he was not such a person. No such evidence was produced. Indeed, in view of the evidence that he was not a reasonable person and the lack of evidence to show that this was his fault, the available evidence tends to place the blame for this ignorance elsewhere. Considering the difficulty of the task of deciding whether an order is lawful or not, officers surely ought to be thoroughly instructed in such problems. Calley's account of his training, however, shows it to have been not only perfunctory but even quite misleading. Calley testified that "all orders were to be assumed legal, that the soldier's job was to carry out any order given to the best of his ability" and that "if I had questioned an order, I was supposed to carry the order out and then come back and make my complaint."[7] Perhaps a "reasonable" person would have seen through this teaching, but Calley appears to have accepted it at face value. A society prepared to turn men like Calley into officers incurs an additional responsibility to make clear to them the distinctions they are supposed to draw particularly if society seriously intends later to charge them with failure to do so.

The Army's reluctance to press charges of atrocities or war crimes, together with the perfunctoriness of its instructions in what are war crimes and its pursuit of policies involving "free fire zones" and "search-and-destroy missions," may well have created in Calley and others a conviction that the Army was not taking its own rules on war crimes very seriously or did not view these activities in its own definition of war crimes.[8]

If Colonel Kennedy was right in his interpretation of "criminal responsibility'' (and there is no doubt that this is a correct interpretation of the law), then Calley really was guilty of murder as charged. If doubts remain about this interpretation of ''criminal responsibility,'' then equally there is doubt about Calley's guilt as charged.

Guilt and Responsibility

Even if Calley is criminally responsible in the sense explained, does this show that he is responsible for My Lai? Does it show that he is solely responsible for it? It seems not. The question ''Who is responsible for My Lai?'' is not the same question as ''Who is guilty of murdering people at My Lai?'' The statement that ''Calley was guilty of murdering people at My Lai'' does not mean or even imply that ''Calley is responsible for murdering people at My Lai.'' A person may well be ''guilty but insane'' but could hardly be ''responsible but insane.'' If he were insane, he would not be ''responsible for (any of) his actions'' and so could not be responsible for murder. A person may be guilty of committing a crime, as perhaps Fagin's boys were of thieving, yet somebody else may be responsible for the crime, that is, for *their* committing it. Whatever Fagin was guilty of, and whatever the children were responsible for, it was not thieving; yet the children were guilty of thieving, and it was *their* thieving that Fagin was responsible for. Similarly, from the fact that Calley was guilty of murdering these civilians, it does not follow that he was responsible for murdering them, since someone else may be responsible for *his* murdering them. At the same time, the fact that Calley was guilty of murdering these people does not mean that he is *not* responsible for murdering them either: his guilt is compatible with both his responsibility and his non-responsibility. Even if others are responsible for *his* murdering them, it may still be true that he, too, is responsible for murdering them.

Determining who is guilty of a certain act is thus quite a different matter from determining who is responsible for it. ''Guilty of something'' does not mean the same thing as ''Responsible for something.'' Moreover, the ''something'' in question is never the same type of thing. ''Who is guilty of X?'' can be asked only about doings, and only about the agent's doings at that, never about events. ''Who is responsible for Y?'' can be asked only about events, never about doings. ''Who is responsible for doing X yesterday?'' is simply not a well-formed question.[9]

This last point is easily overlooked because other similar questions are perfectly in order, such as "Who is responsible for Smith's doing X yesterday?" or "Is Smith responsible for doing X yesterday?" We can ask these two questions because they make clear that we are inquiring into the responsibility for Smith's doing X yesterday and that we leave open the question of whether the person responsible is Smith or someone else. By contrast, the question "Who is responsible for doing X yesterday?" implies that the subject of the sentence refers to the person doing X. "Smith is responsible for doing X yesterday" implies that the action Smith is responsible for is *his* doing X. The question "Who is responsible for doing X yesterday?" thus implies the false assumption that the person who did X *must* also be responsible for doing X.[10]

The Concept of Responsibility

What, then, is this further question we raise when we inquire into whether a person who has done something, who may even be guilty of a certain crime or act of wrong-doing, is responsible for it and perhaps for other things as well? We can quickly dispose of the claim that, since the non-combatants were killed by projectiles from weapons fired by Calley, he himself must be responsible for these deaths and so for the worst outrages at My Lai. If this were true, then the gunners in the artillery and the advancing troops firing into the village must be equally responsible, and so must their bullets and their weapons. But from having been physically responsible for executing the firings and the destruction, it does not follow that all these men, let alone the projectiles and the weapons, should be *held* responsible for their actions and the resultant deaths. What, then, is the difference? When is it true that if a person is responsible for something it is appropriate to hold him responsible for it; when not?

Explanatory and Practical Points of View

The difference in interpreting responsibility is tied to differences between two types of practical points of view. Looking for who or what is responsible is an activity conducted from one of these points of view. By contrast, when we seek understanding or explanation of something, we have a different point of view.

Thus suppose that, during a prolonged trip abroad, Jones undergoes a vasectomy without telling his wife. A year after his return his wife becomes pregnant. He could understand this on the assumption that she was unfaithful to him. If he has enough evidence to dismiss this explanation, he still cannot understand her pregnancy if his model of what happens after vasectomy leads him to believe that it is impossible for him to impregnate her. He does not understand what has happened until he has a clearer grasp or picture or model of what is involved in vasectomy. Jones may not, however, be satisfied with merely understanding the pregnancy of his wife. When he asks who or what was responsible for that pregnancy, he implies that he is speaking from a practical, not merely an explanatory, point of view. He implies that he is looking for something, control of which would enable one to produce or prevent such impregnations by vasectomized males.

Causal and Agent Responsibility

The individual practical point of view from which we sometimes raise questions of responsibility is that of an individual who confronts his environment with a view to tampering with it for his personal ends. From such a point of view, the events to be expected naturally, divide into those wanted and those unwanted by the individual, and the information he seeks is in the nature of "know-how," telling him what he must or can do to bring about wanted events and to prevent unwanted events. Such general know-how can be couched in terms of responsibility. Thus the notion that "faulty brake linings, icy roads, and poor construction of steering mechanisms *are* responsible for car accidents" implies that any person who regards car accidents as undesirable and so desires to prevent them must be sure to have good brake linings and to avoid icy roads and cars with faulty steering. In saying that a faulty brake lining *was* responsible for some accident which has already occurred, one is simply applying such general knowledge to a particular case. When we adopt this point of view, then, we pick out as responsible for something those things which we, the users of the information, will want to modify in order to prevent events unwanted or bring about events wanted by us. No thought is given to the permissibility or otherwise of tampering with the things responsible, or about doing something to rectify the situation brought about by the responsible factor. We can indicate responsibility ascriptions from this point of view by the expression "(causal) responsibility."

In a social application the practical point of view can be that of a member of an organized group bent on tampering with the environment as a collective agent in order to improve upon it. By their behavior any number of the members of such a group are or can be factors contributing to the coming about of wanted or unwanted events which would not come about otherwise—that is, if they behaved differently or were not there at all—or to the prevention of such events which otherwise would come about. From the point of view of a member of such a community, it is therefore a much more intricate business to determine what must be changed if unwanted events are to be prevented and wanted events to be brought about. In our society this involves the following important social practices and institutions.

First, we lay down for our society as a whole the considerations on the basis of which certain sorts of events are to be regarded as wanted and others as unwanted ("socially wanted-unwanted"), quite independently of whether they are wanted or unwanted from the point of view of this or that person. Thus the pollution of a given privately owned stream by an industry in the neighborhood is unwanted from the stream-owner's, though not from the industrialist's, point of view; it may be wanted or unwanted from the society's point of view, depending upon the relative importance to it of the industry's product and of the cleanness of the stream.

Next, we make clear (in ways described below) what each person *must* do or not do towards bringing about the most important socially wanted events and preventing the socially unwanted events. We can call this procedure "assigning to each his responsibility to society." This by implication also tells the individual what he or she may and may not do towards bringing about personally wanted events and preventing personally unwanted events. Thus if pollution of a certain stream is socially unwanted, then the industrialist may not continue manufacturing his product which he personally wants if this involves polluting that stream.

Another thing we make clear in our society is what measures may or will be taken against those individuals who do not discharge their responsibility to society. We can call this "society's responsibility to the wronged." Such measures include punishment, compulsory medical, psychiatric, or reformative treatment, and compulsory indemnification of those who have incurred loss, damage, injury, harm, or suffering as a result of a person's failing to discharge his responsibility to society.

Finally, we assign to appropriate authorities the task of taking rectifying measures when unwanted events do occur or wanted events do not occur. I shall call this "society's responsibility to the unfortunate." It has become plain in recent years that making the individual who is responsible for the damage pay for it may not protect members of the society from unwanted events as effectively as arranging, say, for compulsory insurance. Once the primitive idea is given up that all socially unwanted events are to be blamed on some agent, we are more ready to consider other and more bountiful sources from which the unfortunate and the wronged may derive relief.[11]

From the individual practical point of view, then, we can ascribe responsibility "(casual) responsibility" to events (explosions, collapses), things (gas furnaces, houses), or persons (repair men, residents), but we cannot say that these things were responsible *to someone,* nor that they should be *held* (except in the innocuous sense of *"considered"* or *"believed to be"*) responsible. From this point of view, we can say only that a person *was* responsible for something that has already happened, not that he *is* responsible for it. Such responsibility cannot be *assigned* or *assumed* or otherwise *acquired.* We can assign responsibility only to persons: only persons who have had the sort of responsibility for something which can be assigned can later be *held* responsible for something that happened, and then only if its happening shows that they failed in their assigned, assumed, or otherwise acquired responsibility; and only persons who have failed in this responsibility can *be* responsible for something that has happened.

Despite the greater number of things one can say about responsibility from the social rather than from the individual practical point of view, *ascribing responsibility* to an x for something y that has already happened, comes to the same thing in both cases, namely, singling out an x which satisfied these two conditions: (1) x has a property, φ, such that the event y would not have happened in those (normal) circumstances in which it did happen if x had not possessed φ; (2) when we want to prevent (or reduce the likelihood of) the recurrence of events of the same type as y, then, of all the things with properties like y in the respect specified in (1), it is x which it is best, all things considered, to change so that it no longer has the property φ. Of course, the grounds on which a given x can be said to satisfy condition (2) will be very different when ascribing responsibility from these two different practical points of view. The most obvious differences concern the status of x, the characteristic φ on account of which x can have responsibility ascribed to it, and the way in which any properties of x may legitimately be changed to produce the desired result. When we adopt the social practical point of view, we employ many safeguards to protect those to be declared and later held responsible. Nobody can have responsibility for some past occurrence ascribed to him unless that occurrence can be attributed to a failure in his responsibility to society, that is, his failure in a task he could have performed and knew he was required to perform; he cannot be held responsible for it except by persons to whom he was responsible for his failure; he can be subjected to corrective measures only if he failed to give a satisfactory answer when held responsible; and there are only certain carefully circumscribed forms of corrective measures to which he may be subjected, for the sake of ensuring that he will not bring about socially unwanted events or prevent socially wanted ones, or for the sake of rectifying states he has already brought about.

In considering ascriptions of responsibility from the social, practical point of view, we need to avoid confusion by distinguishing "causal responsibility" and "agent-responsibility," though most of the time it will not be necessary to add this qualification. This explains why we want to say that the artillery gunners, the blindly firing infantry, Meadlo and Calley—but not Medina—were responsible, that is, (causally) responsible, for the deaths of many civilians; but the gunners, the infantry men and perhaps Meadlo are not, whereas Calley and perhaps Medina are, responsible, that is (agent-) responsible, for these deaths. The question now arises how we would answer these latter questions.

The Dimensions of (Agent-) Responsibility

This type of responsibility involves at least two persons, the person *who* is responsible for something and the person *to whom* he is responsible. The former has a certain task to perform, which I shall call his "(task-) responsibility"—what he is "(task-) responsible for." Performing that task is discharging, not performing it is failing in, his (task-) responsibility. The person to whom he is (task-) responsible also has a task, namely, to *supervise* the person who is (task-) responsible to him, or to *hold him responsible* when he is failing in his (task-) responsibility. This task may in turn be a (task-) responsibility for which the second person is (task-) responsible to a third and so on, till we come to someone who is thus (task-) responsible to society, as is the Commander-in-Chief of the Armed Forces or the Board of Trustees of a State University. But there need be no such chain of responsibility: everyone of us is (task-) responsible directly to society for a lot of things, such as ensuring that our taxes get paid.

Holding a person responsible consists of making him give an account of how he has handled his task responsibility. If he has discharged it, then no more needs to be done. If he has failed to discharge it, then he is responsible for the failure; that is, he must answer why he failed. We can say in such a case that he is "(answerable-) responsible" for it. Suppose the placement officer of a department is the person (task-) responsible to the department for getting students placed; then he is (answerable-) responsible to the department for students *not* getting placed, that is for his failure to get them placed. That he is (answerable-) responsible means that he must explain why he failed and that, to be in the clear, he must give an exonerating, exculpating or, at least excusing answer. If the explanation is inculpating, then his failure is culpable, he *is* "(culpable-) responsible" for his failure. The task of *holding him* responsible for his failure then proceeds to the next step, the taking of appropriate rectifying measure by the person to whom he is responsible; perhaps dressing him down, admonishing, reprimanding, warning him, perhaps even firing or punishing him.[12]

It is now clear why we think that the gunners and infantry men are not, while Meadlo, Calley, and Medina may well be, (agent-) responsible for the deaths of these non-combatants; we are inclined to think the former did not, while the latter did, fail in their (task-) responsibility; the first group did discharge their responsibility to society, while the second group did not.

Our (Task-) Responsibility

How, then do we become (task-) responsible? There seem to be three different ways: deliberately *assuming* responsibility, as when Jones' brother, after the death of Jones and his wife in a plane crash, assumes responsibility for the orphaned children; or being *saddled with* responsibility by the circumstances, as when the oldest son is saddled with the responsibility for his siblings after his parents' death; or having responsibility *assigned* to one, as when a court assigns responsibility for the orphaned children to an official guardian. But in the end, all three ways are dependent on society's authority to determine how individuals come to have (task-) responsibility.

If we accept these observations about the social, practical point of view which underlies the idea of (agent-) responsibility, then it is easy to see what must be the principle underlying society's methods of allocating (task-) responsibility to its members. It must be to modify their natural behavior patterns with a view to reducing the number of socially unwanted events and increasing the number of socially wanted events. In our society we employ two simple ways and a more sophisticated one for accomplishing this end. The first includes spelling out and prohibiting certain modes of behavior: those which necessarily aim at certain socially unwanted events, whether these aims are reached, as in the case of murder, or whether they are not, as in the case of attempted murder; and those which, like driving above certain speed limits, do not necessarily involve aiming at socially unwanted events but nevertheless frequently bring them about. Ths first method also includes spelling out and requiring certain other modes of behavior: those which prevent unwanted events from occurring, such as helping another person in need when the need is urgent and when one is in a good position to offer help. The second method involves the setting up of certain minimal standards of circumspection, caution, forethought, and care, concerning the accidental or unintended bringing about or prevention of certain socially wanted or unwanted events, and then requiring of everyone that in his own activities he observe these minimal standards of care. The point of this is that observation of these standards would increase the incidence of wanted and diminish that of unwanted events, while ignoring them would have the opposite effect.

The third and more sophisticated method differs from the first two in that it not merely imposes certain *curbs* on people's natural aims, for the sake of thereby preventing some events and bringing about others, but makes it the prime role of certain persons to devote their energy, knowledge skills, and ingenuity to the task of bringing about socially wanted and preventing socially unwanted events. The function of the police, for instance, is not merely to help in carrying out the task of bringing to account those who have already failed in their responsibility under the first two heads, but also by their presence to deter and perhaps forcibly stop some who in their absence might well proceed to do so.

Calley's Responsibility

What was Calley responsible *for?* He was found guilty of murder, but this implies only that he intentionally did something he should have known was a crime. If he had had a mental disease adversely affecting his ability to judge and choose, he would not have been "responsible for his acts," *any* of his acts; he would have been not "accountable," and so not *responsible for* commiting the criminal acts he was found *guilty of* committing. However, he was found not to have had such a mental disease and so he was responsible for committing these crimes.[13] Since his murders involve the deaths of non-combatants, he is also responsible for these deaths. What does this come to?

That he is responsible for committing these crimes implies that he satisfies all the conditions for the proper application to him of "retributive" measures designed to rectify in a certain way the disturbance brought about by his crimes. Retributive measures, as we understand this term, are those measures to be applied to a person when he has failed in that most important part of his responsibility to society which specifies what socially undesirable events he must not aim at and what standards of care he must not fall below. They are designed to bring home to him the error of his ways and to bring about a change. Punishment is often said to serve this end, though it is doubtful whether it actually does. By contrast, that Calley is responsible for *the deaths* of these people only implies that he satisfies all the conditions for applying to him a different type of rectifying measures, namely, those designed to restore conditions as far as possible to those prevailing before these deaths. I shall say that when a person satisfied either of these two sets of conditions, he is "(liable-) responsible." Both these uses of "(liability-) responsibility" imply that the rectifying measures to be taken would be at the expense of someone whose fault it was that conditions need restoring to an earlier superior level.

Individual and Group Responsibility

The question now arises, however, whether Calley alone was guilty of murder and he alone (liable-) responsible for the deaths of non-combatants; and whether he was the chief culprit. Are not other individuals more blameworthy? Did not others bear a greater share of the responsibility? Were we not all of us collectively responsible? But then again, does it even make sense to say that one man is responsible for what another does? Is not this as confused an idea as getting rid of one's guilt by killing a scapegoat? And are there really degrees of responsibility? Must we not say, rather, that a person is either responsible for something or he is not, and not that he has a certain higher or lower degree of responsibility for it?

Degrees and Other Dimensions of Responsibility

Let us note, in passing, that it is misleading to think of guilt as having degrees. "He is guilty" means "He committed the act," that is, the act of which he is accused. He can only be either guilty or not guilty, not more or less so. Of course, there are different degrees of intensity of a person's guilt feelings, that is, the feelings experienced by the average person when he or she acknowledges the justice of an accusation against him. When two people guilty of the same thing have guilt feelings of different intensity, we can say that one "feels guiltier" than the other. When it is also appropriate for one to have stronger guilt feelings than the other, we want to infer that one must be guiltier than the other. This is misleading, however, since it is a conflation of four different matters: the "magnitude of the guilt," i.e. of the crime; the "degree of culpability," i.e. the measure of available extenuations and aggravations; the "degree of blameworthiness," which is a function of the first two; and the "extent of his (liability-) responsibility," which is a function of many things. Thus, Meadlo and Calley were both guilty of murders on a large scale; hence the magnitude of their crimes was much the same. But Meadlo *felt* a lot guiltier though he was less culpable than Calley, since he acted on repeated and insistent orders by a superior officer standing over him and since he was less qualified than Calley to judge the lawfulness of these orders. Meadlo therefore was less blameworthy than Calley, and the extent of his (liability-) responsibility was more limited than Calley's.

But are there really degrees of responsibility? Was Calley more responsible for the deaths for which *he* was responsible than Meadlo for those deaths for which *he* was responsible? Was Calley *very* responsible for them and Meadlo only a *little* or *mildly* so? Or are there no degrees of responsibility?

Here we must distinguish between the various uses of "responsibility" already distinguished: "accountability" (as in "Calley was responsible for his actions"), "(task-) responsibility," "(answerability-) responsibility," and "(liability-) responsibility." There are degrees of accountability: in this sense a person may have full or only diminished responsibility or none at all. A person's diminished responsibility altogether exempts him from (task-) responsibility for certain things or creates excuses for failure in certain (task-) responsibilities. By contrast, it does not make sense to speak of degrees of (task-) responsibility or (answerability-) responsibility though, as we have seen, it does make sense to speak of degrees of (culpability-) responsibility. Lastly, we cannot speak of degrees of (liability-) responsibility, but we can think of one person's (liability-) responsibility as greater than another's because he is liable *to* a greater burden than the other. Thus when we compare people's responsibility "in magnitude" we must remember that it is (accountability-) responsibility and (culpability-) responsibility that vary in degree, (task-) responsibility and (answerability-) responsibility that vary in extent, and (liability-) responsibility that varies in the magnitude of the burden.

External and Internal Responsibility

In the case of (task-) responsibility we can, however, think of responsibility *as shared* equally or unequally, among a number of people. Hence, though there is no question of the degree of (task-) responsibility or (answerability-) responsibility or (liability-) responsibility, there is a question of one's share in the total responsibility for that for which one is, together with others, responsible. We can, in such a case, speak of "joint responsibility." The members of an appointments committee may have joint responsibility for making appointments, each member bearing an equal share of that responsibility. Let us call this the committee's "external responsibility." When the committee fails in its external (task-) responsibility, then it is (answerable-) responsible to certain persons and can be held responsible for this failure by the person(s) *to whom* it is responsible, say, the Senate. If the committee has no chairman, then each member has an equal share in the common tasks. Call that a member's "internal responsibility." If a member can show that he has discharged his internal (task-) responsibility, then he is not (liable-) responsible for, does not bear any share in the (liability-) responsibility for, the Committee's failure in its external (task-) responsibility. Where the committee has a chairman, the external responsibility is usually divided up among its members in different and unequal ways, the chairman taking a much heavier load of the (task-) responsibility than the others as well as being solely (answerable-) responsible for the committee's failure. However, the members are internally (answerable-) responsible to the chairman. Thus when such a committee fails in its (task-) responsibility, it is the chairman who is answerable to the Senate, and he will therefore attempt to prevent failure by overseeing the members' work.

A chairman is thus "responsible for" the members of the committee in that he is held responsible for those failures of the committee which are failures in the internal responsibilities of its members. It is therefore desirable that he should have authority to direct its members, perhaps power to discipline them if necessary.

When we speak of "being responsible for Jones," we mean being a group member (answerable-) and/or (liable-) responsible for any failure in Jones' internal (task-) responsibility, and usually also being (task-) responsible for seeing to it that Jones discharges his internal responsibility. Masters are in this way responsible *for* their servants, officers *for* their subordinates, and the represented *for* their representatives. Of course, guardians of insane wards are not (task-) responsible for getting their wards to discharge their internal responsibility, for such wards do not have any. Such guardians have all the external responsibility, and, since there are only two members in this group and one of them is not accountable, no one has any internal responsibility at all.

In some complex groups, such as the army, church, corporation, or trade union, whose structures involve a hierarchical chain of responsibility for subordinates, we find a corresponding hierarchical chain of authority over the subordinates. In such groups everyone is responsible *to* his superior and responsible *for* his subordinate. In such a group, the chief bears external (answerability-) responsibility for the groups are not, however, completely protected from external (answerability-) and (liability-) responsibility. The chief need not take the rap for all their failures. He can, by an investigation of the behavior of his subordinates, place the (culpability-) responsibility and so the external (liability-) responsibility on some person lower down in the hierarchy if he can show that he himself, and the commanders between him and that person can show that they themselves, discharged their internal (task-) responsibility. Thus the question of who was responsible for the slaughter at My Lai is essentially the question of whether or not Meadlo, Calley, Medina, and the officers above them failed in their internal (task-) responsibility. If Meadlo need not but Calley ought to have known that the order Calley claimed to have been given by Medina and passed on to Meadlo was unlawful, then Meadlo did but Calley did not discharge his internal (task-) responsibility. Hence Meadlo does not, but Calley does, bear a share in the external (liability-) responsibility for the slaughter. If Medina gave the order to "waste" the men, then he too failed in his internal (task-) responsibility; and, as mentioned before, those who are (task-) responsible for officer training may be said to have failed in their internal (task-) responsibility for enlightening officers on what are war crimes and what are unlawful orders. Again, those who conceived of "free fire zones" and "search-and-destroy" operations may well have failed in their internal (task-) responsibility if these strategic concepts involve the certainty or high risk of killings and devastations which are contrary to international law. If so, then these persons, who have failed in their internal (task-) responsibility, also bear some part, perhaps even a large part, of the external (liability-) responsibility for My Lai.

The Sovereign People

A further extension of responsibility occurs in societies which are democratic. For in such societies, unlike those which, for instance, subscribe to the "Divine Right of Kings," it is the people who are "sovereign." This sets up a new supreme authority to which the government is construed as being internally responsible, though it is one to which it is notoriously difficult to give institutional form. Thus, in a democratic society the members play two quite different and opposed roles, and so does the government. While as subjects the members of the society occupy the lowest rank in the political order, as sovereign they "collectively" occupy the highest rank and are therefore responsible *for* its subordinates, including the government and its organs. While as ruler of its subjects the government occupies the highest rank of the political order, as servant, representative, or agent of the sovereign body of citizens it is subordinate and responsible to that sovereign.[14]

When speaking of "group responsibility," we must therefore make distinctions among three types of cases: those cases in which it is a group (such as the German people or the Waffen SS, or the U.S. army) which is held responsible *for* the acts of certain individuals; those cases in which it is certain individuals (such as Hitler or the Commander-in-Chief) who are held responsible for the acts of a group, such as a country's declaration of war, an army's invasion of a country, or a battalion's preparatory artillery barrage; and those cases in which a group (such as a business or a church) is held responsible for the acts of another group (such as an organization of watchmen or a university).

The final question concerns cases of the last kind. It is simply the question of whether we, the American people, the sovereign, should conceive ourselves as being "collectively" responsible, that is, externally (answerable-) responsible, to some potential tribunal, such as that which was set up at Nuremberg after World War II and (liable-) responsible for the massacre at My Lai.[15]

We are considering the question of the external responsibility of one group, American civilians, for the acts of another group and its members, the American army. We have already noted that the Army's chief is (answerable-) responsible to the government for failures in the (task-) responsibility of the Army, but that he can escape (liability-) responsibility for such failures in the internal (task-) responsibility of his men if he can show that he discharged his internal (task-) responsibility. Now, if we are as a group (answerable-) responsible for our government and for the Army it uses to carry out its policies, then all of us are—as a group, not individually—(answerable-) responsible for failures in the Army's (task-) responsibility. It seems, then, that one could justifiably maintain that we are so responsible, for the government is internally (answerable-) responsible to us, the sovereign. Because we sit in judgment on its policies at election time, it is easier and less risky for us than for members of most other kinds of societies to convey to the government our criticism of its policies.

Suppose, then, that we really are in this way "collectively" (task-) responsible for ensuring that governmental policies are morally acceptable, that various sections of the Army, including several officers of Charlie Company and others, were (liable-) responsible for these massacres; that unlike the Army brass who have demonstrated that they have not failed in their (task-) responsibility, "we" are all externally answerable for these individual failures which jointly produced the army's failure in one of its (task-) responsibilities, namely, the prevention of war crimes. Given all this, what was the internal (task-) responsibility of each member whose discharge constituted the discharge of *his share* of the sovereign's external (task-) responsibility for the prevention of war crimes? Those who have protested against the war or its more obnoxious strategies, those who have engaged in acts of civil disobedience, or those who have become conscientious objectors, have surely done much towards discharging that internal responsibility. Even those who have supported the war have not, of course, *ipso facto* failed in their internal responsibility, for supporting a war is not the same as sharing in the responsibility of war crimes.

Who, then, has failed? No doubt there are many ways in which one can fail. Let us simply take an example. Let us assume that there is a certain attitude towards the lives of others, particularly those of other cultures, which is not uncommon among soldiers anywhere, and that, under the sort of pressure to which Calley was exposed, this attitude leads almost inevitably to war crimes. It is summed up in the slogan "A few gooks more or less—what's the difference?" Those who put victory above everything else, who at most pay lip service to international law, who would cover up war crimes, who can see no difference between unavoidable killings of non-combatants and deliberately executing them to avoid inconvenience, who advocate methods of indiscriminate mass killing and destruction—these are on the way to adopting the attitude I mean. Those who see the connection between this attitude and the proneness to war crimes under conditions of strain, yet themselves adopt that attitude and encourage it in others, fail in their internal responsibility and I believe can be said to bear a share—collectively a not inconsiderable share—of the responsibility for the massacre at My Lai.

Notes

1. Richard Hammer, *The Court Martial of Lt. Calley* (New York: Coward, McCann & Geoghegan, 1971), p. 17.

2. Such miscalculations appear to have occurred not infrequently. Cf. e.g. two articles by Ernest van den Haag, who investigated U.S. war crimes in Vietnam during the spring of 1971, which appeared in *National Review,* Oct. 22, esp. pp. 1171–3, and Nov. 6, 1971.

3. Hammer, *op. cit.,* p. 10.

4. For details concerning the law, see Arthur Everett, Kathryn Johnson, Harvey Rosenthal, *Calley* (New York: Dell Publishing Company, 1971), ch. 13 and Hammer, *op. cit.* For relevant discussions, see Richard A. Wasserstrom, ed., *War and Morality* (Belmont, California: Wadsworth, 1970) and Richard A. Wasserstrom. "The relevance of Nuremburg," *Philosophy and Public Affairs* (Fall, 1971).

5. Hammer, *op. cit.,* p. 178.

6. Everett, et al., *op. cit.,* pp. 206–207.

7. Cf. Hammer, *op. cit.,* pp. 240 ff.

8. Cf. the report on war crimes by Ernest van den Haag in *National Review* (Oct. 22 and Nov. 6, 1971, pp. 1172–1173, 1128–1231).

9. 'Who is responsible for supplies?' is a well-formed question, but only because it does not inquire into responsibility for something particular which has already happened, but inquires into what I call "(task) responsibility."

10. For the benefit of those interested in recent discussions of this topic, I should say that this appears to be the oversight which led Hart into saying that with utterances such as "He did it" (e.g., "He hit her") *"we confess* or *admit* liability, make accusations, or *ascribe* responsibility." (H. L. A. Hart, "The Ascription of Responsibility and Rights," *Proceedings of the Aristotelian Society* 1948–1949. Section III.) "He did it" never ascribes responsibility for something: when the vase lies broken on the floor, "He did it" may well ascribe responsibility for "it," the vase's having been smashed. But "He hit her" is not a suitable substitute for "He did it," because it contains no "it" for which this remark can by implication ascribe responsibility to the hitter. "He did it" can simultaneously do two jobs: identify a doer of an unspecified

doing implied to be relevantly related to "it" and ascribe responsibility for "it" (not the doing) to the doer. "He hit her" can do only one job, namely, identify the hitter. It must leave open the question of who is responsible for his hitting her: it may not be he at all but his guardian, or she may have only herself to blame.

The same mistake is made by Joel Feinberg, *Doing and Deserving* (Princeton, N.J.: Princeton University Press, 1970), pp. 137–139, who argues, quite correctly, that Hart did not, after all, make a mistake when he said "he hit her" can be "ascriptive," for "sometimes we have the action, so to speak, in our hands, and we want to know . . . whom to pin it on." (*Ibid.,* p. 137). Feinberg is, however, wrong in thinking that *ascribing an action* to someone is *ascribing responsibility* for the action to him. It is false to say that " 'It was Mary who smiled" ascribes the responsibility *for smiling* to Mary." (*Ibid.,* 139). "It was Mary who smiled" cannot simultaneously ascribe to Mary the action of smiling and the responsibility for that action. When we want to ascribe a deed to someone by identifying him as the doer, what we "have in our hands" is only a *type* of action, *smiling,* something that is not a particular action until it is "pinned down" to some agent. When we want to ascribe responsibility for some action to someone, what we must have in our hands is a particular action, something already pinned down to some agent. This does not of course mean that we must know the agent's name or anything else about him. We may ask who is responsible for the killings of certain people by unknown killers, but even then the question is not about the identity of the killers. (When the Yablonski killers will have been identified, we shall know who killed the Yablonskis, we shall know who is guilty of those killings, but we still may not know who is responsible for these killings, for these killers' killing of the Yablonskis.)

11. For arguments against this approach, see e.g. Ernest van den Haag, *op. cit.,* pp. 1176, 1227–1228, 1232.

12. Those who desire a fuller account may consult H. L. A. Hart, *Punishment and Responsibility* (New York: Oxford University Press, 1968), esp. Ch. IX. My views can be found in two articles: Richard T. DeGeorge, ed., "Responsibility and Freedom, *Ethics and Society* (New York: Doubleday, 1966), pp. 48–84 and Myles Brand, ed. "Responsibility and Action," *The Nature of Human Action* (New York: Scott-Foresman, 1970), pp. 100–116.

13. Hammer, *op. cit.,* ch. 16.

14. Cf. Jean Lacques Rousseau, *Social Contract,* Bk. 1, Chs. VI, VII.

15. I ignore the fact that there is not now such a tribunal, just as the Allies then ignored the fact that there was no such tribunal when the crimes were committed.

14

Racism and Moral Pollution

Anthony Appiah

1987

In recent years South Africa has figured large in public moral discourse all around the world; men and women who appear to agree about little else have joined, with varying degrees of sincerity, in condemning *apartheid*. Many people and many states have sought to express their moral distance from racism by seeking practical dissociation from the South African Republic but there is no doubt that the struggle in the Republic exercises a particular fascination on the moral imagination of the West. This fascination derives, I think, from the fact that the system in South Africa represents, in a very pure form, the institutional expression of an ethical system that has been officially expelled from most of the industrialized world. *Apartheid* shocks us Westerners because, in a modern industrial city like Johannesburg, run by people whose form of life is very like that of contemporary Europeans and North Americans, there operates—until recently without excuse—an ethical system whose immorality most of us no longer feel we need to argue. For most Westerners now believe that race is not a legitimate basis for moral distinctions between persons.[1]

It is as well to begin by reminding ourselves why this has not always been so. In his justly well-known *Short History of Ethics*, Alasdair MacIntyre seeks to show how "moral life changes as social life changes."[2] One dimension of change that he identifies is a gradually increasing tendency to assess agents for their intentions rather than for the consequences, intended or not, of their actions. MacIntyre traces this change between the Homeric period and ours. Thus, he reminds us of W. H. Adkins's observation, apropos of Homeric Greece, that "to be *agathos* one must be brave, skillful and successful in war and peace; and one must possess the wealth and (in peace) the leisure which are at once the necessary condition for the development of these skills and the natural reward of their successful employment."[3] *Agathos*, of course, is the "ancestor of our *good*." But it is unimaginable for us that such a term could express the primary concept of moral assessment. The reason is two-fold.

First, as *Oedipus Rex* should remind us, it requires us to take too little interest in what the agent is attempting to do, rather than what he or she actually achieves. An agent who intelligently pursues a desirable goal may fail to be *agathos* simply as the result of bad luck—or, as the Greeks might have preferred to say, of the Fates. And second, we no longer believe that what makes people good depends in the required way on what MacIntyre calls their "socially alloted function."[4]

This second change has often been observed by anthropologists and historians of law. Maine's claim that the history of the law displays a movement from *status* to *contract*, involves a recognition that we have come to see the obligations of citizens as increasingly dependent on the life they have chosen rather than the position into which they were born. Anthropologists speak of the move from *ascribed* to *achieved* status. We no longer recognize the fact that someone was born a woman or a slave or a Jew as grounds for requiring of them different behavior (or as warranting different treatment) from that appropriate to a man, or a free citizen, or a person born into a Christian family.

It is, of course, for these reasons that we find racism and sexism morally unacceptable. Each involves a denial of the basic claim, expressed so clearly by Kant, that, from the perspective of morality, it is as rational agents *simpliciter* that we are to assess and be assessed. For us, what matters is not who you are but what you try to do.

These concerns intersect with the concerns of this issue of *The Philosophical Forum* because the South African regime is racist. An ethical system which regards race—or any other ascribed status—as a morally relevant characteristic offends against the Kantian conception of morality. This fundamental change of view is reflected in the appeal to us of doctrines of *contract* and *consent* as the foundations of political obligation, even though well into our own millennium, every European ruler could claim the service of his or her subjects by right, without the fiction of the tacit consent of the people.

To the extent that our rejection of the South African system represents our opposition to the ethics of status and ascription, it confirms what MacIntyre sees as a basic tendency of the history of Western ethical thought. Yet South Africa also raises questions about the extent to which we have moved along another of the dimensions of the ethical that MacIntyre identifies. Recent discussion of the issue of divestment raises what will be the major point of this essay: namely that there are ways in which we have not (all) moved from assessing agents by the consequences of their acts towards assessing them by the consequences they intend.

Nobody supposes the claim that we have moved towards allowing a greater role for intention in our moral assessments entails that we now suppose that a person is immune from criticism for an unintended consequence of an act. We require that people have reasonable grounds to believe that their acts will have the consequences they intend. It is no defense to moral (or legal) responsibility for the death of another person that we did not intend it, if our acts could reasonably have been predicted to put other people's lives at risk. But if a person reasonably believes that their acts will have good consequences, then we are inclined not to criticize them when their best laid schemes "gang a-gley"; indeed, we are likely to offer them sympathy rather than to ascribe them blame. To assess action in this way is, in a certain respect, to close the gap between the point of view of the critic and the point of view of the agent. In a world of assessment by intentions, we see the act retrospectively as the agent saw it prospectively, and judge him or her accordingly.

This change from an assessment of consequences to an assessment of reasonable intentions derives, I think, from a deeper change. Among the pre-classical Greeks and many more recent traditional societies elsewhere, people may be stigmatized for their unintended association with evil. A person who has been involved with an outcome that is seen as undesirable may be seen as polluted by that association, even if he or she took all the care in the world to avoid it. One kind of case involves a person who unintentionally breaks a ritual taboo; ancestors and gods will be seen as justified in bringing misfortune on such a person, however fine their intentions. Oedipus cannot claim in his defense that he did not know Jocasta was his mother—incest is incest, intended or not. Furthermore, in Homeric Greece, as in many traditional societies, it was accepted that suffering for whole families or lineages might legitimately be caused by ancestors and gods as the result of the acts, intended or not, of another lineage member. Here, too, is a case where suffering was seen as merited, even though the evil that warrants it was not the agent's doing.

It is natural, I think, to see what warrants suffering in these cases (*we* should hardly call it "punishment") is not so much what we call "guilt" as a kind of *pollution*, which I shall dub "taint." Indeed, in many traditional societies the ancestors and the gods revoke the threat of suffering once the agent engages in ritual cleansing of some sort. What is required is not remorse or repentance, but the reestablishment of a certain kind of order; an order that is seen as deriving not from culture but from the deepest structure of reality. The laws of taboo and the consequences of a breach of taboo are largely indifferent to human intentions and beliefs.

It is hardly necessary to add that these are notions that modern Westerners reject. If the paradigm for the earlier phase in the West is the ethical world of Homer, the paradigm for the later one is, surely, the view codified in utilitarianism. For the utilitarian, what is right is what has the best consequences for sentient beings, independent of their ascribed status, and the agent acts well if he or she takes care in trying to bring these consequences about. Someone who meets this condition is acting rightly, and if bad fortune means that the actual consequences fall short of the intended ones, there is no space for guilt or punishment or reproach.

Wise utilitarians will not say that this implies there is no space for a different moral emotion, namely, regret. As Bernard Williams (who is, however, no utilitarian) has observed:

> The constitutive thought of regret in general is something like 'how much better if it had been otherwise'. . . . In this general sense of regret, what are regretted are states of affairs, and they can be regretted, in principle, by anyone who knows of them. But there is a particularly important species of regret, which I shall call 'agent-regret', which a person can feel only towards his own past actions (or, at most, to actions in which he regards himself as a participant). In this case, the supposed possible difference is that one might have acted otherwise, and the focus of the regret is on that possibility, the thought being formed in part by first-personal conceptions of how one might have acted otherwise. . . .
>
> The sentiment of agent-regret is by no means restricted to *voluntary* agency. It can extend far beyond what one intentionally did to almost anything for which one was causally responsible in virtue of something one intentionally did. Yet even at deeply accidental or non-voluntary levels of agency, sentiments of agent-regret are different from regret in general, such as might be felt by a spectator, and are acknowledged in our practice as being different. . . . The lorry driver who, through no fault of his, runs over a child, will feel differently from any spectator. . . .

> Doubtless, and rightly, people will try, in comforting him, to move the driver from this state of feeling. . . .[5]

We understand the driver's feeling—indeed, we should probably be appalled if he failed to display agent-regret. But we do not regard him as guilty; and in comforting him we must try, at least, to get him to distinguish agent-regret from guilt.

Regret can have a place even in the utilitarian scheme of things because it is a feeling that expresses and strengthens our desire for the good. The utilitarian can want us to regret the bad, even where we did not mean to bring it about, because it is because we abhor evil and desire good that we care to maximize utility at all. We can even suppose that, with sufficient ingenuity, the specific character of agent-regret could be given such a justification.

Notice, however, that though regret, in general, and agent-regret, in particular, may lead us to wish we had known to act otherwise, they do not reflect a belief that we *ought* to have acted otherwise, given what we knew. Regret is an ethical response, perhaps even a moral one, but it is not a response which has anything to do with our judgment of what the agent should have done. It belongs, if I may put it this way, to the context of assessment and not to the context of decision.[6]

* * *

Status to contract, ascribed to achieved status, consequences to intentions, pollution to guilt: each of these is part of a single recognizable transition in the history of Western ethical ideas. I say "ethical" and not "moral" ideas because though these changes all belong to the ethical dimension, the dimension of the critical evaluation of human life and action, the earlier phases differ in their conceptual geography so substantially from ours, that we should be loath to call them "moral" at all.

This story I have been telling seems plausible enough. There is, no doubt, much truth in it. But I want to argue in the remainder of this essay that there is a *prima facie* case to be made that some of our moral language remains committed to a notion of taint, and that in a way which belongs to the context of decision and not merely to the context of assessment. I shall offer a different argument for the claim that a symbolic dissociation from *apartheid* might be right—the claim which has often been justified in the actual debate by arguments from taint. The argument I shall offer belongs more securely in the moral world that MacIntyre identifies as distinctively modern.

As I say, I raise the problem in this issue of *The Philosophical Forum*, because this notion of pollution is displayed in some of the thinking about the issue of South African divestment. I am not going to be unreservedly enthusiastic about the way the notion is mobilized. And so I should say here that I do not think that this argument offers the best grounds for divestment in the present situation. My project is philosophical, not political: though the sort of argument I am going to discuss is central to the political debate over divestment, *I* regard it as marginal to the real issues. Because of the issue on which I want to focus, I shall consider a particularly "pure" case, where taint may be invoked as the *determining* consideration in the context of decision. In the context of the divestment issue, this is going to be somewhat misleading, precisely because, as I say, far from being a determining consideration in that case, I think it a marginal one. It is important to bear this in mind in what follows.

Suppose, then, that the facts were these.

CASE I: We are considering, as trustees, divesting a university of shares in a company doing certain kinds of business with the South African government. The company in question provides equipment that the South African government uses to maintain the system of *apartheid*; and we are sure that this therefore contributes to a system of racial exploitation, whose consequences include a great deal of suffering and the abuse—including through wrongful killing—of people's rights. We are also sure of the following claims.

1. Our divestment will not lead anyone in our own institution, or in our own country, or in South Africa, who does not already see that *apartheid* is wrong to come to agree with us that it is wrong. Consequently, we can expect our action to have no effect on the level of political or economic pressure on the givernment there to change its policies for the better, and we have no reason to think that our action will contribute to anybody's moral education.
2. Divestment from the company will make no relevant difference to the outcome of South Africa. Other people without our scruples will buy the shares, and even if the company were to refuse to provide its equipment, other suppliers would supply equally efficient equipment at about the same cost.
3. If we were to hold on to the shares we should have no influence on the behavior of the company in question that would lead it to

behave in ways that will relevantly affect the South African situation; so that, in particular, threats to divest will have no useful consequences.

4. a) Our position as trustees is no legal barrier to our divesting, in particular because
   b) our institution will not suffer any great losses if we do.
5. The company's other activities in South Africa and elsewhere do not contribute to the sum of human welfare in such a way as to "swamp" the significance of the evil with which they are associated in South Africa.

I place these conditions explicitly here because I doubt that all of them apply in the cases of divestment under actual consideration. Yet, to judge by the arguments offered by some, many people would still be in favor of divesting in these circumstances. The reason they would give is that in maintaining these shares we have "dirty hands." We are associated, through our ownership of the shares with a wicked system; we play a part in it. Our holding of the shares taints us.

Stated thus bluntly the claim is likely to find both proponents and opponents. Rather than trying to decide between them, by an analysis, at the start, of how the notion operates in general, I want to begin by considering some cases. For here, as elsewhere in our moral reflections, we may find our intuitions sharpened by considering a different case which appears to have the same structure.

I propose to consider a particularly distressing case, which constitutes the kind of parallel that is most likely, I think, to persuade the opponents of this argument. It needs to be distressing because the situation in South Africa is regarded by proponents of the argument (in my view, rightly) as particularly distressing. I am not concerned here with persuading those who refuse to accept the relevance of the dirty-hands argument because they do not find the consequences of *apartheid* especially worrying.

The key features of the pure case I have been discussing seem to be these:

1. The act we are contemplating is intended to remove us from a certain relation to a series of acts which is morally deplorable.
2. The relation is that we are *profiting from the provision of tools* for that series of acts; though we could make the same (or nearly the same) profit without providing those tools.
3. Nevertheless, the act we are contemplating will make no differ-

ence to the outcome; except that agents other than ourselves will profit from the provision of those tools.

Here is a case with this structure.

CASE II: I sell hunting knives on a block where there is another store which does this also. The owner of the other store is quite indifferent to the interests of others. I am in an upstairs room from which I can witness the following events. A gang of youths is torturing a member of another gang. Finally the leader of the gang says to one of its members: "Go buy a knife and we'll kill him." I know enough about the gang to know this is not mere bravado. They mean to do it. I also know that there is nothing I can do that will stop them. I will call the police, of course, but by the time they arrive it will be too late. Were I to interfere myself I would merely risk being killed also. I call the police, and then I hear the bell in the shop below. I go down. The youth who has been instructed to buy the knife comes in and asks me to sell him one. He makes no menaces; if I do not give him a knife he will simply go down the block to the other store. Let us suppose, further, that these knives sell extremely well and are in short supply: if I don't sell it to the youth, it will certainly be gone tomorrow. I have no significant economic incentive to sell it.[7]

The question is whether I have any moral reason not to sell this youth the knife. If I do, I will be *profiting from providing a tool* for a morally deplorable act. But if I do not, my competitor down the street will profit (unknowingly, as it happens) from providing the tool. My choice is irrelevant to that aspect of the outcome.

Some people would say, of this case, that it would be better not to sell the knife. If I do, I will be tainted by the action. But to say this is to commit yourself, as I said, to the view that taint is relevant not merely in the context of assessment—the context in which regret would plainly be appropriate—but in the context of decision. That some people believe this is exactly what I said I would show.

Utilitarians will object that the revulsion I will almost certainly feel if I am the kind of person that a utilitarian would want me to be is not, by itself, a reason not to sell the knife. If my selling it would weaken my revulsion, then that would be a consequence worth considering.

Since the other potential knife-seller is already a monster, there is no reason to suppose that his selling a knife will change his moral dispositions for the worse; and, at any rate, so far as I know, he does not have any knowledge of what the knife is for. But since the revulsion is likely, in fact, to strengthen my repugnance to killing—as a matter of psychological fact this sort of blameless involvement in evil often has this effect—then to refuse to sell the knife on account of the revulsion is the kind of moral narcissism that Bernard Williams has suggested the utilitarian might regard as "moral self-indulgence."[8]

The utilitarian accusation is particularly unconvincing here. What is being proposed is that it is right that I should take this horrible circumstance as the occasion for my own moral education, since there is nothing else to be gained from it. The revulsion is a proper response, the utilitarian may say, since, *ceteris paribus,* those who have it will act better, consequentially speaking, than those who do not. But though it is for this reason good that I have this feeling, it will be right to ignore it in this case. Many people have objected to the utilitarians' general picture of moral self-indulgence, that it is psychologically implausible. But, as Williams argues, it is morally implausible also.

> The utilitarian's theory, once he admits the value of these dispositions [such as my revulsion], takes the question 'what is the right thing to do?' a long way away from the question 'what answers is it desirable that people should be disposed to give to the question "what is the right thing to do?" The tension created by this separation is very great, and there is strong pressure, if utilitarianism is to retain any distinct identity *within* moral thought, for it to reject or hopelessly dilute the value of these other dispositions, regressing to that picture of man which early utilitarianism frankly offered, in which he has, ideally, only private or otherwise sacrificable projects, together with the one moral disposition of utilitarian benevolence.[9]

The project of being a certain kind of person, associated, as Williams suggests, with the notion of integrity, might well lead a decent person not to want to be associated in this way with the brutal torture and murder of a human being, even if association would have only the good consequence of increasing his or her revulsion against such killings. Surely, to give a different example, there might be something to criticize in opponents of capital punishment who attended public hangings to reinforce their moral sense? For, as a Kantian might insist, this seems a peculiarly revolting case of regarding others as means and not as ends.

Moral intuitions here diverge: I confess to being of two minds about this case, considered in the abstract, myself. On the one hand, it does seem that there is something to the idea that in this case, it should make a moral difference to me which one of us sells the knife. On the other hand, it is hard to resist the thought that this is just a kind of moral narcissism. Nothing, save the fact that I escape the description.

P: —profits from providing a tool for a morally deplorable act

is achieved; and even that achievement is gained at the price of depriving me of an opportunity for strengthening in a desirable way my forward-looking moral commitments.

Part of this worry is reenforced by the sense that if it makes a difference in this case, whether it is I or the other dealer that provides the weapon, then it may make a difference—and the wrong difference—in cases which are not so finely balanced. If my not satisfying P counts for something, then might it not count for something in a case where not satisfying P has consequences that are otherwise undesirable? Suppose I can poison my knife so that the victim dies swiftly and painlessly, whereas my competitor will not know that this will help, and wouldn't help in this way if he did know. Now I have to choose between avoiding satisfying P, on the one hand, and saving someone a degree of suffering, which in the context of what he is generally experiencing, is bound to be regarded as only a minor achievement. To resist poisoning and handing over the knife here because I do not wish to be involved in the consequences *would* surely be to deserve the accusation of moral self-indulgence.

The theorists of taint are not without resources here. They can insist that in this case it would be right to follow Luther's injunction to "sin bravely." That one will satisfy P is a consideration against the action, but not one that dominates the more urgent need to reduce human suffering. But the question, of course, is whether taint can ever be operative as a morally legitimate motivating reason in cases where other things are not equal. To put the question at its sharpest: is the fact that the victim will die minutes earlier and thus escape some moments of suffering and fear because I, and not my competitor, sell the knife, enough to dominate the argument from taint?

I do not know how to answer these questions. But the fact that they are not easy suggests that those who dismiss the argument from taint may be failing to account for a crucial feature of our moral judgments. If so, I cannot conclude that the argument from taint is ineffective: and if it is not ineffective here, then it might not be so in the case of divestment. In particular, the conclusion that *where it makes no other morally relevant difference* taint of this kind can be a compelling reason, in the judgment of some, should incline such people, if they are small share-holders, to consider whether they ought not to divest, perhaps over a reasonable period, of shares in companies which contribute to *apartheid.*[10]

For the trustee who accepts that CASE II lends support to the moral significance of taint, however, the transfer of the principle that, *ceteris paribus,* one should not profit from the provision of the tools for evil, is not immediate. If the case of the knife-seller depends, in part, on the fact that his integrity is at stake, then we should need to show that there are analogous issues for institutions. But the notion of a university—or any other institution—having integrity *in the sense in which an individual agent could be said to have it* is of dubious intelligibility. Integrity has, in part, to do with the coherence of the projects, the vision, and the significance of a single life; but universities do not obviously have projects, or visions, or significances of the appropriate kind.

Three kinds of considerations seem to support this last claim. First of all, as Milton Wachsberg pointed out to me, many people (though not he or I) believe that a university must display neutrality within a certain range of moral opinion. We are told, for example, that a university should not express an institutional view on public policy questions not having fairly directly to do with education. Different officials, academics, and students may take different views of the rightness of welfare policy or the moral permissibility of abortion, but these are not questions on which the institution, as such, ought to pronounce. This notion of neutrality is not one that prohibits the university from pronouncing on *all* moral questions: it might be right, for example, even according to the proponents of a neutrality principle, that the statutes of universities should expressly endorse non-discrimination on the basis of gender, race, creed, or sexual orientation. But this is because these are matters on which discriminatory views can be regarded as outside the scope of acceptable differences of opinion. Neutrality does not prohibit universities from expressing their abhorrence of *apartheid,* for example, either.

Now the reason the intelligibility of this notion of neutrality threatens the idea that the university can be regarded as falling within the range of non-natural agents to which the notion of integrity applies, is that nobody would claim that an individual moral agent—let alone a person of integrity—should remain neutral on such questions.

I cannot elect as a moral agent to have no opinion on the matter of abortion because neutrality demands it of me. It might be, say, that my role as a judge required me to put to one side my moral views and to apply the law as it stands, even if that meant ruling that people may legally do what I take to be morally wrong; or, less obviously, that my duty as a doctor required me to kill a fetus to save a mother, even though, as a Catholic, I believe this to be wrong. But my duty to act in these cases without regard for some of my own moral views does not entail an obligation not to have, or even to express, those views (except, perhaps, in the courtroom or the surgery, where the expression of these views is itself something that my role prohibits).

This consideration is, no doubt, not one that will compel those who deny the intelligibility of the principle of neutrality—but it *should* compel those who can see the force of the case for the principle, whether they accept it finally or not. But there are, as I said, three considerations against the application of the notion of integrity to institutions; and I find the second consideration more compelling.

Roughly speaking, the second consideration is that it is both intelligible and right that institutions can fail to have coherent purposes. The reason is fairly simple. One kind of incoherence of purpose is to have preferences that are not transitive. For a rational person with coherent purposes who favors A, all things considered, over B, and B likewise over C, will favor A to C also. But it is not too hard to give examples which suggest that a reasonable procedure for deciding what policies a community will follow, might sometimes lead to an outcome where A is chosen over B, B over C, and C over A, even if every individual in that society had transitive preferences. So we can say that if the decision procedure represents the community's "view," then the community has a view which is incoherent in a way that we would regard, in an individual, as irrational. Thus, to take the simplest of a familiar range of examples, suppose three voters, Amy, Bob and Cass, rank three policies, A, B and C as follows:

Amy prefers A to B to C
Bob prefers C to A to B
Cass prefers B to C to A

A majority vote to choose between A and B will select A, between B and C will select B and between C and A will select C.

The fact that majority voting can lead in this way to what are, in effect intransitivities in collective preferences might seem to be simply an argument against majority voting. But Arrow's theorem shows that rational agents, using decision procedures that satisfy apparently minimal conditions of reasonableness, can have collective preferences which are not transitive. Once one has been through Arrow's theorem one can see that this is indeed so, and though the result is a paradox—in the sense of something that is contrary to accepted assumptions or beliefs—it is a paradox that one can come to live with; accepting, after all, that, given the existence of people with radically differing conceptions of what is good, a society may be unable to resolve the disagreements among them by reason alone.

Transitivity of preference for individuals, on the other hand—as I have argued elsewhere[11]—is part of the framework of assumptions about rationality which makes the ascription of intentional states possible. We may allow that real people fail to have transitive preferences, because real people deviate from the path of pure reason: but we cannot, in my view, endorse a conception of reason which encourages such deviations.

Both my view of what Arrow's theorem shows and the claim that transitivity is a norm that characterizes an ideal of individual coherence of preference are controversial: they depend on technical issues which would take us well out of the way here.[12] Anyone who agrees with me on both these questions, however, has a reason to doubt that integrity is a notion that can properly be applied to institutions.

But a third and final consideration is that any detailed attempt to apply the notion of integrity to an institution begins to look first forced and then simply hopeless. We might say, to begin with, that most states lack integrity because their actual policies are inconsistent with their highest expressed principles. Yet, in the end, we shall find ourselves falling back on the recognition that it is a lack of integrity in the decision-makers that raises the real problems. Can we imagine a kind of moral criticism which stigmatizes a state as lacking in integrity while allowing that all of its decision-makers are, individually, people of the highest integrity and consistency of purpose?

That the university has no integrity to lose or gain, however, does not mean there are not issues of integrity at stake. For, if integrity matters at all, the individuals who profit from the university's investments, whether as employees or as students, undoubtedly do have integrities we must consider. A trustee who refuses—rightly in my view—to accept that the university has an integrity to lose, cannot deny the relevance of the integrity of its members. For one's duty as a trustee is to serve the university's purposes, and though, in doing so, one needs to protect the value of its endowment as a means to those purposes, one cannot do that at the price of those purposes as ends. If part of the university's function is moral pedagogy, then for trustees to allow students to be illegitimately associated with evil is to betray their trust.

To the extent that a trustee accepts that moral taint is relevant in the context of decision, he or she is bound to consider whether the association with evil entailed for students and staff by the university's holding shares in companies doing certain sorts of business with South Africa weighs more strongly than the good that comes from holding those shares. But if, in particular, it is true—as Milton Friedman has argued[13]—that, given the relatively small size of the university's portfolio in relation to international capital markets and the general "fluidity of capital," divestment will have negligible costs; and if it is also true, as it seems to be, that universities have no weight as shareholders in influencing a company's decisions, then how can a trustee who believes in taint oppose divestment?

The answer, I think, is that he or she must insist that the logic of taint requires limits. For the other relevant difference between the knife-seller and the member of the university is that his or her connection with the evil is, in some intuitive sense, a good deal less direct. And directness of connection makes a difference to our intuitions about taint.

Return again to the case of the knife-seller, modified, however, by a crucial change of perspective.

CASE III: Suppose, now, that I am not the knife-seller but his partner; and suppose I know him to be a consequentialist. I have all the evidence that the knife-seller had, and, at the moment of choice, I am carrying up a box of knives from the store-room. If I stop where I am on the steps, the knife-seller will get a knife from the top shelf in the store; if I go on, he will take one from the box. The knives are relevantly identical. My choice is not between selling the knife and not selling it, but simply a matter of determining which of two identical knives will be the fatal weapon. Because I am the knife-seller's partner my provision of the knife is part of a pattern of action from which I profit; though, of course, my profit, like his, will be the same whether I bring up this knife or not.

Here, my connection with the wrong is, in two senses, less direct; first, there is a further intervening agent between me and the wrong, and, second, the particular form my profit takes is less directly dependent upon that wrong. It is true that the level of profit of the knife-seller in the first case depended at most marginally on the sale: nevertheless, it is true of him that selling the knife to the youth would determine which particular dollars and cents made up his income, whereas this is not true of me. For whichever knife my partner sold, it would be paid for with the same money.

I think that many people who are willing to argue from taint will find my involvement here less tainting than in the earlier case. That is my intuition also; that is, I believe that if taint matters in CASE II it matters less in CASE III, despite the fact that they are predictably identical in their consequences for the gang's victim.

And this has, I think, two consequences for CASE I. First of all, the relation of a student to the South African investments of his or her university is, in the pure case I imagined, where conditions 1–5 hold, extremely indirect by both these tests. There are many intervening agents, and divestment will make no difference to the particular dollars and cents that constitute the financial basis of the advantage the student gets. (Of course, the associated evil in the case of *apartheid* is a great deal more serious, since it includes instances of torture, and involves the suffering and deprivation of millions.)

But second, and more importantly, it seems to me that the fact that there seems to be relatively little to be said morally against continuing up the steps with the box, undermines the intuition that there was something morally to be said against selling the knife in the first case. There seems to me no principled reason why these differences between the two cases should make a difference. Trying to understand why it seems to make a difference would be an interesting project in moral psychology: but I am skeptical that there is a rationally acceptable basis for the distinction. For if, in particular, the knife-seller's choice is more important than his partner's because it makes a difference which dollars and cents make up their profits, then this notion of directness seems very closely bound up with a notion of evil as contagion—and thus with notions of pollution and taboo rather than of guilt and wrong.

Nevertheless, directness of connection does seem to be part of the logic of taint: and those who believe in it ought to wonder, I think, whether the connection in the case of divestment is direct enough.

* * *

I have been arguing about taint in terms of cases. But there is something to be said for trying to give an abstract characterization of the cases where it might be thought to be relevant to the context of decision. For abstract characterization seems to me to reenforce the skepticism that I feel about the concrete examples. The abstract position seems to be this.

Taint matters when an agent acts in a way which causally contributes to evil. Since in many cases someone who knowingly causally contributes to evil is responsible for that evil, the distinctive character of taint shows up best in two sorts of cases, in each of which that responsibility is in doubt.

In the first, the evil consequence, though foreseen, was recognized by the agent as being a consideration against acting. These are the sorts of cases which Williams considers, where "the agent is faced with a reliable choice between a detestable action and an outcome which is utilitarianly worse: where 'a reliable choice' means that he has a choice between doing and not doing the action, and it is certain beyond reasonable doubt that if he does not do the action, then that outcome, or something yet worse than that outcome, will follow."[14] (Such a case, for example, occurs when one is coerced into doing something awful by a terrorist threat.) In these cases, many people who judge that the detestable act is, all things considered, right, may still feel tainted by their association with it: and this may weigh with them before the act as a reason for not carrying it out.

But the cases I have been considering are of a second kind. Here the awful outcome is causally overdetermined, in such a way that, though, if one acted, one would be causally implicated in the outcome, not acting would not change the outcome relevantly. The difference between acting and not acting is a difference between two ways the evil can occur and not a difference between two degrees of evil.

In CASES II and III, the causal implication is fairly straightforward. The knife-seller and his partner each knowingly play a causal part in getting the knife into the hands of the murderers. In CASE I, the causal implication is somewhat more complex, but one still is involved in providing the resources for evil.

For the consequentialist, the cases of overdetermination will invite the thought that the use of the fact that one will be tainted as a basis for decision involves a confusion between two questions, which the literature on causation plainly shows to be distinct:

1. Did I play a causal role in the outcome?

2. Did I make a difference to which outcome occurred?

Williams's cases invite the thought that the agent who considers taint in the context of decision is confusing the questions:

3. Am I doing something which would normally have bad consequences?
4. Is what I am doing something whose consequences, all things considered, are bad?

In my judgment, these consequentialist accusations of confusion are compelling grounds for skepticism about the application of ideas of taint.

I confess, then, to finding the argument from taint less than impressive. But I said I would offer a different way of explaining the appeal of the argument from taint, that seems to me more obviously compelling in the case of South African divestment. That argument begins by rejecting one central requirement of the pure case I constructed: namely 1. For it seems to me that one way of interpreting the arguments of those who have spoken of "dirty hands" in this context, is to suppose that they start from a recognition of the symbolic dimension of certain kinds of institutional acts.

The thought is something like this. Universities and foundations are institutions which have a special relation to the political climate of a modern state. The pedagogical function of the university includes not merely the training of competent and well-informed technicians but the education of thoughtful and responsible citizens. Foundations express and carry out certain public purposes, purposes whose value they have a secondary function of getting others to recognize. Because of this, where foundations or universities express a moral view, it carries a special weight in public moral discourse.

Publicly dissociating an institution whose official acts carry this special weight from a connection with evil, even where that connection is not itself directly causative of evil, is one way of contributing to the general recognition of that evil. In the context where the issue of dissociation has been raised, not to divest risks the possibility that the institution will be interpreted as not recognizing the evil for what it is. On the other hand, the public expression of revulsion for evil, by this symbolic dissociation, reenforces correct moral feelings in some and creates them in others.

The proper image here is not Macbeth washing from his hands the bloodstains that are the traces of his guilt, but Pilate's washing of his hands: an act which was intended not to save Christ, but to withdraw moral approval for killing him.

And if this is the proper image, then it is an essential part of this view of divestment that it is a public and symbolic act: an act which expresses a moral conviction—and thus is consequentially good if it leads to public recognition of the moral claim and action on it—rather than the purgation of a tainted association with evil.

To see institutional divestment by organizations like universities and foundations this way is to have an argument for it beyond the direct consequences of divestment on the South African situation. But it is also to view the institution as expressing a moral conviction in a way which depends on a public perception that an investment in a company that delivers the tools of *apartheid* is a morally impermissible kind of association with evil. To communicate a belief in a way that depends on a presupposition of this kind is, of course, to leave the presupposition unquestioned; and, therefore, in the present context, to endorse it. For those of us who doubt this presupposition, this rationale for divestment has, then, a price. We shall succeed in contributing to an atmosphere in which our governments will be under pressure to put the South African government under pressure at the cost of endorsing what we regard as an error in moral thought. Whether that price is worth paying is a matter of judgment; but, given the other more directly consequential arguments for divestment, it is a price we do not have to pay.[15]

* * *

I have been examining the case for arguments from taint, both in general and as they might be thought to apply to the issue of divestment in a possible world other than ours. That such arguments figure so largely in public discussion of divestment suggests, as I said at the start, that our moral imaginations have not completed the trajectory implied in the picture of a movement from pollution to guilt. Others, notably Bernard Williams, have argued that there are good reasons for not being simply consequentialist in our morals, and perhaps there are: but I doubt that a belief in taint is one of them.[16]

That is the conclusion I want to draw. I do not want to draw the conclusion that universities and foundations in the United States or elsewhere should not divest; for, as I said, though talk of taint plays a large part in the hurly-burly of discussion about divestment, it seems to me of marginal relevance to the real issues. I take those real issues to be broadly the issues a consequentialist would raise, and to be summed up in the misleading simplicity of the question: All things considered, would we make the world a better place by divesting? This is a question to which I have an answer. But since it is not one for which I have argued, a *Philosophical Forum* is not the place to give it.

Notes

1. Since no rational South African sincerely believes that every non-white person lacks and every white person possesses the moral capacity to behave as a responsible citizen, *aparatheid* depends essentially on what I call "intrinsic racism": the view that the bare fact of race can legitimately be the basis of moral distinctions. I discuss this issue further in my forthcoming *African Reflections*.

2. Alasdair MacIntyre, *A Short History of Ethics,* (New York: MacMillan Publishing Company, 1966), p. 1.

3. W. H. Adkins, *Merit and Responsibility in Greek Ethics,* cited by MacIntyre, *op. cit,* p. 6.

4. *Op cit.,* p. 8.

5. Bernard Williams, *Moral Luck,* (Cambridge University Press, 1981), pp. 27–8.

6. Of course, regret may become relevant in the context of decision because we sometimes know that we or others will regret what we have done, even where it is the right thing to do. History is replete with cases (notably in warfare) where it is right to do something awful. For the utilitarian regret can become relevant here because it will cause a kind of mental anguish, even when it is not associated with guilt.

7. This means that I satisfy a condition corresponding to 4(b) above; there is a marginal loss due to the discounted value of tomorrow's profits.

8. "Utilitarianism and moral self-indulgence" in *Moral Luck (op. cit.),* pp. 40–53.

9. "Utilitarianism and moral self-indulgence" (op. cit.), p. 53.

10. It is possible that some would want to go the way of distinguishing between my selling the knife and my competitor's doing so, on the grounds that *I* am contributing to killing the victim, if I sell it, but only letting someone contribute to killing him otherwise; a distinction correlative to the familiar distinction, urged against consequentialists, between killing and letting die. To insist on such a distinction here, however, is just to restate the argument from taint.

11. Anthony Appiah, *Assertion and conditionals,* (London: Cambridge University Press, 1985: Part I).

12. The best discussion of Arrows theorem of which I am aware is Alfred

A. MacKay's *Arrow's Theorem: The Paradox of Social Choice* (New Haven: Yale University Press, 1980). He also has an excellent discussion of voting paradoxes.

13. Milton Friedman, "Let the protesters themselves divest." An "op ed" piece in the *New York Times,* May 16, 1986.

14. "Utilitarianism and moral-self indulgence" (*op. cit.*), p. 42.

15. We do not have to pay it because most people in favor of divestment hold that it will be consequentially good. Plainly someone who knowingly profits from a failure to contribute to the alleviation of evil, in circumstances where acting would make an important difference, has dirty hands in an uncontroversial sense: they are not so much tainted by their association with evil as responsible for their contribution to it.

16. J. J. Smart and B. A. O. Williams, *Utilitarianism: For and Against,* (Cambridge: Cambridge University Press, 1973).

15

Metaphysical Guilt and Moral Taint

Larry May
1991

Existentialist views of responsibility have often been accused of being extreme and implausible. Existentialists argue, for instance, that membership in a group which causes great harm implicates each member of the group, even those who did not do anything to bring about the harm. Group membership, especially membership in a community, is held to carry with it increased moral responsibility. In this chapter, I wish to analyze the relationship between community membership and moral responsibility. I will defend a social existentialist account of a person's community-based responsibilities.

It is true that existentialist views of responsibility expand greatly the normal realm of things (including attitudes, omissions and even some effects over which one had no control) for which it is appropriate for a person to hold himself or herself responsible. But the view is not so extreme as it might first appear: being responsible is not the same as being morally guilty (which entails moral blameworthiness). Karl Jaspers made a major contribution to this debate when he suggested that there are types of guilt which are based on who one is and not on what one had done. The former type of guilt, which he called metaphysical guilt, does not necessarily translate into moral guilt, but it does entail some form of moral responsibility. In attempting to defend an existentialist account of responsibility I propose that there are levels of being morally responsible which are less severely accusatory than being morally guilty, namely, those that involve shame and moral taint. Establishing these points will hopefully make more plausible the existentialist project of expanding the domain of responsibility.

Specifically, in this chapter, I wish to investigate the legitimacy and status of responsibility attributions which concern what Jaspers called "metaphysical guilt." In the first section I will explore the concept of metaphysical guilt and attempt to identify the moral implications of attributions of metaphysical guilt. In the second section I attempt to link the experience of guilt, especially metaphysical guilt, with the notion of membership in a community. In the third section, I examine those cases where communities contribute to major harms, but where the harm would have occurred even if a particular member did not make his or her contribution. By reference to the concept of metaphysical guilt, I contend that it does make sense to say that the members of these communities are morally tainted by, although not necessarily morally guilty for, these harms. In the fourth section I will briefly take up the question of whether expanding the domain of responsibility to include metaphysical guilt, as existentialists have recommended, is advantageous.

I. The Concept of Metaphysical Guilt

In his book, *The Question of German Guilt*, Karl Jaspers distinguishes moral from metaphysical guilt. The latter is defined as follows:[1]

> There exists a solidarity among men as human beings that makes each co-responsible for every wrong and every injustice in the world, especially for crimes committed in his presence or with his knowledge. If I fail to do whatever I can to prevent them, I too am guilty. If I was present at the murder of others without risking my life to prevent it, I feel guilty in a way not adequately conceivable either legally, politically or morally. That I live after such a thing has happened weighs upon me as indelible guilt.

There are two aspects of metaphysical guilt mentioned in this passage which will form the basis of my expansion of Jaspers' important notion. As I will understand it in this chapter, metaphysical guilt arises out of each person's shared identity, out of the fact that people share membership in various groups that shape who these people are, and that each person is at least somewhat implicated in what any member of the group does. But metaphysical guilt is not merely based on group membership. Rather it arises out of the fact that a person did not but could have (and should have) responded differently when faced with the harms committed by his or her fellow group members. The guilt arises from the fact that nothing is done to prevent the harms or at least to indicate that one disapproves of them. Due to these failures, the individual does nothing to disconnect himself or herself from those fellow group members who perpetrate harms. And while it may be that one is also morally guilty for one's omissions which contributed to the harm, what is important for metaphysical guilt is that one chose to do nothing to distance oneself from the harmful acts of one's fellow humans (or more plausibly, some smaller subgroup of humans). Metaphysical guilt is based not on a narrow construal of what one does, but rather on the wider concept of who one chooses to be.

There is an incomplete form of metaphysical guilt which existentialists have sometimes discussed. Sometimes metaphysical guilt is discussed as if it only concerned group membership and not also a person's responses to the harms of his or her group. In the above quotation, Jaspers comes dangerously close to saying that each of us, merely by being members of the human race, also shares responsibility for all of the harms of the world. And Paul Ricoeur has discussed the concept of "original sin" in which everyone is guilty, "even little children in the wombs of their mothers."[2] Perhaps it is this occasional failure to recognize that metaphysical guilt has two aspects and not just one, which is responsible for the view that existentialists hold to an implausible view of responsibility. Since I do not believe that the incomplete view is entailed by existentialist beliefs, nor a view widely accepted among existentialists, I will not address it in this chapter.[3]

Metaphysical guilt, even in its full and proper meaning, is clearly different from moral guilt. Jaspers illustrates this difference when he says that[4]

> there is no moral obligation to sacrifice one's life in the sure knowledge that nothing will have been gained. . . . But there is within us a guilt consciousness which springs from another source. . . . It is not enough that I cautiously risk my life to prevent it; if it happens, and if I was there, and if I survive where the other is killed, I know from a voice within myself: I am guilty of being still alive.

One cannot move from the feeling of metaphysical guilt to any kind of claim about violating a moral obligation or duty. Being metaphysically guilty does not entail being morally guilty.

Yet, Jaspers does believe that there is a kind of moral strand that is sometimes interwoven with metaphysical guilt.[5]

> And probably every German capable of understanding will transform his approach to the world and himself in the metaphysical experiences of

> such a disaster. How that will happen none can prescribe, and none anticipate. It is a matter of individual solitude.

On my social existentialist account, metaphysical guilt calls forth a certain kind of moral judgment. It forces upon the individual a reassessment of who he or she is. It calls for people to reflect upon and often change their attitudes and dispositions toward the harms of the world, even when it is impossible for these people to effect change now. And by changing one's stance toward the world, one thereby changes oneself. Those who are unaffected by the harms of their communities share moral responsibility, although not moral guilt, for these harms. I believe that shame or taint are those moral concepts most closely connected to metaphysical guilt. To avoid future shame or taint, people must change who they are in the face of their communities' harms. Sartre discusses these issues in some detail under the subject of authenticity.

In *Anti-Semite and Jew*, Sartre defines authenticity as follows:[6]

> Authenticity, it is almost needless to say, consists in having a true and lucid consciousness of the situation, in assuming the responsibilities and risks that it involves, in accepting it in pride or humiliation, sometimes in horror and hate.
>
> There is no doubt that authenticity demands much courage, and more than courage.

Authenticity involves, among other things, being conscious of who one is and taking responsibility for the harms of one's class, one's position and one's situation in the world. To be "inauthentic" is to "deny" or "attempt to escape from" one's condition, to fail to assume responsibility for choosing to be who one is.[7]

Authenticity concerns a kind of responsibility that is neither political nor narrowly moral, if we think of this term as referring to the realm of explicit behavior. But since choice is involved, there is a moral dimension nonetheless. As Sartre says, "the choice of authenticity appears to be a *moral* decision . . . but in no way serving as a solution on the social or political level."[8] Indeed, the authentic person is not necessarily one who changes his or her explicit behavior in light of moral norms. Rather, the authentic person often lacks the ability to change his or her explicit behavior at all, such as was true of Sisyphus who lacked the ability to stop climbing, even though he did have the ability to control how he reacted mentally to his fate.

Nonetheless, there is a moral dimension to authenticity for Sartre, as is true of my own view as well. Sartre devotes a lot of attention to the authentically appropriate kinds of attitudinal response a person should make concerning the life situations he or she faces. It matters whether one accepts one's situation with pride or humiliation, with horror or hate, Sartre tells us. These attitudes and dispositions are of course not merely emotional responses to one's situation. Rather they are clearly meant to be reflectively arrived at. But most importantly, as I will argue, the appropriateness of these dispositions and attitudes is a moral appropriateness. Even when we cannot change the world with our actions, there are other choices, "original choices," concerning what Thomas Flynn called the "criteria according to which we deliberate and decide" how to approach our world.[9]

As I construe it, metaphysical guilt only entails *moral* responsibility if by moral responsibility we mean responsibility for attitudes and character traits as well as for behavior. Inauthenticity involves a failure to see oneself as accountable for who one is, and this is surely a failure of character, indeed a type of cowardice. The authentic person has the virtue of courage and as a result meets head-on his or her faults, or those of one's fellow community members, and regards oneself as at least partially responsible for them. The inauthentic person is metaphysically guilty, but given that being authentic does not involve simple choices of how to behave, moral guilt is often inappropriate.

The underlying principle of existentialist ethics is that one is always morally *responsible* for who one chooses to be, that is, for the choices of attitude, disposition and character, as well as for one's behavior. One needs to become consciously aware of who one is as a necessary, although not sufficient, step toward reflectively understanding and then deciding whether to change one's life. The discussion of authenticity for Sartre, and metaphysical guilt for Jaspers, reveals that people should strive to understand who they are, and to approach the self with a strong enough attitude of accountability that whenever it is possible to change for the better who one is, a person will strive to take necessary steps to change. Here it is vitally important that people regard themselves as accountable for their metaphysical states even at those times when they cannot do that which would change these states.

Authenticity involves a deep feeling of accountability for one's self. Not everyone who is inauthentic or metaphysically guilty is also morally guilty because not everyone can change one's self or one's situation. As Jaspers points out, people are not morally guilty for failing to do those things which have very little likelihood of changing anything. But people are morally responsible for becoming consciously aware of their situations, for only when they are so aware will it be possible to change for the better when change becomes possible. In Sartre's own words:[10]

> if someone gives me this world with its injustices, it is not so that I may coolly contemplate them but so that I may animate them by my indignation, expose them and show their nature as injustices, that is, as abuses to be suppressed.

Of course, being indignant in the face of the injustices perpetrated by one's community does not necessarily lead to an overcoming of those injustices. In normal circumstances, people should do more than merely express indignation. What Sartre is getting at is that no matter how restricted one's options, one still has the choice of the attitude one takes toward the injustices of the world. The choice of whether or not to be indignant is something which occurs deep in the psyche and is almost always a choice that is open to us. If we merely passively accept injustices then we choose to align ourselvese with them, and this is what makes us both metaphysically guilty and morally responsible, although not necessarily morally guilty, for these injustices.

There is an important collective dimension to metaphysical guilt. It is important, morally speaking, that certain evils or harms occur through *my group's* facilitation, even in cases in which there is nothing that my group's members could have done, on our own or even in combination with others, except in the very long run, to prevent these evils or harms. The group solidarity which Jaspers identifies as one of the key ingredients in metaphysical guilt creates a moral taint for all of those members whose group is in any way implicated in evils or harms. To use Jaspers' own example, it is appropriate that all Germans feel tainted by what their fellow Germans did, and such a feeling should persist even in those cases where there was nothing that many of these people could have done differently, in terms of individual or collective behavior, that would have prevented Hitler's reign of terror. In the next section I will attempt to answer the question: what is it about the fact that one is a *member* of a group which is causally responsible for a major harm, that morally taints the members?

II. Guilt and Community Membership

An existentialist account of responsibility can be rendered initially plausible by noting that people often feel pride as well as guilt for what their fellow community members have done. The sheer fact of one's membership in a biologically or geographically defined group is normally not under one's control. But what is under one's control, and hence the subject of appropriate feelings of responsibility, is how one positions oneself in terms of that group. In communities, as in other groups, it is not mere membership that creates responsibility, but how one reacts (behaviorally or attitudinally) to the groups of which one is a member. In this section, I will try to explain why people have feelings of responsibility based on group membership. I leave the question of the appropriateness of such feelings to the next section.

It is undeniable that being a member of a particular community which participates in harmful activity often causes some kind of moral feeling of guilt or taint for the members of the community. I am thinking of such examples as Americans feeling guilty for My Lai, Germans for the Holocaust, etc., even though the individuals who feel guilt could not have prevented the harm from occurring. We are here still in the domain of metaphysical guilt, but now focusing on the lack of effective choices at the community level. And we are now forced to think about moral responsibility in terms that are quite different from the normal model of moral guilt. For if there really was nothing an individual member of a community could have done to prevent the community from participating in a harm, and the individual did not, on his or her own, actually aid his or her community in this participation, moral responsibility, at least understood on the model of individual moral guilt, would be inappropriate.

Racism is, so psychological studies claim, a function of the socialization as well as other forms of social interaction that occurs within groups.[11] Yet it is common for people to say that they feel guilty for such things as the racial violence perpetrated by fellow community members where racist attitudes are commonplace. Merely by sharing attitudes in common, why is it that some members of groups also feel a sense of shared responsibility for what some other members do as a result of having these attitudes? An attitude, of course, is not the sort of thing about which people reach agreement. Indeed, an attitude is not even an undertaking in the sense that it is consciously arrived at, especially where group attitudes are concerned. But the feeling of moral responsibility may still be linked to one's choices. For people make choices about how to regard, or respond to, the dominant attitudes in their communities, and even how to react to the attitudes which they themselves have been initially socialized to form by their communities. Such reactions form the basis for possible changes in who one is. Thus, such guilt feelings do not involve the incomplete view of metaphysical guilt mentioned above. The people who feel guilty in these cases made choices concerning how to react to their own and others' attitudes within the community where these racial harms occurred.

Consider the case of racism in a group such as a university community. Of course most universities have a central decision-making structure, but I will use the term university community to stand for the less formally structured group of students, teachers and staff, who are connected in widely diverse ways, to the central administration. What all of these members of such a community share in common is a culture: a set of intellectual, aesthetic and social influences which continue over time. Cultures bind the members of a group together by providing common experiences and viewpoints, thus perpetuating a form of solidarity of which Jaspers spoke. The intense interaction of ideas that occurs in a culture means that the members of a group in which there is a shared culture identify themselves with the group and in a sense with one another. Of course the identification may be very weak, especially for members who are only on the fringe of the mainstream of the community; and in such cases the group identification may be so weak as not to generate feelings of metaphysical guilt. But I am mainly interested in the experiences of those who do feel such guilt.

When a group develops a culture, then that group is not merely an aggregate, for like a decision-making procedure a culture allows for the amalgamation of individual actions and attitudes into something more than the mere sum of its parts. Most important, cultures are both the products of individual actions and attitude, and also the producers of new actions and attitudes in the world. New attitudes that arise within a culture are often very different from attitudes that would arise among individuals who do not share a common culture. This is mainly due to the cross-fertilization of ideas that occurs, in which a member of the group reacts to the views of fellow members who are perceived as akin to oneself.

The shared attitudes within a community come, over time, to create a shared identification: a shared feeling of solidarity. Just as the members of a community gain a personal sense of pride from the accomplishments of the community as a whole, as well as for the accomplishments of their fellow members, so the members of a community often come to feel shame or moral taint for harms which members of their community have caused. People in communities share more than a sense of the accomplishments within the group, they also share a sense of the failures. This is what generates the sense of responsibility that members of a community feel for the harms in which their communities participate.

The solidarity of a community often creates a shared feeling of responsibility for what occurs within the group. This feeling of responsibility is linked to that part of one's identity which is based on the groups of which one is a member. It is not merely that one is a member of a group within which harmful attitudes, for instance, have become dominant. Sometimes responsibility is based on the feeling that there was something wrong done by one's group members which one could easily have also done. Sometimes there is the feeling that one should have done something to break the chain which links one, as a nonoffending party, to the rest of the group. Of course, a person cannot cease to be ethnically German, but he or she can disavow or condemn what fellow group members believe or are currently doing. Such acts of language or mind may break the chain of responsibility between individual and community. By condemning or disavowing what one's community has done, one changes that part of one's self which is based on how one chooses to regard oneself. Such changes disassociate oneself from one's fellow group members and diminish one's shared responsibility for what those others have done.

As I said above, the existentialist view is sometimes interpreted as holding that even when one had distanced oneself from one's group, there should still be a feeling of moral responsibility for what the group does. The most plausible explanation of this shared responsibility is that solidarity continues to make one identify with what one's group does, regardless of whether one has tried to distance oneself from the acts of one's group. I think that this more extreme version of the view of metaphysical guilt is only partially true. As an actual account of why it is that some people feel guilt in such cases, it is worth attention and seems to contain a germ of truth. But as an account of one's *appropriate* feelings, the account should not be accepted. Jaspers seems to recognize this point when he distinguishes between guilt associated with merely being a member of a group versus guilt associated with condoning what one's group has done.[12]

The examples we have considered so far illustrate the metaphysical guilt which results from one's membership in, and acceptance of, a certain group which has caused harm. The guilt is metaphysical because it has to do with who one chooses to be, in the sense of whether one accepts or rejects such affiliations, rather than what one has actually done. But what is the appropriate moral feeling connected with metaphysical guilt? Moral guilt is appropriate when there is something that a person brought about in the world. Being a causal agent is closely connected to moral guilt. But when a person's causal agency is not in question, or at least when the causal role one played did not make a difference in the world, then moral shame or taint may be the appropriate moral feeling. We are thrust into the domain of responsibility for who one is, and the terms of judgment should be different than those which are addressed to a person's explicit behavior. I explore this point further by turning next to the difficult case of those who feel tainted by the fact that they are a member of a community that has participated in harm, but where there was nothing the member of the community could have done to prevent the harm. A consideration of such a case will allow us to examine what reasons can be advanced for thinking that there are appropriate moral feelings which correspond with metaphysical guilt.

III. The Case of South African Divestment

Consider the case of university investments in companies which support apartheid in South Africa. Anthony Appiah has recently raised the following question:[13] what if, contrary to fact, selling a university's shares in companies doing business with South Africa would make no difference in the world? Assume that some different university or other buyer would arise to purchase the shares of stock of which a given university divests itself. Appiah argues that it is a mistake to think that moral responsibility should be assigned to the members of this community even though some feel tainted by what their community has done.[14] In what follows I will set out Appiah's reasons for holding this view and then I will challenge his conclusions from the standpoint of an existentialist understanding of metaphysical guilt.

Appiah begins by claiming that there is a difference between ancient and modern conceptions of morality. "For us [moderns]," he says, "what matters is not who you are but what you try to do."[15] Taint is a category which is left over from ancient times when people's responsibility was determined by group affiliation. Appiah is generally skeptical of the older tradition, especially because "people may be stigmatized for their unintended association with evil." And, says Appiah, such a person may be tainted or polluted "by that association even though he or she took all the care in the world to avoid it."[16] The ancient conceptions of morality did not properly distinguish behavior from character. Yet, according to Appiah, character is often a function of factors like group membership over which people do not have control. Appiah claims that it is simply anachronistic for people today to rely on this ancient conception.

There is another sense of taint, Appiah tells us, which is distinctively modern but which is not necessarily something we should endorse either. Modern taint is assigned on the basis of a kind of "dirty hands." Appiah asks us to consider the case of those who are members of a university community that owns stock in a company that "provides equipment which the South African government uses to maintain the system of apartheid." In such cases, we, the members, "are associated, through our ownership of the shares with a wicked system; we play a part in it. Our holding of the shares taints us."[17] All that any of us, individually or collectively, can do is to disassociate ourselves from apartheid, but we cannot change it. Here we do engage in a type of behavior; if we are tainted, it is not merely on the basis of who we are. But, while our behavior links us to an evil, Appiah assumes contrary-to-fact that there is no change in behavior on our part which will eliminate that evil. If these are the facts, then, according to Appiah, the existence of the evil is not something which is under our control, and hence it is also not something for which we are morally responsible even if we feel tainted by it.

In the pure case which Appiah asks us to imagine, apartheid will not be diminished by our acts. So the features of the case that concern us are these:

1. The act we are contemplating is intended to remove us from a certain relation to a series of acts which is morally deplorable.
2. We are profiting from this relation; although we could make nearly the same profit without this relationship to apartheid.
3. Nevertheless, the act we are contemplating (working to achieve divestment) will make no difference to the evil of apartheid; except that people other than ourselves will then profit from this relationship.[18]

Even though we feel tainted by our university's continuing participation in the evil of apartheid, it is not appropriate that we hold ourselves morally responsible for this evil in Appiah's view.

Appiah says that it is important for our sense of moral integrity that our actions not taint us with evil, but he does not think that this is relevant for moral responsibility. Appiah thinks that it might be important for people to maintain their sense of integrity even when the changes in behavior necessary for maintaining integrity will not make any other difference in the world. For integrity makes a difference for the agent, and of course this is a difference in the world. If people did not have a sense of integrity, and did not act on that sense, their lives would surely be the worse for it. But this is the only basis that Appiah finds for thinking that these considerations should have any moral sway on our behavior.

There is much more to be said in support of the moral importance of taint than is captured in Appiah's few lines on the value of integrity. Appiah is wrong initially to think that what a person does or tries to do is unrelated to who that person is. Indeed, even if who one is has to do with group affiliations, one is almost always in a position to denounce or condemn one's group. The influence exerted by these groups on one's identity is diminished by one's ability to choose which groups one joins as well as how one reacts to the groups one finds oneself in. Insofar as it is possible to distance oneself from one's group affiliations one is able to exert significant influence on one's metaphysical self in ways that have moral importance. Those individuals that can, but choose not to, distance themselves from their groups which are contributing to harm are metaphysically guilty and also morally responsible for, in the sense of being morally tainted by, the harms caused by their fellow group members or institutions.

There are three notions of taint which can be associated with metaphysical guilt. The most common form, which is closely akin to guilt by association, is based on one's associations regardless of whether one is even aware that one has such associations, such as exist when merely being Jewish is said to make one tainted by what Jews, about whom one knows nothing, in another part of the world have done. Obviously, in this group of cases one's association with evil does not have anything to do with what one chooses to do, and should not normally have much to do with one's moral responsibilities. But the two other kinds of taint, those based on associations one could distance oneself from, and those based on associations which one could end, but which, if ended, would still not make any difference in the world, are much more important morally than Appiah would lead us to believe. For in both cases, it matters that one could cut the link between oneself and these groups and thereby affect one's moral identity.

Consider the case we spoke about in Section One, the case of

Germans feeling guilty for atrocities perpetrated by fellow Germans against Jews in the 1930's and 1940's. What matters is that these people were associated, through the membership in the German race, with those who perpetrated the atrocities. It does not matter whether or not there was anything that most Germans could have done personally to change the outcome. We should not engage in simple "guilt by association." But in the German case, some people were aware of what was happening and could, by the ability that all people had to denounce, or at least disavow, the atrocities, thereby distance themselves from the harm. Given this ability, then at least some of the taint in question remains connected both to what a German tried (or failed to try) to do and to who that German is. And in these cases taint is appropriately seen as a form of moral responsibility for who one has chosen to be. Taint is not merely to be avoided because it disrupts the integrity of the self.

In Appiah's pure case of divestment in South African companies, the same result can be reached as with the case of German guilt. A person almost always has the existential option to disavow the associations in which one finds oneself. As a result, Appiah is wrong to think that in this case there is a great divide between who one is and what one tries to do. These are related notions just as there is a relationship between certain metaphysical states and one's moral responsibility. It is worth noting once again that by this I do not mean to suggest that one is *morally guilty* for these states, since metaphysical guilt does not entail moral guilt. Appiah is right to think that taint, rather than moral guilt, really is the right term for the cases we have been considering. But Appiah is wrong to think that theories of moral responsibility should not have a place for taint. In the final section of this chapter, I will conclude with a brief discussion of the importance of moral taint in a conception of moral responsibility.

IV. Expanding the Domain of Moral Responsibility

One of the most obvious objections to the views I have here articulated is that I have expanded the notion of moral responsibility too far for it to have the motivational force which it previously had when moral responsibility was restricted to behavior for which a person could be said to be morally guilty. Thomas Jefferson once referred to this sort of concern as the fear of "incessant responsibility."[19] This objection perhaps has its greatest poignancy with respect to the discussion of moral taint. According to this characterization, the concept of taint is thought to play a useful role only in that it marks out the field of the non-obligatory but nonetheless ideally virtuous life. In an ideal world we would like not to be associated in any way at all with the perpetuation of harm or evil. We are tainted by these associations, and we regret them, but, so the objection goes, that should be all. We should not think that we have failed in respect to our moral responsibilities. I wish to challenge this view in these last brief remarks.

For virtually every person, individual identity is intimately connected with group membership. From a moral perspective, it is vitally important that people continue to feel motivated to shape and reshape their communities and other groups. When the members of a university community resign themselves to their university's involvement in apartheid, they also resign themselves to be associated with moral evil, and thereby they resign themselves to have their identities shaped in ways they would not choose. Given the importance of communities in shaping a person's moral character, as soon as the individual feels overwhelmingly determined by group affiliations, significant options for moral and social change are cut off.

Let us recall Sartre's remarks about being responsible for being born.[20] We do not choose to be born in the sense of being able to influence the time, place and circumstances of our birth, but there are choices we make concerning our birth that affect our responsibility. Sartre's position has some plausibility in that we do have an "originary choice" about at least some of the facts of our birth. We can resign ourselves to those facts, or we can rebel against them, at least in terms of the attitudes we take toward the facts of our birth. We may be born into a group which has a history of terrorizing its minority citizenry, and we may have no opportunity to change the group's behavior, but we can affect the way that group affiliation shapes our selves. While we cannot deny that we are, say, United States citizens by birth, we can strongly condemn what the United States has done in a particular case, and thereby reshape our selves (perhaps also reshaping what it means for others to consider themselves U. S. citizens).

The existentialist project cannot seriously be slighted for not being important. But it can be slighted for widening our concepts of moral responsibility to such an extent that people no longer feel as strongly motivated to avoid harm as they once did when responsibility was tightly connected only to guilt. Moral taint is certainly not as severe a condemnatory moral category as is moral guilt. And this is as it should be. People must feel motivated, if at all, to avoid directly causing harm to others. But this motivational project is not necessarily weakened by including other "lesser crimes" in the list of things for which people should feel a sense of moral responsibility. People continue to feel strongly motivated to avoid murder even though there are other laws, such as traffic laws, the violation of which is also a violation of our legal obligations.

Even if there were to be a lessening of our sense of motivation to avoid "capital" moral crimes by the introduction of "lesser" moral crimes also to be avoided, there are clearly important offsetting advantages to stressing the avoidance of moral taint. Again, it is necessary to think about the relationship between responsibilities and communities. By feeling motivated to avoid the taint of community-associated harm, people will see their moral responsibilities as calling for involvement in what their fellow community members are doing. Of course, this does not mean that people should invade one another's privacy or seek to curtail one another's "harmless immoralities". Rather, I am only addressing clear-cut harm to others that members of one's community participate in. Moral taint is a concept which emphasizes that people should feel responsible when their fellow community members engage in these harms.

Seeing one's own moral status as interrelated to that of one's fellow group members will negate the tendency to ignore the most serious moral evils: those which can only be thwarted by the collective efforts of communities. The social existentialist emphasis on the moral importance of metaphysical guilt takes seriously our group affiliations and thereby sets the stage for taking seriously our shared responsibility for the great tragedies which our communities have perpetrated.[21]

Notes

1. Karl Jaspers, *The Question of German Guilt,* translated by E. B. Ashton, New York: Capricorn Books, 1961 (1947), 36.

2. Paul Ricoeur, *The Symbolism of Evil,* translated by Emerson Buchanan, New York: Harper and Row, 1967, 269.

3. Those interested in pursuing the view that we are all responsible for everything should consult Herbert Morris' attempt to defend this notion in his essay "Shared Guilt," in his book *On Guilt and Innocence,* Berkeley and Los Angeles: University of California Press, 1976. I have labelled my own view as *social existentialism* to distinguish it from those early existentialist positions which deny the importance of social groups in the formation of the self and in understanding the limits on our moral responsibilities.

4. Ibid., 71.

5. Ibid., 74.

6. Jean-Paul Sartre, *Anti-Semite and Jew,* translated by George J. Becker, New York: Schocken Books, 1965 (1948), 90.

7. Ibid., especially 91.

8. Ibid., 141.

9. See Thomas R. Flynn, *Sartre and Marxist Existentialism,* Chicago: University of Chicago Press, 1984, 8.

10. In *What is Literature?*, translated by Bernard Frechtman, London: Methuen, 1950, 45, Sartre makes a similar point concerning the moral responsibility of the writer: "if the writer accepts being the creator of injustices, it is within a movement that points beyond them to their abolition."

11. One of the classic studies is Gordon W. Allport's *The Nature of Prejudice,* Garden City, NY: Doubleday Anchor Books, 1958.

12. Karl Jaspers, *The Question of German Guilt,* op. cit. 36.

13. Anthony Appiah, "Racism and Moral Pollution," *The Philosophical Forum,* vol. 18, nos. 2–3 (Winter–Spring 1987), 185–202. (Page citations henceforth refer to this anthology.)

14. Ibid., 236. Appiah is hesitant to draw this conclusion and, to be fair to him, his conclusion is quite qualified. But at the end of his essay he does announce that a belief in taint is not a good reason to cease to be a consequentialist.

15. Ibid., 220.

16. Ibid., 221.

17. Ibid., 225.

18. Ibid., 225–26.

19. Thomas Jefferson's letter to Samuel Kercheval, July 12, 1816, reprinted in *Thomas Jefferson on Democracy,* edited by Saul K. Padover, New York: Mentor Books, 1939, 63.

20. See Jean-Paul Sartre, *Being and Nothingness,* translated by Hazel Barnes, New York: Washington Square Press, 1966 (1943), 710.

21. This essay is taken from my book *Sharing Responsibility*. I am grateful to the following for comments provided on various versions of this chapter: Hugh LaFollette, Iris Young, Marilyn Friedman, Rod Bertolet, Bill McBride, Suzanne Duvall Jacobitti and Penny Weiss.

16

Measuring Responsibility

A. Zvie Bar-on
1985

"Collective guilt" is a nasty phrase. We recoil instinctively from the concept expressed by it. Collective indictment appears, at least *prima facie*, synonymous with injustice, vindictiveness, blurring of distinctions.

For all that, history has recorded quite a few cases of communities and even whole nations being condemned collectively. In recent years, moreover, we witnessed (in Vatican pronouncements) a significant act in the opposite direction: a people was acquitted of the collective guilt of deicide, of which it was accused nearly 2,000 years ago, this accusation having brought in its wake senseless hatred between nations and innumerable crimes against the people on whose forehead the mark of Cain had been set for no good reason. Were this the only case throughout history in which collective guilt had been imposed on innocent people, it would be sufficient to make its concept repugnant to us. All the more so, as it is one case among many. Did the Nazis not make collective indictment into a method, a constant component in their refined technique of oppression and destruction?

It is thus obvious that when dealing with the problem of guilt for the enormous crime of the Final Solution, we must be extremely cautious. And yet, the question has to be formulated in terms of collective guilt: is the whole German people guilty, and if so, what is the nature of that guilt? If not, who is to blame for the murder of six million European Jews during the period between 1939 (or perhaps 1933) and 1945? Who is to blame for converting an entire state into a well-oiled machine for executing this murder? A machine which was supposed to go on with the job until the last Jew in the world had been killed. Who then is guilty and what is the nature of the guilt? Trying to answer this question, I have no illusions; it is very complex and I may hope to contribute only partially to its solution. My approach will be to present the responses of three Germans to this problem, to analyze these responses critically and draw some conclusions. The three are Adolf Eichmann, Günter Grass, and Karl Jaspers.

Could Kant Save Eichmann?

I chose to analyze Eichmann's stand on the question of guilt for two reasons. *First*, this is the response of a man who had the top function in implementing the Final Solution. Few are the cases in which responsibility for the genocide of the Jewish people is as clear and unequivocal. *Second*, he was, as far as I know, the only Nazi who, when brought to judgment, attempted to determine the measure of his guilt by general criteria, invoking one of the most influential systems of ethics of our time. This exceptionally bold attempt deserves our utmost attention.

As it happened, there was a considerable difference between Eichmann's claims on this issue at the police interrogation and what he said in the courtroom. The investigator had heard from him a straightforward declaration that *all his life he was trying to follow Kant's philosophy and in particular the Categorical Imperative*. But at the cross-examination in court it became clear that there were two qualifications to this claim: (1) his interpretation of Kant's Categorical Imperative underwent changes in the course of years; (2) with the passage of time changes also occurred in the circumstances of his life which limited, as he came to think, the extent to which he was able to put into action Kant's requirement (as he understood it).

The main change in his interpretation of the Kantian principles was apparently the result of his studying Kant's *Critique of Practical Reason*. Strangely enough, this study took place only when Eichmann was already engaged in implementing the Final Solution. Until then, so he claimed, the Categorical Imperative was known to him merely in its simplified commonsense form. To quote from the proceeding of his trial (Session 105; July 20, 1961):

> *Question:* Is this when you learned for the first time the concept of the Categorical Imperative?

Answer: No, I had known the Categorical Imperative earlier, but it was in a nutshell, in a summarized form. I suppose it could be summarized as, "Be loyal to the laws, be a disciplined person, live an orderly life, do not come into conflict with laws"—that more or less was the whole essence of that law for the use of the little man.

This was Eichmann's "earlier version" of the Kantian principle. At the same cross-examination Eichmann also spelled out his later version of it:

Question: What did you understand by Kantian principles?
Answer: I meant by this that at any time and at any moment my way of life should set an example within the framework of the legislation of the laws . . . This is exactly what Kant said.[1]

As Hannah Arendt pointed out, his later version is "an approximately correct definition of the Categorical Imperative" (according to which my action can be considered moral only if "I can also will that my maxim should become a universal law"), while his earlier version is obviously incompatible with it.[2] We cannot be sure from his reported statements whether Eichmann himself so understood the relation between his two versions. But when he spoke of the circumstances that debarred him from living according to the Categorical Imperative, he had certainly in mind his later interpretation of this principle.

Now, what were these circumstances and what was in them to prevent Eichmann from fulfilling the requirements of Kant's ethics? He gave several answers to this question and they were not wholly compatible with one another. The most adequate answer was presumably the one which had connected the "turning point" of his life with the Wannsee conference in January 1942. Let us recall that this was the conference of the representatives of the top Nazi authorities, at which Heydrich read out the instructions for starting the implementation of the Final Solution. This was evidently the latest occasion on which Eichmann could have fully realized the function that he was to perform (if he did not know it earlier).

He was asked at the trial (Session 79) by his defense counsel, Servatius: "It appears from your remarks in reference to your memoirs as recorded by Sassen and from what you have said now, that you were gratified by this conference. Could you comment on this?" To which Eichmann replied: "Yes, but my satisfaction was of a kind different from that of Heydrich . . . after all the efforts [to find other solutions] I could, thanks to the Wannsee Conference, say to myself, declare myself, that [it is being done] against my will and not according to my plans, that I am not to blame, that like Pontius Pilate who had washed his hands I am innocent. For at that conference hard and fast rules were laid by the elite, the leadership, by the Popes of the Kingdom. And myself? I only had to obey.''

Let us compare this assertion with Eichmann's answer to Judge Raveh during his examination of Eichmann's approach to the Kantian philosophy (Session 105):

> *Question:* In other words, you contend that your activities in connection with the deportation of Jews correspond to the imperative premises of Kantian philosophy.
>
> *Answer:* No, of course not—because what I referred to was not my life under constraint and compulsion. . . . After all, what I did was thrust upon me. What I meant was the situation where I could be my own master, where I could follow my own will and the dictates of my conscience.

The picture drawn by Eichmann in the courtroom is thus as follows. The Wannsee Conference, which sounded the bell for the implementation of the Final Solution, made Eichmann realize that the powerful political and military machine of Germany was embarking upon criminal activity on a vast scale. The plan was not agreeable to him. Admittedly, he believed firmly, just as did his comrades of the National Socialist Party, that the Jewish problem required a drastic solution, *i.e.*, that the German State had to be purged of Jews. Relentless means ought to have been used for that purpose, like terror, persecution, concentration in labor camps, and finally forced deportation (indeed, he had played a leading role in all these activities). But not mass killing! Of that he did not think, that he did not justify.

Were it to be decided by him—so he implied—the Germans would never have used such radical means. However, the *Führer* had decided and given orders—and he had to obey. As a good citizen, and true to the oath he had given to the *Führer* and the SS, he had to obey. It was at this stage that he concluded that he was no longer able to live according to Kant's Categorical Imperative; there were two reasons for this. *First*, the very content of the Final Solution was incompatible with the principle. As he put it in the courtroom (Session 105): ''It could not be within the framework of the Categorical Imperative to kill people by force of arms. . . ." *Second*, the Final Solution was different from his own program, from the course of action which he had adopted out of his free will, and no one acting against his will and intentions could in any sense be considered a "lawgiver" and thus live according to Kant's Categorical Imperative.

It would follow that Eichmann's actions could no longer be considered moral, Kant's principle being taken as the criterion of morality. Yet, whoever had followed Eichmann's reasoning so far was now in for a big surprise: these circumstances, he nonetheless thought, were *not sufficient to incriminate him*. He was convinced that at least one of the two reasons which had obstructed his fulfilling Kant's requirements could at the same time serve as an excuse for his actions contrary to these same requirements. Since he had performed them against his will, but according to orders, it was not he who was responsible for them, but his superiors, and ultimately—the *Führer* alone. Thus, after all his efforts to find a helping hand in Kant's philosophy, Eichmann had to fall back upon the argument used *ad nauseam* by Nazi leaders and commanders of the German armies: the guilt for the crimes of the Germans against Jews, against other peoples, against the whole of mankind, does not taint the German nation, nor the Nazi party, nor even its leadership, but one man alone.

That was Eichmann's tale in Jerusalem. It is open to criticism on several counts. First of all, prior to the Wannsee Conference, did he really act according to his later version of the Categorical Imperative, which we have accepted as its approximately correct interpretation? Of course not. It would be simply ludicrous to describe his Nazi activity up to 1942 as compatible with Categorical Imperative, in particular if we recall one of Kant's alternative formulations of it, according to which a moral person must relate to his fellow-man, be he Christian or Jew, Gypsy or Negro, man or woman, not merely as to a means for his own plans and ambitions, but as to an end in itself. There is hardly any action of Eichmann's party, even before gaining power, there is no law it had initiated, no order its leaders had issued, which does not contradict directly the Kantian conception of ethics in its letter and spirit. It is also beyond doubt that while working out methods and policies for the implementation of the discriminatory laws and orders of the Nazi government, Eichmann showed wholehearted identification with their contents and spirit. He could therefore maintain that he was acting them out as if he were their legislator. But that, on its own, is far from being a sufficient condition for an action to accord with Kant's moral law. Moreover, there is in Kant's philosophy no trace of support for the contention that a man is allowed to forego the Categorical Imperative when pressed to do something against his will and sense of justice. Quite the contrary. Consider, for instance, the parable told in the *Kritik der praktischen Vernunft* (2nd ed., p. 54), where a vassal is ordered by his prince under the threat of death to bear false witness against an honest man whom the prince wishes to destroy. The moral of it is that a man's duty is to refuse to do anything which would harm his fellow man, even if he thereby endangers his future and his life. That, according to Kant, is the measure of a man's true freedom.

Until now we have assumed that Eichmann told the truth in the courtroom. However, the facts established at the trial contradict this assumption. It is clear that Eichmann's activity in the framework of the Final Solution was not against his will, as shown by his enthusiasm, initiative and diligence in carrying out his functions. The strongest evidence is provided by his behavior during the second half of 1944, when it was obvious that the fate of Germany had been sealed, yet Eichmann was feverishly continuing the deportations. Were the whole program contrary to his will, he would certainly have taken advantage of the tendency then prevailing among the leaders of the SS (apparently endorsed by Himmler) to stop the bloodbath, and have thereby returned to a state of "harmony" between himself and the Categorical Imperative. Instead, he continued his Final Solution activities; only that now *he defied the orders of his superiors*.

We are left with the following conclusions. There is no reason to assume that, throughout his Nazi career, Eichmann was at any time acting against his will and convictions. His identification with the Nazi ideology was complete throughout and his actions followed directly from it. There is also no argument to show that these actions were at any time compatible with the principles of Kantian ethics.

There was not and there could not be anything in his "Kantian argumentation" to strengthen his main line of defense, which sought, as we saw, to transmit all the guilt up the ladder of command to its very top, to Hitler alone, or at most to him and the group of his closest associates. This response, which in effect clears the whole German people of guilt, except for one or a few individuals, is not unique to Eichmann. It has been offered by many Germans and non-Germans; but a legion of arguers will not add a whit of validity to the argument.

Grass's Argument in Jerusalem

In the fascinating lecture which Günter Grass gave in Jerusalem, a few years after the Eichmann trial, there was a world of difference from the responses of Eichmann. The address, like all Günter Grass's writings, contained no trace of an intention to whitewash his compatriots or to transfer the guilt from the whole nation onto one man or a small group of men:

> We, the good-natured Germans, the dreamers and the shrewd fellows, the German eccentrics, inventive and industrious—when the order fell "sing together," "join in, everybody," we got up from our revels all over Swabia, Silesia, the Rhineland, and other provinces, and begot a political crime that exceeded all the provincial standards. And as soon as our Reich, which we had called "the third," was defeated, we came back without hesitation, everybody who had lived longer than our destructive arrogance came back to the idylls which were half-ruined, but we were able to repair them. As peasants who in the autumn bury their *mangel-wurzels* in heaps, so did the decent Germans try to bury their past. But the *mangel-wurzel* heaps are scattered about the ground in spring, and then the stench spreads all over the country and no idyll remains safe from the sour vapor. What freezes on the lips is altogether one sentence: the Germans, those who did it and those who let it be done, killed six million human beings. . . . Was it easy to burden the industrious and virtuous citizens with the elaborate program of the Final Solution, which needed participants in knowledge, participants in action, and silent witnesses? The process was dreadfully simple: it was announced in print, prepared according to laws and performed methodically.[3]

A few comments are appropriate to this passionate testimony. First, we may react uneasily to his speaking of the "order" to unleash the Holocaust, since we saw how Eichmann used this concept to transfer the guilt to one man only, who headed the chain of command. Yet, it is clear, both from the above passage and from the rest of the lecture, that it is not an excuse that is sought here, but an *explanation* (in the same lecture Grass condemned the conception "order compels," quoted from Globke, who had taught the Holocaust perpetrators the way to clear their names of guilt). Günter Grass describes colorfully the human landscape of Germany, where a number of traits are mixed together producing provincial creatures "hospitable and harmless, quarrelsome over trifles, always ready to forget themselves in singing, and often inviting the silent stranger to join in the glee." Despite the many differences between the inhabitants of various German provinces, practically all of them have a scale of values headed by the same few virtures: diligence, efficiency, thoroughness, and attention to detail in the performance of duties. This is how Grass explains why, when the "order" came, there were no questions about its sense and justice, but the Germans rose and performed the crime.

Even merely as an explanation of how the genocide came about, however, this appears to simplify matters. The number of Germans who volunteered to do the dirty work and then did it with conviction and overwhelming enthusiasm (as in Eichmann's case) was far too large for what Günter Grass suggests. We cannot ignore the need to search for deeper causes of the behavior of millions of Germans during the Holocaust.

Secondly, we may consider Grass's attitude to the meaning of the crime and the guilt for it. On this he is unhesitatingly outspoken: "the Germans . . . killed six million human beings." This is an unequivocal language of admission. Grass clearly holds that the responsibility for the crime affects *all* Germans, at least all those who were living in Germany at the time. But in what way does it affect them? Certainly not all of them equally. Had Günter Grass meant that all Germans are guilty to the same extent, it would practically not be far from the contention that none (or only one, now dead) was guilty. As a matter of fact Günter Grass *does* indicate distinctions between degrees of responsibility, or measures of guilt, but not so much explicitly and directly as by using expressions like "those who did it and those who let it be done," or "participants in knowledge, participants in action, and silent witnesses." This issue undoubtedly requires a more extensive and detailed analysis, such as will be found in the third response below.

Lastly, there is Grass's remark that the Final Solution was "prepared according to laws." We must again be careful not to imagine analogies with Eichmann's position. The reference to laws was made by Grass to provide a basis not for justification or forgiveness, but for defining the *nature* of the crime; its enormity was increased and not mitigated by its "legalization." Only here too, Grass is not sufficiently precise and univocal. This is especially noticeable in another part of the paper, actually its central part, where he tries to point out the lessons that the new generation should learn from the Holocaust:

> The history of mankind, however hard we try to polish its lights, is also a history of crimes and genocide. Let us keep within the bounds of the European chapter and consider "The Short Description of the Destruction of the West Indies." With a belated shock we read the tale told by the Spanish bishop Bartholomeo de las Casas about the atrocities of his compatriots in Jamaica, Cuba, Haiti, Mexico, Guatemala and Venezuela.

> Without going into details he tells of 500,000 Indians killed on one island, 200,000 on another, of two to three million Indians killed in Mexico. Who will take to heart these matters today? We got used to thinking of this chapter of European history as a gripping and horrifying subject in the school curriculum. There is practically no European nation which did not at one time or another make crime its political ally.[4]

True, at this point Grass warned his audience of a possible misunderstanding: in juxtaposing the Final Solution against numerous crimes from history he did not mean to obscure its enormity. His aim was to combat our getting used to crimes of any kind, and particularly crimes committed against entire nations. Yet, despite this disclaimer, one has the impression that the uniqueness of the Holocaust became lost in Günter Grass's presentation. In this respect too, the third response is much more adequate. It will show that an accurate determination of the character, dimensions, and meaning of the crime is indispensable for delimiting the guilt correctly.

Four Kinds of Guilt

Now to the last position to be examined here, that of Karl Jaspers. He was one of those infrequent philosophers who do not feel exempted from the task of dealing with current problems and seeking answers to questions and challenges presented by living reality. Incidentally, Jaspers stayed in Germany throughout the Nazi period, but dissociated himself from the regime. He was dismissed from his post of professor at Heidelberg University in 1937, but remained in that town, together with his Jewish wife, till the disintegration of the Third Reich.

My analysis of his approach is based on three sources. The first is his book *Die Schuldfrage* (Heidelberg, 1946), a personal and also a national confession, a parallel to which can hardly be found in world literature. The second source is an interview given by Jaspers to the German weekly *Der Spiegel* in 1965, on the eve of the Bundestag debate on the Statute of Limitations in respect of Nazi crimes. The last source is a short address which he sent to the symposium on "The Unsolved Problem," held in Brussels in 1966 with the participation of Jewish and German scholars.

The interviewer from *Der Spiegel* argued that if merely German war crimes were excluded from falling under the twenty-year Statute of Limitations, there would be non-Germans who went scot-free after committing crimes similar to those for which the Germans were still to be punished. This was countered by Jaspers:

> This argument would not have been unwelcome if it were correct. But it ignores the radical difference between war crimes and crimes against mankind. War crimes are against humanity (*die Menschlichkeit*). . . . The pretension to decide which communities and nations are allowed to live on this Earth and which are not, and to materialize this decision by extermination is a crime against mankind (*die menschheit*). . . . Such actions were done to Jews, Gypsies, the mentally ill.[5]

Jaspers continued:

> . . . The realization that what is involved here is a crime of a new type, is the precondition for judging the question of limitations. This question then finds its evident answer when one is clear about four closely related questions. First question: what kind of crime? Mass murder by the authorities, a new crime unprecedented in history. This crime presupposed a state of a new type—the state of criminals. Second question: by what law is [this crime] to be judged? By the law which unites all men, the Law of Nations. Third question: where is the legitimate tribunal to apply this law? So long as there is no institutionalized Tribunal of Mankind, which is the proper place for it, the tribunals are the law courts of those states which declare that the Law of Nations is normative for their own legal system. Fourth question: what punishment? To this unique crime against mankind there corresponds the death penalty, restored after its abolition, as an exceptional punishment for this exception.[6]

Of particular interest in our context is Jasper's answer to the first of his four questions, his defintion of the crime. It should be noted that this stand concerning the crime committed against the Jews and other ethnic groups (which was to be continued, as Rosenberg's plan envisaged, by bringing "order" into Eastern Europe after the final victory of the Nazis) does not agree with the position taken by the jurists who formulated the Convention on Prevention and Punishment of the Crime of Genocide. They held (like Günter Grass) that the history of mankind has known precedents to this crime, while Jaspers maintains forcefully that the Nazi crime was new in its essence, perhaps mainly because it involved the transformation of an entire state into a state of criminals.

My impression is that the philosopher went deeper than the jurists into the specific circumstances of the planning and committing of the crime, that he noticed how the engineers of this crime succeeded in converting a modern state with all its components, such as the military, the economic, the juridical and even the cultural, which included science, into an instrument for criminal acts. Moreover, using his conception of the Nazi crime Jaspers transcended the juridical aspect of judgment and punishment. He used it to determine the measure of *the guilt of his people*. It becomes clear from his analysis that this guilt cannot be contained within the juridical framework of crime, guilt, and punishment.

Jaspers distinguishes between four kinds of guilt, all of which are relevant to the appraisal of the German's responsibility for the Nazi crimes. They are criminal guilt, political guilt, moral guilt, and metaphysical guilt.

Judgment and punishment in courts of justice relate only to *criminal guilt*. Not all Germans can be charged with it, only those who were directly involved in the planning, preparation, or enactment of genocide. It is peculiar to this modern crime of genocide that the guilt for it is attributable to tens or perhaps hundreds of thousands of people. Only if *all* the offenders are fittingly punished for this crime, will the German people be free of the past in which it constituted a state of criminals. As we saw, Jaspers demanded reintroduction of capital punishment just for that purpose, whereas otherwise he hailed its abolition in Germany and in other countries.

Political guilt applies in Jaspers' view to all the citizens of Germany. Every citizen of a modern state is responsible for the actions of its government and administration, unless he speaks and acts openly against them. But, as Jaspers stresses, there was no effective resistance to the regime until 1943. Where is the authority to judge the citizen and punish him for his political guilt? For Jaspers it is in the hands of the victors, *i.e.*, the Allies who defeated the Germans and dictated to them the conditions of their subsequent existence in the political, economic, and cultural fields. Occupation, reparations to be paid, conditions for reconstruction of the economy and culture, poverty and misery—all these are retributions for the political guilt. All the citizens of the state are somehow affected by these measures, and none has the right to complain of their injustice. The guilt is collective and so is the punishment. How long should these measures last and how extensive should they be? No one but the victor can answer this, and he will act as his interests suggest. The division of the state into two Germanies, the annexation of entire provinces by other countries—these are the effects of the collective political guilt.

The sources of *moral guilt* are all those actions and defaults of the

German citizen which implied his support of the criminal regime, whatever the reasons, sincerity, and effectiveness of his support. There is no authority to judge this guilt, except in the conscience of every individual. The individual weighs and measures the extent of his guilt and decides himself what will absolve him, how he has to change and what he has to do in order to atone. But man is a social creature and his spiritual life does not proceed in isolation. Communication with his fellow man, and in this case first of all with his compatriots, is a part of life. It would therefore be natural if mutual persuasion and influence made the processes of soul-searching, repentance, and spiritual renewal interlace and grow into a communal and finally a nationwide experience.

In this connection Jaspers asks whether every German was morally obliged to protect the victims of his country's regime, and in particular to protect the martyrs of the Final Solution. He gives a qualified answer to this question: the obligation existed and its non-fulfillment is a source of moral guilt, yet no man is morally obliged to give his life for his fellow man. In particular, no one is duty-bound to act in defense of his fellow man if it is obvious that the persecuted will not be saved, while the defender will be victimized as well. The mere fact that his Jewish friends were being deported and killed did not bring about moral guilt. The guilt it did generate is of a different kind, it is the *metaphysical* guilt, which Jaspers defines as follows:

> There exists a solidarity among men as human beings that makes each co-responsible for every wrong and every injustice in the world, especially for crimes committed in his presence or with his knowledge. If I fail to do whatever I can to prevent them, I too am guilty. If I was present at the murder of others without risking my life to prevent it, I feel guilty in a way not adequately conceivable either legally, politically or morally. That I live after such a thing has happened weighs upon me as indelible guilt. As human beings, unless good fortune spares us such situations, we come to a point where we must choose: either to risk our lives unconditionally, without chance of success and therefore to no purpose—or to prefer staying alive, because success is impossible. That somewhere among men the unconditioned prevails—the capacity to live only together or not at all, if crimes are committed against the one or the other, or if physical living requirements have to be shared—therein consists the substance of their being. But that this does not extend to the solidarity of all men, nor to that of fellow-citizens or even of smaller groups, but remains confined to the closest human ties—therein lies the guilt of us all. Jurisdiction rests with God alone.[7]

As early as in 1945, in his first public address after the war, Jaspers confessed movingly and dramatically to the metaphysical guilt of himself and of all Germans:

> We, the survivors, did not seek death. When our Jewish friends were taken away, we did not go into the streets and shout until we had been exterminated as well. We preferred to stay alive for a weak though correct reason that our death cannot possibly help. That we are alive is our guilt.[8]

Conclusions

So far we have considered the positions of three Germans with respect to the responsibility for the crime of the Final Solution. How will this contribute to our attempt to answer our original question?

To the question: "Is it justified to apply in this case the notion of collective guilt?", we should give a qualified affirmative answer. It must be qualified because we do not wish to have the very notion of collective guilt whitewashed from its pejorative meaning, whether in the law, in morality, or in the political realm. We plead for an exceptional application in our case because of the entirely exceptional character of the crime, which can be brought under the two headings:
(a) the initiation, planning, and execution of the genocide of the Jewish people within the context of the Rosenberg style "biological reshuffle" of the population of Europe (and later, presumably, of the whole world);
(b) the transformation, for the sake of (a), of the German state, all its economic, juridical, and technical resources included, into a criminal state.

The crime is exceptional, entirely new, without precedent in the history of mankind, and this fact justifies the use of the concept of collective guilt when trying to measure the responsibility for the crime. The application is however qualified. We use for this purpose for two cross-distinctions, one between the direct and the indirect, the other between the personal and impersonal responsibility. The first of Karl Jaspers' *kinds* of guilt—the "criminal guilt"—is both personal and direct; the second, the "political guilt," is indirect and impersonal; while the remaining two—the "moral" and the "metaphysical" (whether they should be separated will be subsequently questioned)—are personal but indirect.

The clearest case is obviously the first one, that of the criminal guilt.

It should be imputed—as Jaspers rightly urges—to every German (indeed, to every human being) who had participated in the initiation, planning, and execution of the Final Solution. The determination of the exact dimension of this kind of guilt, and of the punishment for it, is in the hands of the judiciary authority. Jaspers thinks, we remember, that for punishing this kind of crime—and only for it—the death penalty should be reintroduced (if it was revoked previously). I prefer to leave this question open. I consider proper the maximal penalty allowed by the state, but "death penalty or not"—is a very difficult question which deserves a separate analysis. Anyhow, the responsibility here is personal and direct, the heaviest known in the history of the law, I presume.

At the other end of the spectrum I would place the "political guilt" which is, as mentioned above, impersonal and indirect. But it is very real because of the fact that a whole state was transformed into an instrument of crime. Jaspers says: "Every citizen of a modern state is responsible for the actions of its government and administration, unless he speaks and acts openly against them." He says "modern state," not just "state." What he probably has in mind is that unlike previous times, in the modern state the relationship of a citizen with the state is such that he *nolens volens* has his share in keeping this state alive, even if he is not involved in what is commonly called "political life," does not belong to any political party, does not even bother to leave his house on the general elections day. Even such a person is responsible for the body politic. There is however no good reason available for considering this responsibility a personal one. And since the guilt is not personal, neither is the punishment. The state as a whole is punished and its citizens are affected only so far as their well-being depends upon the state.

We may accept Jaspers' view that in accordance with the nature of political reality the factor which was supposed to punish the guilty in this case was the victor, *i.e.*, the Allied Powers. But Jaspers also ruled that the victorious powers were justified in treating occupied Germany as they liked, in accordance with their own political interests; the Germans had no basis for complaints of injustice. If this means that the policy of the Allied Powers could have been completely arbitrary and not subject to any general criteria of evaluation and criticism, then this stand cannot be accepted. Such a conception would offend the sense of justice of us all, and not only of the Germans. I would therefore modify Jaspers' formula to the effect that the Allies should have acted in accordance with the interests of the whole mankind, or of the family of nations.

This implies that the occupation authorities should have done everything possible to eradicate from Germany—from its institutional and cultural structures—all that could reasonably be identified with roots of totalitarianism, and this includes the simplified "earlier" Eichmannian conception of the Categorical Imperative. Was this accomplished in postwar Germany? In West Germany, denazification proceeded to quite a considerable extent, while in East Germany it seems not to have materialized at all. The new regime there remained totalitarian. This totalitarianism may be different from that of the Nazi regime; it seems however, to be in several respects more dangerous than the Soviet variety.[9]

Problems of a different nature are bound to arise in connection with the other two kinds of guilt. As Jaspers presents the moral guilt of the Germans, a certain incompatibility is revealed within the very concept of moral duty. The line of reasoning runs as follows: the source of the moral guilt of the Germans is any action or forbearance of action, that implied support, in any form, of the Nazi regime. Specifically, this guilt meant responsibility for the lot of the victims of that regime, including of course the victims of the Final Solution. But, asks Jaspers, did this responsibility impose on every German the moral duty of endangering his own life in an effort to save those victims? This question is answered with an unqualified "no." Such an answer is, we should say, not self evident. It requires reasons, justification. That is to say, the limit that Jaspers puts to the moral responsibility of the Germans is theory-dependent. And what theory will justify Jaspers' stand?

This question brings us back to the same ethical theory which Eichmann tried to use for his defense: the Kantian doctrine. According to it one has the moral duty to respect his fellow man, to refrain from offending him, never to treat him only as a means to further one's goals or ambitions. Thus, as we have seen, this theory could not possibly help Eichmann in the hour of his predicament. But alas, this same theory does not make everyone duty-bound to endanger one's own life in order to save one's fellow man from destruction.

Kant's ethical theory can be criticized on this account. It could even be argued that in the conditions of the Nazi terror such an ethical thesis must have played into the hands of the Nazis, providing an ethical excuse for the indifference to the fate of the victims. However, a person who had adopted the Kantian ethics before the Nazis seized power, could have felt it difficult to depart from it when with the change of regime it became inadequate. Should this person have proposed *ad hoc* an altogether new ethics?

This might have been Jaspers' dilemma which he attempted to solve by means of the distinction between the "moral" and the "metaphysical" guilt. If the guilt imputed to every German who did not do his utmost to save his fellow man from destruction did not follow from his moral duty, there is an alternative way of proving it real—by making it follow from the metaphysical fact of human solidarity. Nevertheless, the overall result of Jaspers' argument is unequivocal: every German who lived in Germany during the Nazi rule and did not actively oppose the regime, bears responsibility for the lot of the victims of that regime.

I think that Jaspers' dilemma would be avoided if we did not interpret the moral duty of man in terms of Kantian ethics which leaves outside of morality the (metaphysical) fact of basic human solidarity and co-responsibility. It seems to me more reasonable to combine moral duty with human co-responsibility from the outset and to interpret the one in terms of the other. Still, whichever way we treat these basic assumptions, Jaspers' final conclusion appears to be inevitable.[10]

Notes

1. From the duplicated minutes of the Jerusalem District Court, Criminal Case 40/61 (The Attorney General of the Government of Israel v. Adolf, the son of Adolf Karl Eichmann, Jerusalem, 1961).
2. H. Arendt, *Eichmann in Jerusalem: A Report on the Banality of Evil* (New York: 1963), p. 121. My subsequent analysis of Eichmann's position, however, diverges from that of Arendt.
3. The Israeli newspaper *Ha-aretz,* March 24, 1967.
4. *Ibid.*
5. *Der Spiegel,* March 10, 1965, p. 57.
6. *Ibid.*
7. K. Jaspers, *The Question of German Guilt* (New York: 1947), p. 32.
8. From *Deutsche und Juden, Beiträge von Nahum Goldmann, Gershom Scholem, Golo Mann, Salo W. Baron, Eugen Gerstenmaier und Karl Jaspers* (Frankfurt: 1967), p. 110. There is a striking similarity in Stephen Spender's view expressed during his visit to Israel (*Jerusalem Post,* January 31, 1975): "If Israel were destroyed, it would be a devastating thing for all of us—not physically as bad as for the Israelis, but spiritually quite as bad. If Israel were allowed to go under, we would be in the position of the Germans who allowed the Nazis to slaughter the Jews, we would all be guilty."

9. See in particular Zbigniew Brzezinski, "The Soviet Past and Future", *Encounter,* March, 1970, pp. 3–16, where it is argued that in contrast to Soviet difficulties in absorbing mordern scientific techniques, "the combination of Prussian discipline, German scientific efficiency, and Leninist-Stalinist ideology has made German communism again a model for its Eastern neighbors." (p. 15)

10. I am indebted to the editors of *Philosophical Forum* for their critical remarks which have enabled me to improve my exposition and enforce my argument. An earlier short version of this paper was submitted to the Conference "The Holocaust—A Generation After", held in New York in 1975. A Hebrew rendering of that version was included in the third volume of *Dapim Lkheker Tkufat Hashoah,* Hakibbutz Hameuchad Publishing House, Tel Aviv, 1984.